Law and Philosophy Library

Volume 115

The Law and Philosophy Library, which has been in existence since 1985, aims to publish cutting edge works in the philosophy of law, and has a special history of publishing books that focus on legal reasoning and argumentation, including those that may involve somewhat formal methodologies. The series has published numerous important books on law and logic, law and artificial intelligence, law and language, and law and rhetoric. While continuing to stress these areas, the series has more recently expanded to include books on the intersection between law and the Continental philosophical tradition, consistent with the traditional openness of the series to books in the Continental jurisprudential tradition. The series is proud of the geographic diversity of its authors, and many have come from Latin America, Spain, Italy, the Netherlands, Germany, and Eastern Europe, as well, more obviously for an English-language series, from the United Kingdom, the United States, Australia, and Canada.

More information about this series at http://www.springer.com/series/6210

Carl Wellman

Constitutional Rights -What They Are and What They Ought to Be

Springer

Carl Wellman
Philosophy Department
Washington University in Saint Louis
Saint Louis, Missouri, USA

ISSN 1572-4395 ISSN 2215-0315 (electronic)
Law and Philosophy Library
ISBN 978-3-319-31525-6 ISBN 978-3-319-31526-3 (eBook)
DOI 10.1007/978-3-319-31526-3

Library of Congress Control Number: 2016937981

Printed on acid-free paper

This Springer imprint is published by Springer Nature
The registered company is Springer International Publishing AG Switzerland

Preface

The central purpose of this book is to identify and explain the moral foundations of constitutional rights, the moral reasons that justify recognizing and applying them in the legal system of a nation state. A necessary preliminary is to understand what constitutional rights are. Hence, the first two chapters deal with constitutional law and constitutional rights respectively. I argue that any adequate theory of constitutional rights needs to explain four species of rights: rights of governing institutions, public officials, private persons and associations.

Judges sometimes appeal to moral reasons when they interpret the content of an established constitutional right or decide whether some claimed constitutional right really exists. Hence, there are many references to Supreme Court cases in Chaps. 3, 4, 5 and 6. These illustrate judicial reasoning about how moral reasons succeed or fail to ground an actual constitutional right.

The focus of Chaps. 3, 4, 5 and 6 is ongoing political debates about controversial constitutional rights, some established in United States law and others merely proposed. It is here that the moral reasons for or against any constitutional right are most easily identified and their relevance most clear. Many of these debates are described in some detail and examined with care in these chapters. My examinations are critical, that is, they go beyond merely describing these debates to an assessment of the relative importance of the pro and con reasons advanced and to reach conclusions about whether each of these constitutional rights ought or ought not to be retained in our legal system or introduced into it.

I do not imagine that I can settle any of these debates. My intentions are to assist others to continue the ongoing discussion of controversial rights more reasonably and to reach some theoretical conclusions about when and how moral reasons succeed or fail to justify any constitutional right. Although the focus of this book is on constitutional rights in the United States, my theoretical theses and assessments of the relevant moral reasons will be applicable to the constitutional law of many other nation states.

Contents

Chapter 1
Constitutional Law

Abstract Law is a text-based practice, a practice of creating and applying legally authoritative texts. A practice is defined as a set of social practice rules, rules implicit in some form of established social activity. National law is made and applied by social institutions such as legislatures and courts and administrative agencies by which a society governs itself. Constitutional law is that body of law that constitutes a nation state, primarily by allocating fundamental legal powers. These may be, but need not be, codified in a written document. Even when they are codified, they are supplemented by unwritten law consisting of institutional practices of interpretation and application including constitutional conventions.

Constitutional rights, in the sense that I intend to consider them, are rights conferred by the constitutional law of some nation state. Hence, to understand constitutional rights one must have some conception of the nature of the law of nation states. Fortunately, one does not need any definition of the concept of national law or any specification of the necessary and sufficient conditions of national law. Instead, I will propose what I hope will be an illuminating way of thinking about the contemporary law of nation states.

1 National Law

National law, the law of some nation state, is essentially institutional. It is made and applied by social institutions such as legislatures and courts. This is as true of customary law as it is of statute law and the common law. Customs constitute laws only insofar as they are recognized as legally binding by the law-applying institutions of the society. Even those theorists who reject legal positivism and insist that there is a necessary connection between law and morality distinguish between the natural law that exists independently of social recognition or enforcement and the human law in force in any society. All jurists and philosophers of law agree that municipal law, the positive law of any society, is institutional. This explains why the law of one society is different from and independent of the law of other societies.

The law is also essentially linguistic. Laws, hence the law or the body of laws, are formulated in language, typically in standard formulations. Modern legal systems are primarily text-centered. Their law-making institutions create authoritative legal texts and it is upon these texts that their law-applying institutions ground their

C. Wellman, *Constitutional Rights -What They Are and What They Ought to Be*, Law and Philosophy Library 115, DOI 10.1007/978-3-319-31526-3_1 decisions. The size, complexity and impersonality of modern societies require that most of their law be recorded in written form. Even here, however, oral tradition may play some role in the law. In smaller more intimate societies, especially those in which oral traditions are strong and reliable, the law might be formulated in unwritten language. But some sort of linguistic formulation is necessary if law is to be a social institution, an institution of the society as a whole. This is because it must be communicated at least to the officials in the legal system and, if it is to regulate the conduct of all those subject to it, more widely to the members of the society. Also, law can perform its normative function of providing a critical standard of justified action only if agents and those who react critically to their actions have some shared formulation to which they can appeal in their practical reasoning.

American legal realists are best known for their rule skepticism, their view that the language of the law does not strictly determine judicial decisions. Accordingly, they distinguished between paper rights and real rights and maintained that real law consists in the decisions of the courts. Their insight, especially that of Karl Llewellyn, was that real law is constituted by the ways in which the legal institutions of a society actually function in practice. What they failed to appreciate is the fact that legal institutions could not function, especially in any complex modern society, without authoritative formulations of the laws. A more adequate legal realism must recognize that the law is both institutional and linguistic.

How should one conceive of a more adequate legal realism? I find the answer in a seminal article by Stephen R. Munzer and James W. Nickel entitled "Does the Constitution Mean What It Always Meant?" They argue that its meaning changes by authoritative interpretation because constitutional law is a text-based practice. (Munzer and Nickel 1977, pp. 1029–1062) Thus, the text is central to constitutional law, but its meaning is modified by the practice of legal interpretation. To my mind, this suggests an expanded conception of law in general as a text-centered practice, a practice of creating and applying legally authoritative texts.

When analytic legal philosophers use the expression "a legal system," they usually mean to refer to a body of laws, to the logically structured set of legal norms of some society. But as a legal realist, I conceive of the law of any society in terms of its legal institutions, those institutions by which a society governs itself. In this sense, a legal system is a complex social institution consisting of interacting social institutions such as legislatures, courts, administrative agencies and police forces. Each of these institutions is an organization of individuals acting in their institutional capacities. Their institutional powers are defined by social practices in the sense introduced by John Rawls. "I use the word 'practice' throughout as a sort of technical term meaning any form of activity specified by a system of rules which defines offices, roles, moves, penalties, defenses, and so on, and which gives the activity its structure. As examples one may think of games and rituals, trials and parliaments." (Rawls 1955, p. 3) In my terminology, however, I distinguish between the social institution of a parliament, an organization of legislators, and the practice of legislating, the structured activity of enacting statutes. Thus, the fundamental reality of municipal law consists in the various social practices of making and applying laws--legal rules, principles or standards.

2 Social Practice Rules

The rules that define and structure these practices have come to be called "social practice rules." In their most basic form, social practice rules arise from and are implicit in some form of social activity, such as parenting. In my society, although not in Plato's Republic, it is a practice rule that parents ought to care for their children. That is to say (1) parents usually do provide for the needs of their children, (2) when a parent does not do so, then others react negatively by condemning or even imposing informal penalties upon the deviant parent, and (3) members of the society, parents as well as others, generally think of both the parental actions of caring for one's children and the critical reactions of others to uncaring parents as justified.

Although social practice rules may be and often are explicitly formulated as rules, as general standards of practice, they need not be. But they cannot be implicit in social practice without some use of language. Obviously, when others praise or blame some agent for performing or refraining from some sort of action, they must use language. Less obviously, no agent can think of some sort of action as justified or unjustified without thinking of it as that specific sort of action, which requires classification and thus linguistic categories. Similarly and for the same reason, others cannot take critical reactions to the fact that some agent has acted or failed to act in some manner as justified without at least some sort of linguistic classification.

It is not necessary, however, that what the members of a society take to be justified or unjustified actions and critical reactions actually are justified. Thus in my society, there was the social practice rule that parents may, perhaps even that they ought to, spank their children when their children seriously misbehave. As we said, "spare the rod and spoil the child." But whether this sort of corporeal punishment is justified or whether our critical reactions to parents who did spank their children were justified is controversial. Again, there was a time when one of the rules implicit in our social practice of cohabitation was that the female ought to submit to sexual intercourse whenever her male partner desired her to do so. Although most of us today regard this social practice of female submission to be unjustified, this does nothing to show that a real social rule was not implicit in it. What makes any social practice rule actual is simply social practice in the broad sense that includes the activities of acting on the rule, of reacting critically to those who do or do not follow the rule, and of thinking, correctly or incorrectly, of such actions and reactions as justified.

A practice exists when a systematic set of social practice rules constitutes roles in some form of activity. Thus, in our society there is a practice of parenting with the social roles of parent and child. What it is to be a parent is defined by a number of rules including the following: A parent ought to care for his or her child. It is not wrong for a parent to punish his or her child for misbehaving. And if a parent orders his or her child to do something, then the child ought to so act. These and similar social practice rules seem to impose institutional duties or to confer institutional liberties or powers upon parents. But what is their normative import?

Consider our social practice rule that a parent ought to care for his or her child. Does this social practice rule impose any duty of care upon a parent? Duties are neither objects in our natural world nor some sort of non-natural entities. Duties are positions under duty-imposing reasons. Hence, to say that a duty exists is to say that there is a reason for one or more agents to act in some specific manner and for others to react negatively in the event that they do not do so. Our social practice rule that parents ought to care for their children consists simply in the facts that (1) parents in our society generally do care for their children, (2) when they do not do so, then others generally react negatively to them, and (3) most people in our society believe that these ways of acting and reacting are justified. These facts are not, singly or conjointly, sufficient to constitute a duty-imposing reason. The fact other parents generally care for their children is not in and of itself a reason why any individual parent ought to care for his or her children. Although the fact that others generally react negatively is a prudential reason for a parent to do so also, it is not a reason for others to react negatively in the event that a parent does not so act. Nor is the fact that most people in our society react negatively to parents who do not care for their children in and of itself any reason to react negatively in any given case. Finally, the fact that these patterns of action and reaction are generally thought to be rationally justified is no reason to engage in these patterns of action, for they may not actually be justified. Therefore, this sort of social practice rule does not actually impose any duties upon those who play the social roles they define.

Nevertheless, if some such rule really is justified, then it does indicate a genuine duty. But what imposes that duty is not the social practice rule itself; it is the reason or reasons that justify it. For example, if there is some reason sufficient to justify the actions of parents who care for their children in our society and some reason to justify the negative reactions of other members of our society to those who fail to do so, then that reason or those reasons constitute a duty-imposing reason. And a parent in our society might also have a moral duty to care for his or her child grounded on the fact that by accepting the parental role, perhaps by adopting the child, or by playing that role for some time one has invited others to rely upon one to act as parents in our society are expected to act. To be sure, this moral duty depends upon the existence of the social practice rule, for it is this rule that creates the legitimate expectation one would betray were one to invite reliance and then betray the trust of those who have relied upon one to their detriment. But it is grounded upon the potential harm that any such betrayal risks, not merely on the social practice rule itself.

Similar reasoning applies to other sorts of social practice rules. Thus, our rule that it is not wrong for parents to punish their children does not in itself confer any liberty to do so. To say that a parent has a liberty to punish his or her child is to say that a parent has no duty not to do so. But our social practice rule that it is not wrong for a parent to punish his or her child consists in the facts that (1) parents in our society often do punish their children, (2) that other members of our society generally do not react negatively to them for doing so, and (3) most members of our society believe that these practices of punishing and refraining from negative reaction are rationally justified. But our belief may be mistaken and there may be some reason of which we are unaware or which we tend to underestimate that imposes a duty upon parents not to punish their children. If so, then parents in our society do not really have a liberty to punish their children. However, if our rule is rationally justified, then it does specify a genuine liberty, a liberty conferred by the reason or reasons that justify the rule, not by the rule itself.

Social practice rules define roles in social practices such as parenting. Of course, one cannot play the role of a parent without some child to whom one owes a duty of care. Any social practice defines a set of interrelated roles. An institution consists of a number of persons playing their respective roles. For example, a traditional nuclear family consists of a male and a female parent caring for one or more children. How parents and children are expected to interact is determined by the social practice rules that define the roles of parent and child. But typically each family member plays more than one role. The male adult typically plays the roles of breadwinner and husband as well as parent. The female parent will play usually play the roles of mother and wife and often income earner also. If there are several children, each will play the role of brother or sister as well as that of a child. Variations on the traditional nuclear family are increasingly common. The adults need not be married and there are single-parent families as well as childless couples. Any nuclear family is situated within an extended family of grandparents, uncles or aunts, and other relatives by blood or marriage. Thus, a social institution consists of individuals playing their interrelated and overlapping roles.

3 Legal Institutions

A national legal system consists of the set of interlocking social institutions by which a society governs itself. These are distinguished from the other institutions of the society by the fact that they claim comprehensive and supreme authority. That is, they claim the authority to regulate every kind of action of every member of the society and the authority to modify or nullify any norm of any other social institution. These institutions govern primarily by creating and applying, often enforcing, norms—rules, principles or standards of conduct. These norms are laws in the relevant sense, and collectively they constitute the law of the society.

For a legal realist like myself, real law is the law as it is applied in practice. Hence, law-applying institutions are more definitive of the law than those that create what purport to be legally valid norms. The paradigm examples of law-applying institutions are the courts, both because they are more reflective concerning their procedures of judging cases and because they have the power to review and overrule actions of the other law-applying institutions. However, administrative agencies often hear appeals from their decisions, the police apply the law in their enforcement activities, and law-making institutions like legislatures in enacting statutes and administrative agencies in formulating regulations apply the law when they do so according to what they judge to be the proper procedures.

Courts are social institutions consisting of judges and auxiliary legal officials, each playing their respective roles. Since the primary function of courts is to judge cases brought before them, the role of the judge is central to any legal system. The role of the judge is defined by the social practice rules that govern the practice of judging legal cases. (The social practice rules that govern the practices of judging beauty pageants or baking competitions are presumably rather different.) Normally, the role of a judge will also be subject to various legal norms, but the social practice rules are more fundamental because it is these that define the role subject to legal regulation. Also, real law consists in the general practices of the officials who apply the law, and any social practice rule incorporates how judges and others actually do apply legal norms.

Among these social practice rules are some that specify how judges normally do and presumably ought to identify the law upon which they may ground their judgments. Primarily, these rules will require a judge to identify a legally valid text by its source, the fact that it has been formulated or recognized by some law-making legal institution following the proper procedure. Thus, statutes enacted by a legislature, regulations issued by an administrative agency, or common law rules recognized in previous court cases will normally be taken to be valid law.

Do the social practice rules that define the practice of judging court cases determine what the law is? For the most part, they do. This is because central to any social practice rule defining the role of a judge would be a pattern of action actually practiced by judges and how legal texts are actually applied in practice determines real law. But some judges might deviate from this general practice, in which case what the law really is would be determined by what they actually do, not what the rule says that they ought to do.

Collectively these social practice rules for the identification of the law constitute what H. L. A. Hart called the rule of recognition of a legal system. However my conception of a social practice rule is somewhat different from Hart's. Hence, I do not agree with him that a rule of recognition is conventional in the sense he defined in the Postscript to *The Concept of Law*. "Rules are conventional social practices if the general conformity of a group to them is part of the reasons which its individual members have for acceptance…" (Hart 1994, p. 255) The British rule that operators of motor vehicles ought to drive on the left is conventional in this sense. Although the primary reason for individuals to follow this rule is to avoid collisions, a secondary reason is the fact that most drivers do in fact conform to this rule. Again, the rule of etiquette in my society that a guest should clear her plate is conventional in this sense. The reason for one to do so is in order to show the host that one has appreciated his food and that in our social circles this is how people generally do show their appreciation. But the fact that other judges identify the law in some manner is no reason for any individual judge to do so. In addition to the general practice of judges to identify the law in some specific manner and the general practice of others to react negatively to those who deviate from this practice, the social practice rule that defines the practice of judging legal cases includes the general belief that these practices are justified. Therefore, the reason or reasons for any individual judge to conform to this rule are those reasons, if any, that do in fact justify the practice of identifying the law in the prescribed manner. However, these rules are conventional in the sense that they are customary, based on or in accordance with use or practice.

Applying the law involves much more than identifying legally valid texts. Judges must also select those that are relevant to the case before the court. Relevance depends upon the facts of the case, but also upon the legal issue to be decided. Thus, some laws will bear on questions of the jurisdiction of the court, others on the standing of a plaintiff to sue, and still others on a writ of habeas corpus. In order to decide a case on the basis of the relevant law, judges must determine the import of the selected texts for the case at hand. This obviously requires reasoning from the relevant legal texts and the facts of the case to a specific judgment that will decide the issue before the court. Although most of this reasoning follows the ordinary canons of inference, some will be governed by specifically legal rules such as the principle that an indicted person is innocent until proven guilty or that proof in a criminal trial requires a higher burden of proof than in a civil suit. An equally important part of this judicial process is interpreting the legal texts upon which any judgment is grounded. At this point also some appeal to moral standards may be required, at least when terms like "due process," "equitable," "reasonable" or "cruel and unusual punishment" are used in formulating a relevant legal text. None of this is controversial. What is controversial is the scope of the reasoning essential to any legal system.

The legal institutions of any society are those by which that society governs itself. Could there be a social system that governs merely by the general commands of those in power? I can see no reason to deny that this could be logically possible, but I doubt that it could persist for any extended period if it did not claim to be justified and its claim was not widely, not necessarily generally, accepted by those subject to it. Even if the loyalty of those who enforce these commands could be purchased by giving them special privileges, the general public subject to these commands would not long submit unless they believed the system of government to be justified. Hence, any realistic conception of law will incorporate some claim to rational justification in its theory of a legal system. But there is also a conceptual reason to include some claim to rational justification in one's theory of law. Almost everyone believes that the law can and often does impose legal duties upon those subject to it. Even if this belief is false, surely it is not unintelligible. Therefore, whether or not any legal system does in fact impose legal duties, it must be capable of doing so. But, as H. L. A. Hart has argued, government by commands backed by threats might oblige obedience but could not create any obligation to obey.

However, Hart seems to have believed that a legal system needs to presume only an internal rationality. In his Postscript he suggests that it need claim only that what it demands of its subjects is justified by valid law but may assume that the legal validity of any rule is determined simply by a conventional rule of recognition. (Hart 1994, pp. 256–257) But a legal conclusion derived from unjustified legal texts or its imposition by an unjustified legal institution would not be fully justified. Therefore, any legal system must claim that its practices and their outcomes are justified by external reasons, justifying considerations logically prior to these practices and their legal applications. Although these justifying considerations may include specifically moral reasons, such as the protection of moral rights or the demands of justice, they need not be limited to these. Because a legal system is the means by which a society governs itself, political reasons including utilitarian calculations and the need to compensate for the defects of human nature can also justify legal rules or institutions.

Accordingly, the practice of judging cases that come before a court involves a claim to rational justification. This claim is made explicit in the practice of applying the law by the way in which judges are expected to derive their decisions from legally valid texts. The judicial reasoning formulated in their opinions is internal to the legal system because it takes for granted the accepted practices of identifying legally valid texts and any special rules of application. However, the claim of the courts that their decisions are justified also implicitly presupposes some sort of rational justification on external grounds. The practice of judging presupposes that the practice rules that identify legal texts by their pedigree pick out institutions justified in making the law and that in positing legal texts these institutions tend to reflect the kinds of reasons that would justify the laws that they make.

Just as a court is our paradigm of a law-applying institution, so a legislature is our paradigm of a law-making institution. A legislature consists of a number of individuals acting in their official capacity as law-makers. In a simple legal system, the legislature might be a council of elders or assembly of nobles. Their legislative practices could be defined for the most part by social practice rules somewhat modified by legal regulation. However, the social practice rules that define the legislative practices of the members of the English Parliament or United States Congress are heavily overlaid with constitutional law and their codified procedural rules.

What gives the legislators in any legal system their authority to make laws, to enact statutes that are legally valid texts? This apparently simple question really poses two distinct questions. First, what gives legislators their legal power to enact legally valid statutes? It is the relevant power-conferring rules of the legal system. These are mainly the constitutional principles, written and unwritten, that structure the system of political institutions of the society. These identify those who possess the capacity to legislate, the scope of the statutes they have the power to enact, and the basic procedures required for legally valid legislation. Ultimately the legal force of these power-conferring rules is derived from their acceptance by the officials, primarily judges, who apply statutes in particular cases.

Second, what justifies the rules that confer this law-making power upon the members of a legislature? These will be considerations external to the law but presupposed by the legal system's claim to rational justification. They will be political reasons--reasons concerning who ought to possess political power in a society, how they ought to exercise their power, and what kinds of legal institutions will most effectively promote these political goals. Only if the law-making powers of the legislators are justified by some such considerations will they have political legitimacy, the moral right to exercise their legal powers of enacting statutes.

Although courts are the paradigm institutions that apply the law and legislatures the paradigms of law-creating institutions, administrative agencies both apply and create authoritative legal texts. For example, the Equal Employment Opportunity Commission applies the federal legislation against discrimination in the workplace when it enforces the relevant laws and establishes procedures for appealing its decisions. It also issues rules and regulations with the force of law that, among other things, specify what constitutes discrimination because of sex, because of religion or because of national origin.

Similarly the Internal Revenue Service applies the federal laws imposing income and inheritance taxes when it collects taxes from those subject to these statutes, identifies individuals who have failed to pay what they owe and imposes penalties for nonpayment. And it issues rules and regulations that determine at what times and in what ways one is legally required to submit one's taxes to the federal government.

Practicing lawyers and those who study the law find it useful to distinguish between various bodies of national law such as administrative law, contract law, tort law, criminal law, family law and constitutional law. Presumably constitutional law is that body of law validated by the constitution. What, then, is a constitution?

4 National Constitutions

What is a national constitution? The *Oxford English Dictionary* defines a constitution, in the relevant sense, as "The system or body of fundamental principles according to which a nation, state, or body politic is constituted and governed." But it adds that "In the case of a *written constitution*, the name is sometimes applied to the document embodying it."

This ambiguity, and the confusion it causes, has been noted by scholars both in the United States and in the United Kingdom. Charles A Miller reminds us that:

> Custom dictates that the United States possesses a "Constitution" rather than a constitution. The difference in orthography reflects the fact that the former is a formal written document describing a pattern of legal rules and institutions that function for political purposes. The latter is a pattern of political relationships which may be, but need not be, defined in legal instruments. (Miller 1972, p. 150)

Herbert W. Horwill had previously complained:

> The word 'constitution' has thus come to be an ambiguous term. Whenever the Supreme Court has to decide whether such and such a Congressional enactment is 'constitutional,' the test is its conformity to the fundamental instrument which is known as 'the Constitution,'…By this limitation we are using the word 'constitution' in one sense when we are discussing the government of the United States and in quite another sense when we are discussing the government of any other country, or when we are instituting comparisons between the United States and any other country. We are committing an error in classification which is bound to result in confusion of thought. (Horwill 1925, pp. 15–16)

My hope is that a text-centered conception of law can avoid misunderstandings arising from this ambiguity. Presumably the United States Constitution is the text, or at least the most fundamental part of the text, of the constitutional practice that is the constitutional law of the United States.

Because the text or texts of the constitutional law of any nation state constitute real law only as they actually function in the practices of their governing institutions, the expression "a national constitution" in its more fundamental sense refers to the body of rules or principles that allocate the sovereign power in the government of a nation state. Thus, what is constituted, established or made up by the combination of elements, by any national constitution may be called either the government of a sovereign nation or a nation state. These elements are its governing institutions and, more fundamentally, the offices defined by the constitution.

Thus conceived, a national constitution consists of a system or body of fundamental principles or rules. To understand how these function in legal practice it is useful to distinguish between different kinds of constitutional principles. Let us begin with A. V. Dicey's description of "the true nature of constitutional law."

> The one set of rules are in the strictest sense "laws," since they are rules (whether written or unwritten, whether enacted by statutes or derived from the mass of custom, tradition, or judge-made maxims known as the common law) are enforced by the courts; these rules constitute "constitutional law" in the proper sense of that term, and may for the sake of distinction be called collectively "the law of the constitution."
>
> The other set of rules consist of conventions, understandings, habits or practices which, though they may regulate the conduct of the several members of the sovereign power, of the Ministry, or of other officials, are not in reality laws at all since they are not enforced by the courts. This portion of constitutional law may, for the sake of distinction, be termed the "conventions of the constitution," or constitutional morality. (Dicey 1939, 23–24)

Several distinguished English scholars apply this classification to the constitution of the United States.

For example, Horwell adopts Dicey's classification as (1) (a) rules that have been enacted by statute, (1) (b) rules derived from the mass of custom, tradition, or judge-made maxims known as the common law, and (2) the conventions of the constitution. (Horwill 1925, p. 4) He then explains:

> The moment we begin to compare the English and American Constitutions we are struck by the fact that the most important part of the American Constitution is one to which there is no parallel in the English. This unique element is an instrument drawn up by the Convention of 1787 and modified by nineteen subsequent amendments.... Next come such statutes as fill in the gaps in the fundamental document or develop its instructions in further detail.... This class corresponds to the English (1) (a).... Then there are various rules which are distinguished from the class immediately preceding by being derived not from statutes but from the judicial decisions which are the basis of common law, and from the class that follows by being capable of enforcement by the courts. These correspond to the English class (1) (b).... Lastly, we come to those customs, practices, maxims and precepts which are not enforced by the courts, and which thus correspond to the English class (2). (Horwill 1925, pp. 6–7)

There is a paradox in this classification of constitutional principles or rules. Some of the rules of constitutional law, constitutional conventions, are not really laws.

Can a text-centered conception of law resolve this paradox? Perhaps it can, for constitutional conventions seem to be a very special sort of social practice rules. If so, then they might well define and regulate the roles of officials in the institutions of a national legal system. Horwill mentions as paradigm examples of constitutional conventions the English convention that "The King must assent to any bill passed by the two houses of Parliament" and the American convention that "Presidential Electors shall not cast their votes according to their independent judgment but shall do no more than formally ratify the results of a previous popular vote." (Horwill 1925, pp. 4 & 7) These could well be seen as social practice rules that define the offices of the King and of presidential electors by limiting their constitutional powers. However, it is doubtful that all constitutional conventions can be interpreted in this manner.

There are several ways, not all helpful, of classifying the different kinds of national constitutions. The most common is to distinguish between written and unwritten constitutions. It is frequently said, for example, that although the United States and most other nations have written constitutions, the English constitution always has been and still is unwritten. However, Dicey long ago explained that this is not true.

> There are laws of the constitution, as, for example, the Bill of Rights, the Act of Settlement, the Habeas Corpus Acts, which are "written law," found in the statute-books—in other words are statutory enactments. There are other most important laws of the constitution (several of which have already been mentioned) which are "unwritten" laws, that is not statutory enactments. Some further of the laws of the constitution, such, for example, as the law regulating the descent of the Crown, which were at one time unwritten or common law, have now become written into statute law. (Dicey 1939, p. 28)

Accordingly, the distinction between written and unwritten constitutions is at best very misleading.

Horwill went further when he explained the source of this distinction and the error that infects it.

> In this instance it has become easier for writers on the subject to use the term 'unwritten constitution' in a peculiar and unexpected sense because of the technical meaning given by the legal profession to the term 'unwritten law,' which is applied to case law, or the common law, in order to distinguish it from the 'written law' of positive enactment. The reports of judicial decisions are written, printed, and published, but nevertheless in the terminology—one is tempted to say the jargon—of the profession they are 'unwritten law.' (Horwill 1925, p. 2)

Although the ideal of conceptual clarity calls for the elimination of this misleading classification, it is probably too firmly embedded in the literature to be completely eliminated.

Anthony King has proposed a more nearly accurate way of classifying national constitutions.

> What Britain lacks is not a written constitution, but a *codified* Constitution, a Constitution with a capital 'C', one that has been formally adopted in accordance with some legal process generally acknowledged as appropriate for the purpose. (King 2007, p. 5)

Unfortunately, this proposal has to date been largely ignored.

Another common and much less misleading classification is the distinction between entrenched and unentrenched constitutions. A national constitution is entrenched when its alternation or elimination requires more than the exercise of normal law-making powers. Clearly the United States constitution is strongly entrenched for a very complex and politically difficult process is required for its amendment, but because Parliament can modify the English constitution simply by enacting a new statute, it is unentrenched. The only obscurity remaining is that there are various degrees of entrenchment so that in some nation states it requires very little more than the usual legislative action to amend the constitution.

One of the most important distinctions is between federal and unitary constitutions. A federal constitution is one in which the sovereign power is divided between a central government and the governments of a number of smaller units, such as provinces or states within its territory. In contrast, a unitary constitution is one in which the central government holds all the sovereign power and any subdivisions are merely local administrative agencies.

Finally, let us not forget the sixth sense of "constitution" defined by the Oxford English Dictionary: "The mode in which a state is constituted or organized; especially, as to the location of the sovereign power, as a *monarchial, oligarchical*, or *democratic constitution*." Although this classification is not much used these days, it is common to distinguish between democratic and undemocratic constitutions and to debate the requirements of democracy.

5 Constitutional Law

What distinguishes constitutional law from other kinds of law such as criminal or tort law? It is tempting to believe that it is that body of law authorized by the constitution, but all law in any national legal system derives its authority from the constitution. Nor will it help to distinguish between direct and indirect derivation of authority because much constitutional law, such as the United States law concerning the constitutional right to privacy, is derived from the text of the United States Constitution only via decisions of the Supreme Court. Once more let us turn to A. V. Dicey for the answer:

> Constitutional law, as the term is used in England, appears to include all rules which directly or indirectly affect the distribution or the exercise of the sovereign power in the state. Hence, it includes (among other things) all rules that define the members of the sovereign power, all rules which regulate the relation of such members to each other, or which determine the mode in which sovereign power, or the members thereof, exercise their authority. (Dicey 1939, p. 23)

Most authorities on English constitutional law adopt some version of this definition.

However, Thomas C. Grey reminds us that because the word "constitution" is ambiguous, so is the term "constitutional law."

> British constitutional statutes, and the entirely statutory constitutions just mentioned, differ from the ordinary norms of the legal systems, not by virtue of their legal force or their origin, but by virtue of their subject matter. Constitutional norms in this sense are, roughly, the most important of the rules that define, distribute, and restrict the institutions and powers of government. But this characterization should not be thought of as stating necessary conditions for describing something as a constitutional norm. Other norms with the status of fundamental law, particularly those placed in a document labeled a constitution, are often quite properly characterized as constitutional in character. (Grey 1979, p. 193–194)

Thus, there are two concepts of constitutional law, one applicable to the law of a nation state with a codified constitution, like the United States, and another applicable to the law of every nation state whether its constitution is or is not codified. To my mind it is the latter, the conception defined by Dicey and many others, that is more useful for the understanding of the nature and functions of constitutional law in any national legal system.

Although it is the fact that it constitutes the political and legal system of a state by allocating the powers of sovereignty that defines constitutional law, Joseph Raz reminds us that constitutional law typically has several other important properties. (1) It is usually, although not always, entrenched. That is, it cannot be changed or abolished merely by the usual legislative process. (2) Whether or not it is entrenched, it is stable. "It is and is meant to be of long duration: It is meant to serve as a stable framework for the political and legal institutions of the country…." (3) It is fundamental. It provides the foundation of the entire legal system because all other parts of the law of any nation derived their validity from its constitutional law. And (4) It is superior to all other law. "This means that ordinary law which conflicts with the constitution is invalid or inapplicable." (Raz 1998, p. 153) Although none of these properties is a necessary condition for the existence of constitutional law, each of them contributes greatly to the way in which constitutional law functions in any legal system.

What the scope or reach of constitutional law is very unclear. A passage in the decision of the Supreme Court of Canada in the Patriation Case is relevant here.

> A Substantial part of the rules of the Canadian constitution are written. They are contained not in a single document called a constitution but in a great variety of statutes some of which have been enacted by the Parliament at Westminster…or by the Parliament of Canada…or by the provincial legislatures such as the provincial electoral acts. (Supreme Court of Canada 1981, p. 876)

This passage is doubly illuminating.

First, it shows that the constitutional law in any nation with a federal constitution includes both the constitutional law of the central government and that of its provinces, as in Canada, or states, as in the United States. This is because in any federal government the sovereign power is divided between the central government and the governments of its main subdivisions. Hence, the law that allocates the sovereign power within that nation state must include both federal and provincial or state constitutional law.

Second, the example of relevant provincial legislation cited, electoral acts, is revealing. Just as there cannot be a parent without a child, so there cannot be any government without a population to be governed. This reminds us that in any democratic government, one of the constitutional offices is citizenship. Citizens share in the sovereign power of a democratic nation state by virtue of their power to vote for public officials and their power to hold public office. It is these basic rights that give reality, to various degrees in different constitutions, to the notion of the sovereignty of the people.

What remains unclear is whether the rules that govern the offices and procedures of the political parties lie within the boundaries of constitutional law. No doubt there are usually laws regulating the functions of political parties in the government. Obvious examples are laws determining the procedures for nominating candidates for public office and others regulating permissible donations to the campaign expenses of candidates. But whether these allocate any part of the sovereign power of the nation state to political parties remains in doubt. Here, as in many other places, the line between the legal and the merely political seems indeterminate.

Although constitutional law is almost always stable and often entrenched, it does change. In the United Kingdom, the constitution can be modified by means of the ordinary legislative process. A recent example is the *Human Rights Act of 1998* that extended the power of the courts of the United Kingdom to include petitions grounded on the *European Convention on Human Rights*. British courts can also initiate, but not necessarily complete, change in constitutional law. In *A and Others v Secretary of State for the Home Department*[1] the Law Lords held that the indefinite detention of foreign prisoners in Belmarsh without trial under section 23 of the *Anti-terrorism, Crime and Security Act 2001* unnecessarily discriminated against foreigners and was therefore incompatible with the *European Convention on Human Rights*. (House of Lords 2004, p. 47). Because of the supremacy of Parliament in the constitutional law of the United Kingdom, this did not in and of itself change the Constitution. But it did, paradoxically, prompt Parliament to enact the *Prevention of Terrorism Act 2005* that extends the power of the Home Secretary to include the indefinite detention of anyone of any nationality.

Although the United States Constitution of 1789 is entrenched and therefore cannot be modified merely by ordinary legislative action, the constitutional law of the United States can change in a variety of ways. Most obviously the original Constitution has been modified 27 times by amendments proposed by Congress and ratified by the legislatures of the several States. However, because this procedure is politically difficult, most basic changes in the constitutional law of the United States are made by the Supreme Court. Clear examples are decisions recognizing rights, such as the right of interstate travel or the right to privacy, not mentioned in the text of the Constitution. But subsidiary portions of constitutional law, such as the electoral law, can be changed merely by federal or state legislation.

Codified constitutions, statutes and judicial decisions are all written and published. Hence, there are a variety of texts normally central to the constitutional law

---

[1] Stepnen R. Munzer and James W. Nickel, "Does the Constitution Mean What It Always Meant?" 77 *Columbia Law Review* (1977), pp. 1029–1062.

of any nation state. This is usually recognized by lawyers and students of the law in the United Kingdom, but much less often in the United States. It is typically assumed that the constitutional law of the United States is contained in a single document, The United States Constitution. However, we can now see that this is not true. As real law, as the text-centered practice of constitutional law, United States constitutional law also includes the texts of many decisions of the Supreme Court and of some statutes that allocate parts of its national sovereignty.

American Legal Realists rightly insist that these texts constitute real constitutional law only as they are applied by the legal institutions of a nation state. Paradigmatically, this is by decisions of its courts, most authoritatively by its highest court or in some nations by a special constitutional court, either upholding or denying the legal validity of some statute or administrative regulation. But these court rulings would be insignificant were they not in turn applied by other kinds of legal institutions. Thus, the British Parliament applied its prior *Human Rights Act of 1998* when, in response to the finding of the Law Lords that its statute permitting the indefinite detention of only foreigners suspected of terrorism was discriminatory, it replaced that statute with the Prevention of Terrorism Act of 2005. And the Home Office presumably applies the relevant constitutional texts when it continues to detain or releases suspects in accordance with them.

In the United States, both federal and state courts apply the texts of the relevant constitutional law when they hold that some contested statute or regulation is or is not null and void because it violates one or more of these texts. But courts are by no means the only legal institutions that apply the texts of United States constitutional law. A President occasionally veto a bill passed by both houses of Congress because he judges it unconstitutional. After each national census, State legislatures normally redraw the boundaries of the districts for the election to the House of Representatives in order to respect Article I, Section 2, Clause 3 of the United States Constitution that reads in part: "Representatives…shall be apportioned among the several states…according to their respective Numbers…." And school boards apply the text of *Brown v. Board of Education*[2] (Supreme Court 1954) when they integrate the public schools they administer.

Where do constitutional conventions fit into the text-centered practice conception of law? Constitutional conventions are customary ways of acting by the officials in a legal system that are generally taken to be morally, but not necessarily legally, required. Although as ways of acting, they are unwritten rules, they may be reduced to writing by scholars who describe some system of constitutional law, in statements made by members of a government, or even when referred to in statutes. Nevertheless, there are no canonical formulations of constitutional conventions as such so that they do not constitute legally authoritative texts of the legal system. (Supreme Court of Canada 1981, p. 880) However, they are social practice rules and as such constitute as essential part of constitutional law as real law, for they regulate the exercise of the legal powers of officials who apply the texts that are legally authoritative. They typically limit the discretion of officials in exercising

[2] John Rawls, "Two Concepts of Rules," *Philosophical Review*, vol. 64 (1955), p. 3, Note 1.

broadly-defined powers conferred upon them by the legal texts of constitutional law. Examples would be the United Kingdom convention that the Crown must assent to any bill passed by both Houses of Parliament and the United States convention that judges should defer to the executive on political questions.

Are constitutional conventions laws? This question is ambiguous. If it is asking whether they are constitutive rules in a legal system, the answer is "yes." They are social practice rules that normally determine how legally authoritative texts are applied by the officials in that legal system. According to any version of legal realism, they are legal rules. But if one is asking whether they are legally authoritative texts to be applied by the courts, the answer seems to be in the negative. Two reasons are advanced to explain why constitutional conventions are not, strictly speaking laws. First, the legal validity of any rule is grounded upon its source in some legislative act, judicial decision or ratified Constitution, but constitutional conventions are not posited in any of these ways. (John 1999, p. 19) And second, constitutional conventions are generally in conflict with the legal rules that the courts are bound to enforce. This is because these rules confer broad discretionary powers but constitutional conventions limit the exercise of these constitutionally established rights. (Supreme Court of Canada 1981, pp. 880–881).

Nevertheless, courts do occasionally take constitutional conventions into consideration in their decisions. Thus the Supreme Court of Canada in its advisory opinion in the *Patriation Case* held:

> We have reached the conclusion that the agreement of the provinces of Canada, no views being expressed as to its quantification, is constitutionally required for the passing of the "Proposed Resolution for a joint Address to Her Majesty the Queen respecting the Constitution of Canada" and that the passing of this Resolution without such agreement could be unconstitutional in the conventional sense. (Supreme Court of Canada 1981)[3]

And in the United Kingdom a conventional duty of confidentiality by members of the Cabinet was considered in concluding that members of the security and intelligent services have a similar legal duty. (House of Lords 1976)[4]

What does this text-centered social practice analysis of constitutional law reveal that might help one to understand constitutional rights? First and foremost that because what defines constitutional law is the way in which it allocates the sovereign power in a nation state, the primary constitutional rights in a nation are the power-rights of those who hold offices in its legal system. Therefore, any comprehensive and balanced discussion of constitutional rights in any nation state must include both the governmental rights of its officials and the civil rights of those subject to its laws. In addition it shows that although constitutional rights may be grounded on a codified Constitution, they can also be grounded on other legally authoritative texts such as judicial decisions, statutes or even administrative regulations. This in turn explains how constitutional rights can be created, abolished or redefined without any amendment to "the Constitution." Finally it shows that

---

[3] Carl Wellman, *Real Rights*, New York & Oxford: Oxford University Press, 1995, pp. 48–50.

[4] H. L. A. Hart, *The Concept of Law*, Second Edition, Oxford: Clarendon Press, 1994, p. 255.

someone might abuse a constitutional right by exercising it in a way that, although entirely legal, is unconstitutional because it violates a constitutional convention.

References

Dicey, A. V. (1939) Introduction to the Study of the Law of the Constitution, 9th edition. Macmillan and Co. London.

Grey, Thomas C. (1979) Constitutionalism: An Analytic Framework. In Constitutionalism. J. Roland Pennock and John W. Chapman (eds). New York University Press. New York.

Hart, H. L. A. (1994) The Concept of Law, 2nd edition. Clarendon Press. Oxford.

Horwill, Herbert W. (1925), The Usages of the American Constitution. Oxford University Press. London.

House of Lords (1976) Attorney-General v. Blake (Jonathan Cape Ltd. Third Party). QB 752.

House of Lords (2004) A and Others v. Secretary of State for the Home Department. UKHL 56.

King, Anthony (2007) The British Constitution. Oxford University Press. Oxford.

McGrath QC, John (1999) The Harkness Lecture: The Crown, the Parliament and the Government. Waikato Law Review 7:1–22.

Miller, Charles A. (1972) The Supreme Court and the Uses of History. Simon and Schuster. New York.

Munzer, Stephen R. and Nickel, James W. (1977) Does the Constitution Mean What It Always Meant? Columbia Law Review 13: 1029–1062.

Rawls, John (1955) Two Concepts of Rules. Philosophical Review 64: 3–32.

Raz, Joseph (1998) On the Authority and Interpretation of Constitutions: Some Preliminaries. In Constitutionalism: Philosophic Foundations, Larry Alexander (ed.). Cambridge University Press. Cambridge.

Supreme Court of Canada (1981) Re: Resolution to Amend the Constitution. 1. S.C.R. 753.

Supreme Court (1954) Brown v. Board of Education. 347 U.S. 483.

Chapter 2
Constitutional Rights

Abstract Constitutional rights are rights defined and conferred by constitutional law. A legal right is a complex of Hohfeldian elements: legal liberties, claims, powers and immunities. A real right, if respected, gives dominion, freedom and control, over some core legal position upon the right-holder in any confrontation with one or more second parties. The most fundamental constitutional rights are the power-rights of the governing public officials and institutions, but they have constitutional liberty-rights, claim-rights and immunity-rights as well. Other constitutional rights are those of private individuals and associations of private individuals.

What is the nature of constitutional rights and how do they function in the constitution of any nation state? Larry Alexander suggests, but does not explicitly assert, a partial answer to these questions.

> Constitutions, as I said, lay down the ground rules for governance. They "constitute" the government. They set up structures, offices, and lawmaking procedures. Constitutions such as the U.S. Constitution and the Canadian Charter also entrench "rights." (Alexander 2011, p. 4)

This is an important truth about national constitutions, but the word "also" is misleading. It suggests that constituting a government and entrenching rights are two independent enterprises. But in any constitution that does both, this is not the case.

It might seem to be so because the "Bill of Rights" is only one part of the *United States Constitution* and the *Canadian Charter of Rights and Freedoms* is a document much later than the more fundamental *Canadian Constitution Act*, also known as the *British North American Act*. However, constitutional law constitutes or establishes a government by defining and allocating legal powers, especially the various legislative, executive and judicial powers, to the offices in a nation state. And the primary function of civil rights in constitutional law is to limit, and thereby partially define, these legal powers. Hence, constituting a government and conferring constitutional rights are two aspects of one and the same enterprise.

On a more philosophical level, allocating constitutional powers and conferring constitutional rights might seem to be very different kinds of enterprises because many constitutional lawyers assume that powers and rights belong to conceptually distinct categories. In this respect they follow Wesley Newcomb Hohfeld and others

C. Wellman, *Constitutional Rights - What They Are and What They Ought to Be*,
Law and Philosophy Library 115, DOI 10.1007/978-3-319-31526-3_2

who insist that in the most appropriate and strict sense only legal claims constitute legal rights. However, some jurists and philosophers of law advocate broader conceptions of rights and others reject any Hohfeldian analysis of rights. Hence, one must determine what conceptual framework is most appropriate for a theory of rights before deciding precisely how constitutional powers and constitutional rights are related.

1 Rights

Because I take legal rights as my paradigms of rights of all kinds, I must take Wesley Newcomb Hohfeld's analysis of the legal language of rights seriously. Through a systematic survey of legal publications, he demonstrated that jurists and judges use the expression "a right" to refer indiscriminatingly to four different legal relations—privileges, claims, powers, and immunities. (Hohfeld 1919, p. 71) Although Hohfeld preferred the term "privileges," I will use the term "liberties" because this has become standard usage in the legal and philosophical literature. Because he assumed that these are fundamentally distinct legal relations with nothing in common, he believed that the legal language of rights is ambiguous and thereby defective. However, H. L. A. Hart and others have denied this and developed theories of rights general enough to explain liberty-rights, claim-rights, power-rights and immunity-rights (Hart 1982, pp. 162–193).

My own theory of rights is along very much the same lines. It seems to me that one can define the content of any right with more precision and better understand how it actually functions in a legal system by analyzing it in terms of the legal positions Hohfeld identified. The most relevant ones are the following: (1) A legal liberty is simply the absence of any contrary legal duty. Thus person P has a legal liberty of doing act A if and only if P has no legal duty not to do A. For example, I have a legal liberty to drink wine before dinner because where I live there is no law against drinking wine, although I do not have any such legal liberty when I visit an Islamic country that prohibits drinking alcoholic beverages. (2) A legal claim is the logical correlative of a corresponding legal duty of some second party. Person P has a legal claim against person Q that Q do act A if and only if Q has a legal duty to P to do act A. Paradigmatically to say that a creditor has a legal claim to repayment against the debtor is simply to say that the debtor has a legal duty to repay the creditor. (3) A legal power is the ability to bring about some change in the legal situation by performing some operative action. Thus P has the legal power to effect some legal consequence C if and only if were P to perform operative act A, then C would be in effect. For example, to say that I have the legal power to give one of my books to a colleague means simply that if I do something like handing a book to my colleague and say "here, this is yours," then my legal property right in the book is thereby extinguished and my colleague becomes the legal owner of the book. (4) A legal immunity from some legal consequence C is the logical correlative of the absence of any legal power of one or more second parties to effect C. I have a legal immunity from losing my ownership by any unilateral act of another such as grabbing my book and saying "Now this is mine." Possession may be nine-tenths of the law, but it is not the whole story.

One might be tempted to identify each of these legal positions with a legal right, but this would be a misunderstanding. H. L. A. Hart argues that:

> But it is not at all clear that lawyers or anyone else would speak of a completely naked or unprotected liberty as a right, or that any useful purpose would be served if they did. The state of nature, if worth describing at all, can be described adequately in other terms. As far as organized society is concerned there would be something not only strange but misleading in describing naked liberties as rights: if we said, for example, that a class of helots whom free citizens were allowed to treat as they wished or interfere with at will, yet had rights to do those acts which they were not forbidden by the law to do. All the very important points in Bentham's doctrine distinguishing between liberty-rights and rights correlative to obligations can be preserved by treating bilateral liberty as an essential *element* in the analysis of liberty-rights but only constituting a liberty-right in conjunction with a perimeter of some protecting obligations or duties. (Hart 1982, p. 173)

Again suppose that the creditor's legal right to repayment consists in nothing more her legal claim against the debtor that he repay her. It would then be possible for the debtor to extinguish her claim merely by saying "I hereby cancel my debt to you." Of course this is not possible because in any legal system in which legal claims are real rights, the debtor has no legal power to cancel his debts in this manner. What examples such as these show is that it is a mistake to identify a legal right with a single legal position because any real right holds against one or more second parties and it requires more than a single legal position to hold firm against others.

One understands legal rights best by conceiving of them as complexes of Hohfeldian legal positions that, if respected, give dominion over some core position upon the right-holder in any confrontation one or more second parties. Dominion is here understood to involve both freedom and control. A few examples should help to clarify this abstract formulation. (1) As one would expect, the core element in my legal liberty-right to drink wine before dinner is my legal liberty of drinking wine before dinner. However, this constitutes a real legal right only in conjunction with a variety of associated legal positions. These include duties of noninterference such as the legal duties of others not to restrain my motions by force and not to deprive me of my property without my consent. Since it is not a mandatory right, it also includes a liberty of not drinking wine before dinner if I choose not to do so. Similarly (2) the core of the creditor's legal claim-right to repayment is simply her legal claim against the debtor that he repay her the amount due by the due date. But this legal claim holds against the relevant second party, the debtor, only because the creditor also has a legal immunity against having her claim cancelled by any unilateral act by the debtor or, in fact, any other person who might presume to intervene on the debtor's behalf. Moreover, the creditor's right typically also includes her legal power to cancel the debt and her bilateral legal liberty to do so or not do so as she chooses. Thus, it is these associated legal positions that together confer dominion, freedom and control, over the defining core of this legal right upon the right-holder. Again (3) my legal power-right to give one of my books to a colleague consists of more than my legal power to do so. Associated legal positions include my bilateral legal liberty to exercise or not exercise this core legal power as I choose and my claim to noninterference against anyone who might force me to exercise it against my will. Lastly (4) although the defining core of my legal immunity-right against being deprived of my property right in my book is simply my immunity against losing my property right by any unilateral act of another, the full right involves other essential legal positions. These include my legal power to transfer ownership to some second party, my legal liberty to exercise or not exercise this legal power as I choose and duties of others not to force me to exercise it against my will. To my mind some such Hohfeldian analysis of legal rights is most useful for the purposes of legal theory. (Wellman 1985, pp. 121–158)

This conception of rights is readily applicable to other species of institutional rights such as the rights of students under the rules and regulations of a College or University and even the morality rights conferred upon the members of some society by its code of moral rules. More controversially, I have argued elsewhere that there are non-institutional moral analogues of the legal positions distinguished by Hohfeld. Thus, I have the moral power of creating a moral duty to meet a colleague for lunch at the Faculty Club by promising to do so. By this act I also confer upon my college a moral claim that I meet her for lunch at the agreed time. However, if my colleague later releases me from my promise, then I have a moral liberty to refrain from meeting her at the Faculty Club at the agreed time. If such moral positions do exist, then presumably one can and should interpret non-institutional moral rights as complexes of moral positions that, if respected, confer dominion over some defining core upon the right-holder in face of one or more second parties who might refuse or resist her attempt to exercise or enjoy her right. I will presuppose this general Hohfeldian conception of rights in what follows.

2 Constitutional Rights

What distinguishes constitutional rights from other kinds of rights? Constitutional rights of the sort under consideration here are one species of legal rights; they are rights conferred by the constitutional law of a nation state. Because constitutional law can be grounded on a variety of legally authoritative sources, they may, but need not be, mentioned in or implied by a document such as the *United States Constitution*. And because constitutional law is that special body of law that allocates the sovereign power of a nation state, they have some role in that allocation.

By their very nature, constitutional rights are fundamental. They are elements in the foundation of the legal system of a nation state because they function in the identification and definition of the law-making powers and, thereby, determine the validity of all the bodies of national law built upon them.

As real rights, constitutional rights are justiciable, appropriate for judicial interpretation and application. This normally implies that the holder of a constitutional right has the power to petition some court or analogous institution to prevent the violation of or obtain a remedy in the event of violation of such a right. Often other parties will also have standing to challenge some alleged exercise or enjoyment or infringement of a constitutional right.

Because constitutional rights are designed to be stable, they are usually, but not always, entrenched. However, this entrenchment may be more or less firm in two respects. First, the judicial review of legislation regarding its constitutionality may be stronger or weaker. Thus, if the United States Supreme Court holds that some statute is unconstitutional, it becomes null and void and not subject to reenactment by Congress. However, if a Canadian court finds that some statute violates the *Canadian Charter of Rights and Freedoms*, the federal Parliament or a provincial legislature that enacted that statute may expressly declare that it shall remain operative notwithstanding. Second, it may be more or less difficult to extinguish or restrict a right enumerated in some constitutional document. Historically the *United States Constitution* has been amended only by a two-thirds vote in both Houses of Congress followed by ratification by the legislatures of three-fourths of the states. But the power of the Israeli Knesset to alter the *Basic Law: Human Dignity and Liberty* (1992) is restricted only by Section 8 limiting the purpose of any law or regulation that violates any of the rights protected by this basic law and Section 12 that forbids the government to weaken any of these rights merely by enacting an emergency regulation.

In order to understand how constitutional rights function in any national legal system, one must distinguish at least between liberty-rights, claim-rights, power-rights and immunity-rights. A few examples from United States law will illustrate these four modalities. (1) The First Amendment to the *United States Constitution* guarantees the liberty-right to freedom of speech of individual citizens and corporate bodies such as newspapers or motion-picture companies. Its defining core is the legal liberty of saying, writing or publishing any opinion one wishes. Natural or artificial persons have this liberty simply because almost any law or regulation that would purport to deny this freedom would be null and void. The word "almost" indicates that this liberty is not unlimited. It does not protect libel, seditious speech, or speech that creates a clear and present danger of inciting violence. As a real right, this core legal liberty is protected by associated legal positions. More important are the legal immunity against any legislation that would deny the exercise of this legal liberty and the legal power of petitioning a court for a remedy in the event of prior restraint of free speech or punishment for having spoken freely.

(2) The Fifth Amendment confers on individual citizens and corporate bodies of citizens the claim-right to just compensation in the event that their property is taken for public use. Its core is obviously the legal claim of citizens or groups of citizens to be paid just compensation for any property taken for public use. Originally this constitutional right held only against the federal government, but after the incorporation of the Bill of Rights into the Fourteenth Amendment, it now holds also against state and local governments. Associated legal positions include the legal power to petition a court in the event that a governmental agency takes one's property without fulfilling its duty to pay just compensation, the legal liberty to exercise this power

of petition if one chooses, and the legal immunity against having one's core claim to just compensation extinguished by any federal or state legislation.

(3) In any democracy, citizens have a power-right to vote in elections for most of the basic public offices. In the *United States Constitution* this right is conferred piecemeal by Article I, Section 2, Clause 1 (for the House of Representatives), the Seventeenth Amendment (for the Senate) and the Twelfth Amendment together with the constitutional convention that electors will vote for the persons chosen by the voters in their respective states (for the Presidency). The state constitutions have a variety of provisions that confer the right to vote on their resident citizens. The defining core of this right is the legal power of voting in federal, state or local elections. This is a power, rather than a liberty, because the act of voting changes the legal situation by increasing the number of votes for some candidate for public office. However, one associated position in this power-right is the bilateral liberty to exercise or not exercise the power to vote as one chooses. (In Australia the right to vote does not include this bilateral liberty because its citizens have a legal duty to vote). Other important associated positions are the citizen's legal immunity against having his or her right to vote denied or abridged on account of race, color, or previous condition of servitude (conferred by the Fifteenth Amendment) or by any legislation that denies the equal protection of the laws (the Fourteenth Amendment).

(4) In some nations, citizens have an immunity right against double jeopardy, against being tried twice for the same offence. In the United States this right is conferred by the Fifth Amendment and therefore originally held only against the federal government and regarding only the most serious offences. However, a series of decisions by the Supreme Court have now extended this right to hold against state governments and regarding any crime or misdemeanor. (Library of Congress 1973, pp. 1093–1105) In addition to its defining core immunity, this constitutional right against double jeopardy includes a legal claim against the federal and all state courts not to be tried twice for the same offence, and a power to petition a court to have any second conviction declared null and void.

These examples show that not all constitutional rights are claim-rights or even neatly divided between the two categories of rights and freedoms. There are at least four species of civil rights—liberty-rights, claim-rights, power-rights and immunity-rights. In another respect these four examples all fall within a single class of rights, civil rights. They are rights possessed by persons, either individual persons or corporate bodies of persons. However, constitutional law also, and primarily, confers rights upon individuals or corporate bodies of persons as officials in the government. These might best be termed "governmental rights" because they are rights a natural or artificial person possesses that authorize or enable them to govern in some society. Examples are not hard to find.

(1) The President of the United States has a constitutional liberty-right to detain and confine persons suspected or convicted of committing an act that violates federal law. Were a private person or most other public officials to detain someone against his or her will, this would, with the exception of a citizen's arrest, be either a crime or a tort or both. But the President has a legal liberty of so doing by virtue of his or her duty under Article II, Section 3 to "take care that the laws be faithfully

executed." (Library of Congress 1973, pp. 549–551) This duty implies the legal liberty of doing, through his or her agents, whatever is necessary to enforce the law of the land including detaining and confining persons. The defining core liberty in this right is supplemented at least by the legal duties of others not to prevent or hinder the President from exercising this liberty to detain and confine, the legal power to delegate this liberty to his or her subordinates and an immunity against having it extinguished by any federal or state legislation.

(2) Article I, Section 6 of the *United States Constitution* confers upon Senators and Representatives a claim-right to compensation for their services. This claim-right holds against the Treasury of the United States. It is protected at least by an immunity against having this claim extinguished by any act of the President or any of his or her agents.

(3) The President has a bilateral power-right conferred by Article I, Section 2 to sign or veto bills passed by the House of Representatives and the Senate. Presumably others have a duty not to coerce the President to either sign or veto against his or her will and certainly he or she has both the liberty to exercise this power as he or she chooses and an immunity against having the core power to sign or veto extinguished by any act of Congress.

(4) Members of Congress have an immunity-right against criminal prosecution or civil suits for any speech or debate in either House conferred by Article I, Section 6 of the *United States Constitution*. Associated elements include the legal power to petition a court to quash any indictment or dismiss any suit brought against one for anything one said or wrote while acting as a member of Congress, a bilateral liberty to exercise or not exercise this power as one chooses and an immunity against having the core immunity extinguished by any act of any branch of the United States government.

In addition to constitutional rights that individuals possess as officials, there are constitutional rights of corporate bodies of officials. For example, (1) the Department of Justice has the liberty-right of exercising the delegated Presidential liberty to detain and confine persons suspected or convicted of committing an illegal act. Although the President could withdraw this liberty-right, the Justice Department is immune from having it extinguished by federal or state legislation.

(2) One of the most important constitutional rights of Congress is the power-right to regulate commerce "among the several States" conferred upon it by Article I, Section 8, Clause 3 of the *United States Constitution*. The defining core of this right is the legal power to pass bills that regulate interstate commerce, although these become laws only if and when signed by the President or, in the event of a veto, passed with a two-thirds majority in both Houses of Congress. An associated legal position is the liberty of Congress to exercise this core power as it chooses. Although any State has the legal power to challenge the constitutionality of any law that presumes to regulate interstate commerce on the grounds that it is ultra vires, Congress has an immunity against having its core power extinguished or diminished by any State action.

(3) The States (and their residents) have an immunity-right against export duties. This right is conferred by Article I, Section 9, clause 5 of the *United States*

Constitution. Its defining core is an immunity against any tax or duty levied by the federal government on any article exported from any State. Associated positions include the power of petitioning a court to declare any federal legislation imposing an export tax or duty unconstitutional, a liberty of exercising or not exercising this power as they choose, and an immunity from any federal legislation that would purport to extinguish or limit this right.

These are only a few of the constitutional rights in the legal system of the United States, but they are sufficient to illustrate three classifications that are relevant to our present purposes. First, civil rights are constitutional rights individual persons or groups of persons possess by virtue of their membership in a nation state and governmental rights are rights an individual official or corporate body of officials possess by virtue of holding some public office in a government. Second, individual constitutional rights are rights that a natural person possesses either as one subject to a legal system or as a holder of public office and corporate constitutional rights are rights that some corporate body holds either as a governing institution or a private organization. Third, within each of these four classes of constitutional rights, one should distinguish between liberty-rights, claim-rights, power-rights and immunity rights because the modality of any constitutional right determines how it can function in any legal system.

3 Why Both?

In the United States, books and journal articles on constitutional rights typically treat only civil rights. Indeed, in this legal literature the expressions "constitutional rights" and "civil rights" are virtually synonymous. There are genuine advantages to defining one's subject-matter in this way. It provides a more limited and homogeneous subject-matter. This in turn enables one to achieve a higher level of competence concerning one's subject and to avoid complexities that arise from the relationships of disparate bodies of law.

Why, then, might one choose to expand the scope of constitutional rights to include both the civil rights of private persons and the governmental rights of public officials and governing institutions? One reason is to avoid a common conceptual misunderstanding. Lawyers and philosophers of law often assume that the rights of private citizens and the powers of public officials are fundamentally different because rights and powers belong to distinct conceptual categories. To be sure, not all powers constitute rights. Nevertheless, some powers are defining cores of power-rights on any broad Hohfeldian conception of the nature of rights. And adopting this conceptual framework for the analysis of legal and moral rights enables one to understand how rights really function in the law of any nation state.

The primary function of civil rights in the constitutional law of any nation state is to limit the governmental rights of those who govern the society. This is because the most important reason to include civil rights in any constitution is to protect those subject to the law from the abuse of public power. Hence, one can understand

and evaluate the civil rights in a national constitution only in relationship to the rights it confers on the governing institutions and officials in that society. To understand how civil rights limit governmental rights one must see how they are applied in legal practice. And to evaluate civil rights one must balance the reasons that justify their recognition and maintenance against the reasons that justify the recognition and enforcement of the governmental rights they limit.

Civil rights and governmental rights are real rights only insofar as they are applied in the legal practices of a nation state. And the practice of the courts clearly shows how the constitutional rights of private persons and the constitutional rights of the government are essentially related. For example, in *Schenck v. United States* the Supreme Court established the clear and present doctrine by balancing the defendant's right to freedom of speech conferred by the First Amendment against the right of Congress to provide for the common welfare conferred by Article I, Section 8, Clause 1 of the United States Constitution.

> Words which, ordinarily and in many places, would be within the freedom of speech protected by the first Amendment may become subject to prohibition when of such a nature and used in such circumstances as to create a clear and present danger that they will bring about the substantive evils which Congress has a right to prevent. (Supreme Court 1919, p. 48)

And in *Hamdi v. Rumsfeld*, the Supreme Court weighed the President's right to detain persons claimed to be enemy combatants against the individual's civil right to liberty.

> It is beyond question that substantial interests lie on both sides of the scale in this case. Hamdi's "private interest...affected by the official action," *ibid.*, is the most elemental of liberty interests—the interest in being free from physical detention by one's own government.... (Supreme Court 2004, p. 52)

And

> On the other side of the scale are the weighty and sensitive governmental interests in ensuring that those who have in fact fought with the enemy during a war do not return to battle against the United States. As discussed above, supra, at 10, the law of war and the realities of combat may render such detention both necessary and appropriate, and our due process analysis need not blink at those realities. (Supreme Court 2004, p. 531)

In real law, civil rights and governmental rights are mutually limiting. Therefore, one can fully understand civil rights only in relationship to governmental rights.

Any nation state needs sufficient authority to pursue the most important purposes of government effectively and at the same time the governed urgently need protection from the most serious abuses of governmental power. Hence, in determining how to best meet these two needs, one must balance the reasons for instituting any governmental right against the reasons for limiting it by one or more civil rights. To assess how this can best be accomplished, one must understand the nature and value of both civil rights and governmental rights. Hence, the justifications of civil rights and governmental rights are interdependent.

For example, the reasons that justify the civil right to freedom of speech are essentially related to the reasons that justify the governmental right to prevent substantive harms.

Freedom of speech is needed for the self-realization of the individual person, for one develops a full personality and character by self-expression in word and action. Freedom of speech is also a necessary means to the discovery and confirmation of truth in the sciences and more generally in all knowledge. Hence, it is needed to provide private citizens and public officials with the information they need to best perform their civic duties. And it enables citizens to hold public officials accountable for the exercise of their governmental power-rights. On the other hand, the government needs the right to prevent substantive harms to those subject to its laws to ensure its moral legitimacy. Because any effective government requires the use of coercion to enforce its laws and coercion is prima facie wrong, a government is legitimate only if it exercises its power-rights in a way that protects its subjects from greater harms, especially the violation of their civil and human rights. And the strength of this reason for establishing a governmental right to prevent substantive harms depends in large measure upon the value of the civil and moral rights this governmental right enables it to protect. Thus the moral justifications of these civil and governmental rights are interdependent.

Similarly, the reasons that justify the governmental right to detain individuals who are claimed to be enemy combatants are essentially related to the reasons that justify the civil right to liberty. The primary duty of any legitimate government is to protect its citizens from military attack because any such attack threatens the rights of its subjects to life, personal security, property and even liberty. Hence, as Commander-in-Chief the President ought to have a constitutional duty to prevent armed attacks upon the citizens. Presumably any duty-bearer ought to have whatever rights are necessary to carry out his or her duties. And detaining those who may well be enemy combatants is necessary to fulfill the duty to prevent armed attacks upon the citizens. Hence, the President ought to have a constitutional right to detain such persons. Central to the civil right to liberty is the freedom to move about without interference. Hence it implies the right not to be confined or detained. One reason that justifies this aspect of the civil right to liberty is that detention in jail, prison or comparable facility are typically harsh and impose suffering upon the inmates. More importantly, detainment disrupts and devalues one's personal relationships with family or friends. It also prevents one from pursuing most of the long-term projects that give meaning and value to one's life. Accordingly, the justification of the governmental right to detain persons claimed to be enemy combatants depends upon the reasons that justify the civil right to liberty and any other rights threatened by attacks by enemy forces.

Finally, this interdependence of the reasons that justify civil rights and governmental rights enhances the normative coherence of the legal system. Neil MacCormick argues that legal coherence requires more than mere non-contradiction. It requires that laws hang together or make sense as a whole. As an example, he refers to Italian laws that some time ago imposed different speed limits for different makes and types of cars. He then asks:

> Do such laws fail to make sense? And if they so fail, why do they so fail? My answer to that is that they fail to make sense if there is no common value which the enactment of such laws serves....Consider: there are three ends which statutes limiting driving speeds may promote, all of which we may suppose to be of serious social value: the safety of road users; economy in the use of fuel; and prevention of excessive wear and tear of road surfaces. If the colour of cars is purely a matter of taste,...it seems doubtful whether any speed limit differential between differently coloured cars could possibly subserve effectively any such end as those envisaged above. (MacCormick 1984, pp. 235–236)

Regarding the laws of a legal system as a whole, he then explains:

> I conclude that the coherence of norms is a matter of their 'making sense' by being rationally related as a set, instrumentally or intrinsically, either to the realization of some common value or values; or to the fulfillment of some common principle or principles. At the level of the highest-order principles or values there is the further requirement of coherence: that, after allowance for the fulfillment of priority rankings of principles and/or values we consider that in their totality they express a satisfactory form of life, and one that it would be possible for human beings, as human beings are, to live. (MacCormick 1984, p. 238)

I would add only that it should be a possible and satisfactory form of life for human beings living in society with one another. The interdependence of the reasons that justify civil and governmental rights, and the balancing of various values that this requires, ensures that a legal system as a whole promotes a valuable form of life for persons living in society with one another.

Therefore, it seems worthwhile to supplement the traditional treatises that limit their discussion of constitutional rights to civil rights by a publication that considers governmental rights as well as civil rights to be constitutional rights. Moreover, this seems entirely appropriate because both classes of rights are conferred by the constitutional law of a nation state or some subordinate unit in that nation.

References

Alexander, Larry (2011) What Are Constitutions and What Should (and Can) They Do? In What Should Constitutions Do? Ellen Frankel Paul, Fred D. Miller and Jeffrey Paul (eds.). Cambridge University Press, Cambridge.

Hart, H. L. A. (1982) Essays on Bentham. Clarendon Press. Oxford.

Hohfeld, Wesley Newcomb (1919) Fundamental Legal Conceptions as Applied in Judicial Reasoning. Yale University Press, New Haven CT.

Library of Congress (1973) The Constitution of the United States of America: Analysis and Interpretation. U. S. Government Printing Office. Washington D. C.

MacCormick, Neil (1984), Coherence in Legal Reasoning. In Theory of Legal Science. Alexander Peczenik, Lars Lindahl, and Bert Van Roermund, (eds). D. Reidel Publishing Company. Dordrecht.

Supreme Court (1919) Schenck v. United States. 249 U.S. 47.

Supreme Court (2004) Hamdi v. Rumsfeld. 542 U.S. 507.

Wellman, Carl (1985) A Theory of Rights. Rowman & Allanheld. Totowa NJ.

Chapter 3
Constitutional Institutions

Abstract Because the primary function of a constitution is to constitute a government, the primary constitutional rights in any national legal system are the rights of its governing institutions. This chapter provides a critical assessment of the reasons for and against the institutions of federalism, the separation of powers, a presidential system, a bicameral legislature, exclusion, cloture, and judicial review. It ends by distinguishing between more and less basic justifying reasons.

Although broadening one's conception of constitutional rights to include both governmental and civil rights is potentially valuable, it defines a subject so broadly as to challenge one's competence and tempt one to superficial treatment. Therefore, in any discussion of this topic, one needs to focus on some limited dimensions of this subject matter. I will focus upon constitutional rights in the legal system of the United States and the moral reasons that might justify them. However, any justification of a constitutional right must recognize that there are somewhat different rights that might have been chosen and, thereby, requires some consideration of alternative constitutional rights in other legal systems. Moreover, I will leave the most detailed and precise interpretation of those rights I discuss to lawyers and emphasize instead the moral dimensions of constitutional rights.

Because the primary function of a constitution is to constitute a government, the primary constitutional rights in any nation state are the rights of the governing institutions established by its legal system. Hence, let us turn our attention first to corporate governmental constitutional rights in the United States. These are the rights conferred by United States constitutional law upon governing organizations such as the national and state governments as complex wholes and, within each, their respective administrative agencies, legislative bodies or courts.

1 Federalism

The *United States Constitution* establishes a federal government, that is, a complex government in which the national sovereignty is divided between a national government and the governments of the several states. It does this by a conferring a variety of corporate constitutional rights upon national institutions and other such rights

C. Wellman, *Constitutional Rights -What They Are and What They Ought to Be*,
Law and Philosophy Library 115, DOI 10.1007/978-3-319-31526-3_3

upon state institutions. A description of a small sample of these rights should be sufficient to indicate how federalism is built into constitutional law. This should in turn enable one to assess the moral justification, or lack of it, of federalism.

Article I, Section 8, Clause 1 of the *United States Constitution* begins: "The Congress shall have the Power to lay and collect Taxes…." This confers upon the national legislature the constitutional power-right to tax individual persons and private corporations throughout the territory of the United States. This is a power-right because its defining core is the legal power of Congress to enact legislation requiring individuals or corporations to pay the amounts prescribed therein and, through agencies to which it has delegated its constitutional power, to collect taxes. Like any real right, it includes more than its core legal position, in this case at least a legal liberty to exercise its power to tax and a legal immunity against having its power to lay and collect taxes extinguished by any individual or institution.

Article I, Section 8, Clause 3 of the *Constitution* reads in part: "To regulate Commerce with foreign Nations, and among the several States…." This famous, or infamous, interstate commerce clause clearly confers upon the national Congress the power-right to enact legislation that imposes requirements upon all those who engage in interstate commerce. However, it has been interpreted by the United States Supreme Court to authorize Congress to enact laws that are only indirectly, if at all, related to commercial activity, for example the operation of motels and local restaurants (*Heart of Atlanta Motel v. United States*, 379 U.S. 241 (1964)). And although the police power is for the most part reserved to the states, the Supreme Court upheld, among others, the Lindberg law punishing the interstate transportation of kidnapped persons. In addition to its defining constitutional power, this right includes at least the legal liberties of exercising its power to regulate and a legal immunity against having this power extinguished.

Article II, Section 2, Clause 1 begins: "The President shall be Commander in Chief of the Army and Navy of the United States…." Together with Article I, Section 8, Clause 1 that reads in part: "Congress shall have the power to…provide for the common Defence," this clause implies the general power-right of the national government to create military forces and to employ them to defend the vital interests of the United States. Although the full extent of the President's legal power-right as commander-in-chief is controversial, no constitutional lawyer could deny that some such power-right exists. Presumably it also includes at least the legal liberty of exercising this military power and an immunity against having it extinguished by Congress or any other national or state institution.

Section 1 of the 14th Amendment reads in part: "No State shall make or enforce any law which shall abridge the privileges or immunities of citizens of the United States; nor shall any State deprive any person of life, liberty, or property, without due process of law; nor deny to any person within its jurisdiction the equal protection of the laws." Then Section 5 confers upon Congress the power-right "to enforce, by appropriate legislation, the provisions of this article."

Together these two sections confer upon the national government the constitutional power-right to enact and enforce criminal legislation to protect individuals from state violations of their privileges or immunities as citizens or their civil rights to due process and the equal protection of the law. Today the largest part of the national criminal law that is constitutionally valid consists of enforcements of these civil rights.

Article VI, Clause 2 reads in part: "This Constitution and the Laws of the United States which shall be made in Pursuance thereof…shall be the supreme Law of the Land…." This provision confers upon the national government an immunity-right against having any of its legislation nullified by any state or combination of states. Although the South Carolina Ordinance of Nullification of 1832 declared the United States tariffs of 1828 and 1832 unconstitutional and therefore null and void and the states' rights doctrine of nullification persisted until the Civil War, it is now a dead issue. In addition to its core immunity against nullification, this national constitutional right includes a liberty to disregard or even resist any attempted state nullification and a power of the United States Supreme Court to declare any state legislation purporting to nullify a national law unconstitutional.

As federal, the *United States Constitution* also confers rights upon the several states. Because Articles I and II contain no clauses conferring the police power upon either the national legislature or the President, and among the limitations upon state powers in Article I, Section 10 none prohibits the traditional police power of the states, presumably the states retain the right to police their respective territories. This is confirmed by the 10th Amendment that reads: "The powers not delegated to the United States by the Constitution, nor prohibited by it to the States, are reserved to the States respectively, or to the people." The defining core of this state right is the legal power to place restraints upon the personal freedom and property of persons for the protection of public safety, health and morals or the promotion of the public welfare. As usual, it also contains the legal liberty to exercise this constitutional power and an immunity against having this power extinguished by any action of the national government or any other state.

Similarly because the states have traditionally levied and collected taxes within their respective territories and Article I, Section 10 of the *Constitution* contains no prohibition of their doing so, presumably the states retain their power-right to tax, Again, this is confirmed by the 10th Amendment. The defining core of this constitutional right is the legal power to lay and collect taxes, and it also includes a liberty of exercising this power and an immunity against its extinguishment.

Article II, Section 2, Clause 1 begins: "The President shall be Commander in Chief of the Army and Navy of the United States, and of the Militia of the several States, when called into the actual Service of the United States…." And the 2nd Amendment declares: "A well regulated Militia, being necessary to the security of a free State, the right of the people to keep and bear arms shall not be infringed." Although the interpretation of the right of the people to keep and bear arms remains controversial, there is clearly a constitutional right of the several states to have militias. The core of this right is the power to create and support militias. Presumably it also contains a legal liberty to use these militias to preserve the security of their respective populations and an immunity against having this power extinguished by any action of the national government.

Article I, Section 9, Clause 1 reads in part: "The Migration or Importation of such Persons as any of the States now existing shall think proper to admit, shall not be prohibited by the Congress prior to the Year one thousand eight hundred and eight…." Although this provision of the *United States Constitution* is now a dead letter, until the civil war it conferred an immunity-right upon the original thirteen states against any national legislation that might limit their liberty to admit persons, whether slaves or free persons, to their respective territories.

These are only a sample of the corporate constitutional rights in United States law. But they are sufficient to illustrate the way in which the *United States Constitution* constitutes a federal government by dividing the corporate governmental power-rights between national and state institutions, each protected against the other by constitutional immunity-rights. One might ask, and some do, whether our constitution establishes the proper balance between the governing powers of our national and state institutions and whether it defines the power-rights it confers in the best manner. However, any comprehensive answers to these questions would be far too detailed and voluminous for this chapter. Let us instead ask simply whether a federal government is more justified than the alternatives for the United States under present circumstances.

One alternative is a confederation, a government in which a number of states retain their sovereignty but confer important powers on central governing institution in order to promote their shared purposes. The classic example is the Confederation of the thirteen original American states after the revolution but before the ratification of the *United States Constitution*. The European Union is a contemporary example. Many argue that a federal government is preferable to a confederation because of its greater military strength. Thus K. C Wheare explains:

> Communities have been led to desire union from a variety of reasons. But in the modern federations some factors seem always to be present. A sense of military insecurity and of the consequent need for common defence; a desire to be independent of foreign powers, and a realization that only through union could independence be secured…. (Wheare 1946, p. 37)

And William Riker advances a general explanation of the origin and purpose of federalism in the same terms.

> The politicians who offer the bargain desire to expand their territorial control, usually either to meet an external military or diplomatic threat or to prepare for military or diplomatic aggression and aggrandizement….The politicians who accept the bargain, giving up some independence for the sake of union, are willing to do so because of some external military-diplomatic threat or opportunity. (Riker 1964, p. 12)

Military security does constitute a very valuable advantage of federalism over a confederate government when a sovereign state needs to meet serious military threats as the United States does today.

A federal government also seems more conducive to prosperity than a confederation. Alexander Hamilton suggests that this is uncontroversial.

> The importance of the Union, in a commercial light, is one of those points, about which there is least room to entertain a difference of opinion, and which has in fact commanded

> the most general assent of men, who have any acquaintance with the subject. This applies as well to our commerce with foreign countries, as with each other. (Hamilton 1961, p. 65)

Sujit Choudhry and Nathan Hume, among others, explain that "A federation also can be understood as a common market that is larger and more efficient than one in which international borders impede the flow of goods, services and capital." (Choudhry and Hume 2011, p. 360) Their language reminds one that the European Union, although a confederation, also provides a common market. However, the fact that the respective European states have independent, often conflicting, monetary policies, has led to a recent economic crisis approaching an economic breakdown. Very probably a federal government would have been able to regulate interstate commerce so that the euro would not be so seriously threatened by the economic policies of Greece, Spain and Italy. More generally, a federal government has greater capability than a confederation to foster economic growth and stability in a world of vastly expended international trade and international corporations.

A third advantage of a federal government over a confederation is its greater ability to reduce pollution and the consequent environmental damage. Although this is one of the most urgent contemporary problems, the individual sovereign states in a confederation have little interest in imposing costs upon their own industries that are polluting the atmosphere or streams of neighboring states and no ability at all to control pollution of their own territories but generated from other sovereign states in their confederation. There are, then, at least three important advantages of a federal government over a confederation for a number of contiguous states coexisting in our contemporary world.

However, it might well be that a unitary government, a government in which all the governing powers of a sovereign state belong to a single central government, would be even better able to promote these military, economic and environment goals than a federation. What, then, are the advantages of a federal government over a unitary government?

The traditional argument for a federal government rather than a unitary one is that the division of powers between the national government and the state or provincial governments will protect the liberty of the people because each level of government will have the power to prevent abuses by the other. Obviously a federal government is neither necessary nor sufficient to prevent the serious violation of individual rights. The United Kingdom, that has a unitary government, has for centuries respected the individual liberties of its subjects; and the Soviet Union during the regime of Joseph Stalin grossly violated human rights in spite of its federal constitution. But perhaps a properly constituted federation will by its very nature protect liberty. Because the *United States Constitution* reserves the police power to the states, the national government should not be able to tyrannize over its subjects by enacting arbitrary criminal statutes that oppress its opponents. And for those who regard this protection as inadequate, it includes the *Bill of Rights*. On the other hand, the state constitutions also contain bills of rights, and the 14th Amendment gives the national government the power to prevent the states from abridging the privileges or immunities of its citizens or depriving any person of life, liberty or property without due process of law or denying to any person the equal protection of the laws. However, William Riker observes that our federal government has not always ensured the benefits of liberty to its subjects. He even asserts regarding federalism that "The main beneficiary throughout American history has been the Southern whites, who have been given the freedom to oppress Negroes, first as slaves and later as a depressed caste." (Riker 1964, p. 152) In practice, the protection of liberty depends primarily, not on federalism, but on a democratic regime and a citizenry with a high respect for individual rights.

At this point, many could argue that a federal government will promote democracy much more than will a unitary government.

> Once formed, a classical federal system is believed to offer numerous advantages over a unitary state. For example, it is thought to bolster democracy by guaranteeing the existence of a tier of regional governments. It not only ensures another set of offices to elect and contest and thus increases the number of opportunities for political participation; it also improves the quality of political participation by empowering relatively small political communities, in which citizens are more likely to have more in common, individual votes and voices are likely to have more influence, and representatives are likely to be more responsive to their concerns in various ways. (Choudhry and Hume 2011, p. 360)

One might add that these regional governments improve representation by providing training grounds and stepping stones for those who may later represent their constituents in the national institutions. On the other hand, a unitary government, like that in France, can and often does include a tier of regional governments to encourage democratic citizenship and train leaders for national office. However, one should recognize that because the states in our federal government possess their own constitutions and independent legal powers, they offer more opportunities for serious political activity to their residents and are better training grounds for national office-holders.

Some argue that the division of powers within a federal government enables it to be more efficient than a unitary one.

> Classical federalism is also said to enhance efficiency in various ways. The existence of two tiers of government allows a diverse society to allocate responsibilities and assign liabilities in a manner that improves the quantity and quality of public goods by engineering a closer fit between those who benefit from them and those who bear the cost. Those goods like military defence, that the regions might fail to produce adequately can be assigned to the central government, while those that depend on local knowledge and preferences, like education and perhaps some aspects of environmental regulation, can be left to the regions.... (Choudhry and Hume 2011, p. 360)

Once more one must recognize that a unitary government of any considerable size can and probably will have both regional governments and a central government. Hence, it is hard to see how or why a federal government will necessarily be more efficient than a unitary one.

A fourth alleged advantage of a federal government over a unitary one is that it offers more secure regional governments to experiment with differing solutions to public problems.

> Public problems are sufficiently complex, and policy-makers' judgment is sufficiently fallible, that rarely is the one right answer obvious--even in the rare case where a single solution, once discovered, turns out to fit every State. As States or member countries innovate, their experience informs not just their own policy choices but those of other States as well. The freer regions are to experiment independently, the deeper will be the common well of expertize about what works and what doesn't. (Donahue and Pollack 2001, p. 75)

Federal governments give greater freedom of independent experimentation because the powers of the regional governments are not merely delegated from a central government that limits and can even withdraw them, but conferred by a constitution that divides the powers of governing between two levels of government and cannot be changed by any unilateral act of the national government. Contemporary examples in the United States come readily to mind. Although the federal law defines marriage as a union of one male and one female, several states have recognized same-sex marriages. And although our national "war on drugs" policy has long been a dismal failure, federal law still criminalizes both the provision and the possession of marijuana, while some states are permitting the medical use of that drug. What is relevant here is not whether these state experiments are improvements in our legal system but that federalism enables them to experiment more freely than would be possible in a unitary government.

A related advantage of our federal system is that it consists of two layers of constitutional law. Each state has its own constitution, often containing provisions similar to those in the *United States Constitution*, and its own system of state courts. Therefore, legal issues of constitutional significance often originate in state courts and the reasoning of state judges provides plausible arguments to enrich the reasoning of federal judges when they must decide similar cases.

Finally, a federal government may be better able than a unitary one to protect diversity in a pluralistic society.

> Typically, federal arrangements allow a minority within a large domain to be a majority within a smaller, territorial sub-unit. Within the sub-unit, that minority-turned-majority can exercise a range of powers to protect its special needs and promote its special interests (be they linguistic, religious, ethnic, cultural, or economic); and the sub-units themselves, or the members thereof, are entitled to various forms of representation in, or influence over, federal institutions at the center. (Norman 1994, p. 79)

Although a unitary government can and sometimes will delegate legislative and other powers to regional sub-units, as the United Kingdom has delegated limited legislature powers to Scotland, Wales and Northern Ireland, these powers are not fully secure because they are subject to parliamentary control. The ability of a federal government to protect diverse segments of its society is sometimes an important advantage over a unitary government. However, this is true only when the internal minorities are for the most part located within distinct regions of the national territory. This may have been the case in the United States when the Southern slave states had very different social and economic institutions from those in the Northern free states, but these conditions no longer exist.

Turning to the other side of the ledger, are there any serious disadvantages of a federal government compared to a unitary one? Wayne J. Norman, an advocate of federalism for the protection of national minorities, recognizes that "...by according majoritarian powers to a national minority within a sub-unit, a federal system almost inevitably creates new minorities (for example, those who are not members of the federally protected national minority) within the same sub-unit." (Norman 1994, p. 80) And William H. Riker reminds us regarding federalism that "The main beneficiary throughout American history has been the Southern whites, who have been given the freedom to oppress Negroes, first as slaves and later as a depressed caste." (Riker 1964, p. 152) Hence, a federal government, in contrast to a unitary one, gives regional governing institutions the power to violate the moral and civil rights of members of some minorities. However, this power is limited in the United States by its constitution civil rights such as those in our Fourteenth Amendment.

A second disadvantage of a federal government is that its division of powers between a national government and its regional governments motivates a race to the bottom regarding welfare programs to meet the needs of the impoverished. First, the national government will shift its responsibilities regarding poverty to the regional governments because:

> National politicians can get credit for cutting government expenditure and avoid being blamed for ineffective poverty programs that help those who seem undeserving. The problems of meeting the genuine needs of the poor and unfortunate are left to governors, mayors, and other state and local officials. (Peterson 1995, pp. 180–181)

Unfortunately the regional governments lack the resources to fund poverty programs adequately because in a federal system:

> Considered "horizontally," or in terms of the relationships between state governments, the multiplicity of states and the constitutionally guaranteed right of citizens to relocate from one state to another, to trade goods and services, and to shift capital across state borders results in a vigorous competition among the states for mobile business investment and taxpayers. Such interstate competition constrains state taxation, spending, and administrative expenses. (Briffault 1994, p. 1314)

However, a unitary national government might be similarly motivated to shift the burden of poverty programs to its regional governments.

Everything considered, is a federal government better than either a confederation or a unitary government for the United States? In our contemporary world, it is preferable to a confederation primarily because it offers much greater military security and economic opportunity. It also has a greater ability to reduce environmental damage. However, a unitary government would have the same advantages over a confederation.

A more difficult question is whether a federal government is preferable to a unitary one. The traditional argument that by a constitutional division of powers between the central government and regional governments it protects liberty more securely is invalid. In fact, this division of powers often enables regional governments to oppress members of internal minorities. It is a social and political culture that respects individual rights that protects real liberty. Our federal government does provide a greater freedom for regional governments to experiment with solutions to pressing social problems than a unitary government would. And the parallel state constitutions and courts provide illuminating reasoning to assist federal judges in deciding analogous constitutional issues. Although it divides the powers of governing in a way that motivates the national politicians to impose the main burden of welfare programs upon the regional governments that because of the national mobility of people and corporations lack the resources to deal effectively with the needs of those in poverty, the same would be rue in a unitary government. The most important advantage of a federal government could be its ability to protect ethnic, religious or linguistic minorities threatened by the majority political forces in a diverse society. However, this advantage exists only when the members of any such minority are for the most part clustered within some well-defined region of the national territory which is not the case in the United States. On balance, it seems that a federal government is preferable to a unitary one in the United States under contemporary circumstances.

2 The Separation of Powers

The *United States Constitution* reflects two principles often believed necessary for the preservation of liberty. One is that the legislative, executive and judicial powers must be allocated to separate branches of the government. The other is that each branch of the government must have the power to check any attempted abuse of power by the other branches. Thus, as Madison explained, it ought to and did combine a partial separation of powers with a control by each of the branches over the others. (Madison 1961, p. 325) It attempts to respect these two principles primarily by the way in which it defines and confers corporate governmental power-rights.

Article I, Section 1 of the *Constitution* reads in part: "All legislative Powers herein granted shall be vested in a Congress of the United States…." Presumably if all legislative powers are vested in Congress, then the executive and judicial branches are granted no legislative powers. Hence, there seems to be a separation of powers in the national government. Then Section 8 defines the legislative power-rights conferred on Congress. The most important of these are the power-rights to lay and collect taxes (Clause 1), to borrow money (Clause 2), to regulate interstate commerce (Clause 3), to coin money (Clause 5), to establish post offices and post roads (Clause 7), to establish tribunals inferior to the supreme court (Clause 9), and to raise, support and make rules for armed forces (Clauses 12–14). However, any abuse of these powers could be checked by the power-right of the President to veto any bill passed by both houses of congress (Article 1, Section 7, Clause 2) or the power-right of the courts, especially the Supreme Court, to declare legislation null and void because contrary to the United States Constitution (implied by Article III, Section 1). Together these constitutional corporate power-rights are intended to provide a balance between the three branches of the government.

Article II, Section 1, Clause 1 begins: "The Executive Power shall be vested in a President of the United States of America." Because the President is not a member of Congress, this seems to establish a clear separation between the legislative and executive powers. Section 2 then defines the power-rights of the President. These include the power to act as commander-in-chief of the armed forces, to consult with the principal offices of the executive departments, to grant reprieves and pardons (Clause 1) to make treaties, and to appoint ambassadors, judges and other officers of the United States (Clause 2). However the power to act as commander-in-chief might be limited by the power of Congress to declare war (Article I, Section 8, Clause 11), the powers granted by Clause 2 are limited because they require the advice and consent of the Senate, and any abuse of the powers granted by either clause could be declared ultra vires by the courts because unconstitutional. Here again the *Constitution* establishes a separation of powers together with a system of checks and balances.

Article III, Section 1 reads in part: "The judicial Power of the United States shall be vested in one supreme Court, and in such inferior Courts as the Congress may from time to time ordain and establish." Thus, the judicial power-rights are conferred on corporate bodies, the courts, separate from the Congress and the President. Nevertheless, the President and Congress have some control over the courts because of the power of the President, with the advice and consent of the Senate, to appoint judges. However, their ability to check any abuse of power by the courts is very limited because judges hold office during good behavior rather than for limited terms and shall receive a compensation which shall not be diminished during their continuance in office (Section 1).

Is this allocation of governmental power-rights a good model for other nation states? Ought every national constitution to separate the legislative, executive and judicial powers and establish a system of checks and balances? Montesquieu, cited by Madison as an authority on the separation of powers, (Madison 1961, pp. 325–326) asserted that it is necessary for the protection of liberty.

> When the legislative and executive powers are united in the same person, or in the same body of magistrates, there can be no liberty....There would be an end to everything, were the same man or the same body, whether of nobles or of the people, to exercise those three powers, that of enacting laws, that of executing the public resolutions, and of trying the causes of individuals. (Montesquieu 1966, pp. 151–152)

However Bruce Ackerman suggests that laissez-faire adherents should not be entirely happy with the way in which American-style separation of powers has protected fundamental negative rights and adds that activist liberals recognize that government has no monopoly on tyranny and that citizens may be just as easily deprived of their birthright freedom by ignorance, poverty, and prejudice. Hence because government failures to act resulting from the separation of powers can threaten those fundamental interests, they will take an even dimmer view of any strict separation of powers. (Ackerman 2000, pp. 723–725) I would add that the United Kingdom, where the Prime Minister and members of the Cabinet are also members of Parliament, has an excellent record regarding the protection of fundamental rights. Therefore, the separation of powers is not necessary for, and may even inhibit, the full enjoyment of liberty.

Another reason to establish a separation of powers is that this might well enhance democracy. Were the legislative and executive powers conferred upon a single institution, even a bicameral legislature like Parliament, the people would elect its members in a single election. But when the executive and the legislature are separate institutions, then in a democratic regime, each will be selected in a separate election. (Ackerman 2000, pp. 640–644) This gives the people two opportunities to choose representatives who reflect their interests and two opportunities to hold them responsible. On the other hand, it requires two elections to replace officials who fail to meet the needs of the public, whereas in a parliamentary system a vote of no-confidence results in an election with a relatively clear focus on a controversial political issue.

A third justification for instituting a separation of powers is that this increases the competence of public officials. (Ackerman 2000, p. 640 and Vile 1998, p. 16) The executive, legislative and judicial functions of government require different abilities not often found in any one person or body of persons. An executive must be able to deal with the details of administration and in cases of emergency to act quickly and decisively. A legislator should act only after considered deliberation, take a more general view, and have the ability to weigh various, often conflicting, social values. A judge should have the ability to identify and interpret a variety of legal sources and to recognize both how general rules or principles apply to the case before the court and how any decision of the court will apply to future cases. This is probably the strongest reason in favor of the separation of powers, although how well it promotes professional competence in practice remains controversial.

Unfortunately, there are also reasons against incorporating any strict separation of powers into constitutional law. First, it is inapplicable to the modern bureaucratic state. Regarding the United Kingdom, H. W. R. Wade explains the necessity for Parliament to delegate legislative power to administrative agencies (Wade 1982, pp. 734–735) and report that:

> There is no more characteristic administrative activity than legislation. Measured merely by volume, more legislation is produced by the executive government than by the legislature. All the orders, rules, and regulations made by ministers, departments, and other bodies owe their legal force to Acts of Parliament, except in the few cases where the Crown retains original prerogative power. (Wade 1982, p. 733)

Bruce Ackerman maintains that the Founders of the *United States Constitution* failed to consider the problem of administrative legislation.

> But this silence should not be excused as an excuse for modern constitutional lawyers to ignore the problem or, worse yet, to imagine that the Founders resolved a problem that they did not know that they had. Constitutionalists should, therefore, extend their thinking to embrace the distinctive structural problems involved in controlling the fourth branch of government: the bureaucracy. (Ackerman 2000, p. 691)

Surely administrative agencies such as the Internal Revenue Service, the Social Security Administration, and many others must enact rules and regulations with the force of law. How, then, can there be any strict separation between the legislative and executive powers in the United States or, indeed, in any modern nation state?

Another alleged disadvantage of any strict separation between the executive and legislative branches of government is that it undermines administrative competence by politicizing the bureaucracy. Bruce Ackerman explains why this happens:

> With the presidency separated from congress, high-level bureaucrats must learn to survive in a force-field dominated by rival political leaders. Because both the president and congressional barons brandish powerful weapons for disciplining disobedient servants, only the most naïve bureaucrat would suppose that the ethic of "neutral competence" can serve as the best survival strategy....The politicization of the bureaucracy is enhanced by a second feature of the separationist system. As we have seen, one of its hallmarks is the possibility of entrenching legislation beyond the next electoral cycle. Although it may be tough to pass a law, it is also hard to change it. As an enacting coalition searches to protect its initiative from easy revision, personnel policy will be high on its list of entrenching devices. If the coalition can appoint ideological soul-mates to leading positions in the infant agency, these civil servants will be in a strategic position to fight a two-front war against future congresses and presidents. (Ackerman 2000, pp. 699–700)

Although this reasoning is cogent, one might wonder how seriously this disadvantage should be taken. One might even argue that any such politicization enhances democracy by rendering bureaucrats indirectly responsible to those who elect the President and the members of Congress.

Because the members of the Constitutional Convention of 1787 were so concerned with the threat of tyranny, the *United States Constitution* establishes both the separation of powers and a system of checks and balances. Consequently, as past and recent history remind us, political differences between the President and Congress far too often result in a deadlock during which no bill enacted by Congress can survive a presidential veto or an impasse between the two houses of Congress so that no proposed legislation can be passed by both the House and the Senate. Nor can the administration act to resolve any pressing social problem, for it lacks the required authority that Congress refuses to provide. Montesquieu recognized this possibility but assumed that reasonable politicians would resolve their disagreements.

> Here, then, is the fundamental constitution of the government we are treating of. The legislative body being composed of two parts, they check one another by the mutual privilege of rejecting. They are both restrained by the executive power, as the executive is by the legislative. These three powers should naturally form a state of repose or inaction. But as there is a necessity for movement in the course of human affairs, they are forced to move, but still in concert. (Montesquieu 1966, p. 160)

Unfortunately, he failed to recognize how often politicians persist in unreasonable actions. This may not seem so serious to those who believe that those govern best who govern least. But in our modern world where national governments have inevitably taken on a vast range of social responsibilities, governmental inaction will at best leave urgent needs unmet and at worst result in democratic disaster as when a frustrated president dissolves the legislature and installs himself as a dictator. The very real possibility of such deadlocks is the most serious reason not to embody the separation of powers together with a system of checks and balances in any national constitution.

On balance the disadvantages of the separation of powers considerably outweigh its advantages. It does little if anything for the preservation of liberty and may or may not enhance democracy. However, it may contribute a little to increase the competence of public officials by its specialization of labor. Nevertheless, any strict separation of powers is inapplicable to the modern bureaucratic nation state, probably undermines competence by politicizing the bureaucracy, and frequently results in socially harmful deadlock. This raises the question of whether a parliamentary system of government is preferable to a presidential one, the next subject for our consideration.

3 A Presidential System

The Administration of the United States consists of the President, the Vice-President, the Cabinet (the heads of the major departments), the departments and other administrative agencies, including the so-called independent agencies such as the Securities and Exchange Commission and the Federal Reserve System.

The President is the CEO of the federal government. Article II, Section I, Clause 1 of the *United States Constitution* begins with what appears to be a straightforward provision: "The executive Power is vested in the President of the United States of America." This suggests that the President has an unlimited constitutional power-right to administer the affairs of the federal government as he or she sees fit. Presumably, the President could and should delegate the relevant portions of this executive power to the several departments and agencies that carry out the administration of public affairs. If so, each federal agency would possess a constitutional power-right to administer some portion of the federal executive power. However, things are not that simple. The several departments and agencies are established by Congress and the functions of each are specified, typically very broadly, in the legislation that creates it. Therefore, the line between the constitutional power-right of each agency and its statutory power-right is often controversial.

The situation is complicated by another provision of the *Constitution*. Article II, Section 3 reads in part: "…he shall take Care that the Laws be faithfully executed…" This imposes upon the President a constitutional duty to take whatever actions are necessary to carry out and enforce federal constitutional and statute law, including the statutes that establish the federal administrative agencies. This implies that the President has whatever constitutional rights are necessary to carry out this duty. Presumably he or she could delegate relevant portions of these constitutional rights to the various administrative agencies.

The constitutional rights delegated by the President tend to predominate over the legislative limits on the statutory authority of the Department of Defense. Article II, Section 2, Clause 1 begins: "The President shall be Commander in Chief of the Army and Navy of the United States…." Although it is the Congress and not the President that has the constitutional power-right to declare war, Congress and the courts have generally been reluctant to restrict the actions of the President, the

Department of Defense and the armed forces when it comes to emergencies calling for military action.

Article II, Section 2, Clause 2 begins: "He shall have power, by and with the Advice and Consent of the Senate, to make Treaties,... and with the Advice and Consent of the Senate, shall appoint Ambassadors...." Then Article II, Section 3 reads in part: "...he shall receive Ambassadors and other public Ministers...." These imply that the President has whatever constitutional power-rights and liberty-rights are necessary to conduct the diplomatic affairs of the United States. Presumably the President could and should delegate corresponding rights to the Department of State. However, these diplomatic constitutional rights of the President and the Department of State are much more limited by Congress, especially the Senate, than those of the Department of Defense.

Similarly, each of the other administrative departments and agencies will possess both constitutional rights delegated by the President from his or her executive power and statutory rights conferred by Congress in the legislation by which it established it. The scope of the constitutional rights will vary from agency to agency, but presumably it will be narrower regarding the so-called independent agencies.

The *United States Constitution* establishes what has come to be known as a presidential system of government. This is a form of government in which (1) the executive power is possessed primarily by a president and the administrative agencies he or she supervises and (2) the administration is strictly separated from the legislature and relatively independent of legislative control. The former has been explained briefly above. The latter depends upon two additional provisions of the *Constitution*. Article I, Section 6, Clause 2 reads: "No Senator or Representative shall, during the Time for which he was elected, be appointed to any civil Office under the Authority of the United States...; and no Person holding any Office under the United States, shall be a member of either House during his Continuance in Office." This ensures that there can be no overlap between the members of the legislative branch and the executive branch of the government. Then Article II, Section 4 reads: "The President, Vice President and all civil Officers of the United States shall be removed from Office on Impeachment for, and Conviction of, Treason, Bribery, or other high Crimes and Misdemeanors." This provides the President, Vice President and the heads of the administrative departments with an immunity-right against being removed from office merely because any disagreement over administrative policy, thus ensuring a considerable measure of independence from Congress.

A parliamentary system of government, such as that in the United Kingdom, is different in both respects. The Prime Minister and the members of the Cabinet, who head the main administrative agencies, are members of parliament. And they normally lose their offices upon a parliamentary vote of non-confidence. There is a debate in the legal and philosophical literature between advocates of a presidential system and those in favor of a parliamentary system. However, the historical record shows clearly that each kind of administration has worked well in some countries and under favorable circumstances but failed dismally in other nations and under different circumstances. Therefore, it is a mistake to evaluate these systems of government in general. Instead, let us ask whether the United States is justified in retaining its strong presidential system under present circumstances.

Any thorough evaluation of our presidential system of administration must consider both traditional justifications and contemporary reports of its strengths and weaknesses. Why, then, might we want to retain our presidential administration? (1) It enables the citizens to choose the chief executive. As Alexander Hamilton argued: "It is desirable that the sense of the people should operate in the choice of the person to whom so important a trust was to be confided…." (Hamilton 1961, p. 458) Although he justified this by an appeal to republicanism, we would consider this a requirement of democracy. However the sense of the people also operates in the choice of any prime minister, although indirectly through their votes for the members of parliament. But Juan J. Linz, who favors a parliamentary system, admits that: "On the other hand, presidential elections do offer the indisputable advantage of allowing the people to choose their chief executive openly, directly, and for a predictable span rather than leaving that decision to the backstage maneuvering of the politicians." (Linz 1990, pp. 56–57) However, it is not clear whether this gives the citizens much more control over the choice of their chief executive. For one thing, they must choose between candidates nominated by political parties that may or may not operate very democratically. And in a parliamentary system, they usually know in advance who will become prime minister in the event that their chosen party forms a cabinet.

(2) The President is directly accountable to the citizens. Hamilton also argued: "With a positive duration of considerable extent, I connect the circumstance of re-eligibility…The last is necessary to enable the people, when they see reason to approve of his conduct, to continue him in his station, in order to prolong the utility of his talents." (Hamilton 1961, p. 487) Or, of course, to vote him out of office if they disapprove of his handling of the administration. However, Linz points out that in a presidential system the president may not be eligible for reelection, that he or she may be able to shift responsibility for any failures to the legislature and that the voters cannot hold the president accountable until the end of a fixed term, typically of 4 years. (Linz 1994, pp. 12–14) Nevertheless, a president who runs for reelection is directly accountable to the electorate and cannot be shielded from their disapproval by any parliamentary action or inaction.

(3) The primary executive power is vested in one official, the President. Alexander Hamilton regarded this as one of the most important virtues of our Constitution.

> That unity is conducive to energy will not be disputed. Decision, activity, secrecy, and dispatch will generally characterize the proceedings of one man, in a much more eminent degree, than the proceedings of any greater number; and in proportion as the number is increased, these qualities will be diminished. (Hamilton 1961, p. 472)

Granted that unity is required in order to administer the many activities of any government effectively, Bert A. Rockman reminds us that:

> Hamilton's writings preceded the development of mass-based party organizations that could infuse energy into a collective executive—which is, after all, more characteristic of parliamentary systems. For, other things being equal, parliamentary systems tend much

> more than presidential ones to have the characteristics of collective action. (Rockman 1997, pp. 50–51)

This is probably because even the most energetic president will often have his or her policies frustrated by Congress, but a prime minister can usually count on the full cooperation of parliament. What matters is unified action by the government as a whole, not merely the unity of the executive branch.

(4) The President holds office for a fixed term of considerable duration, 4 years in the United States. Alexander Hamilton explains why this is desirable.

> Duration in office has been mentioned as the second requisite to the energy of the executive authority. This has relation to two objects: To the personal firmness of the Executive Magistrate in the employment of his constitutional powers; and to the stability of the system of administration which may have been adopted under his auspices. (Hamilton 1961, p. 481)

Granted that a weak or dithering president is undesirable, firmness in a president can become obstinacy and prevent compromise when any administration must cooperate with a Congress that has a mind of its own. Stability in an administration is also desirable, both to enable it to undertake and complete long-term projects the value of which may not be clear in the early stages and to enable individual citizens and business organizations to plan their activities on the basis of reliable predictions of governmental policy. On the other hand, Juan J. Linz points out that the fixed term in a presidential system of government imparts an undesirable rigidity. It divides the political process into fixed segments unrelated to changing circumstances or to any loss of confidence by the electorate or their representatives. (Linz 1994, pp. 8–9) Moreover, empirical studies show no strong correlation between political stability and either a presidential or a parliamentarian system of government.

(5) The chief executive is independent of the legislature. Hamilton emphasized one aspect of this independence.

> Another and no less important desideratum was, that the executive should be independent for his continuance in office on all, but the people themselves. He might otherwise be tempted to sacrifice his duty to his complaisance for those whose favor was necessary to the duration of his official consequence. (Hamilton 1961, p. 460)

This independence is established by the chief executive's 4-year term established by the *United States Constitution*. However, a strong presidency also requires that the chief executive be independent of the legislature in his or her exercise of the executive powers. Presumably this is also established in the *Constitution* because it establishes the separation of the executive, legislative and judicial powers of government. However, this is not so. To be sure, the incompatibility clause (Article I, Section 6, Clause 2) does ensure that no member of Congress can hold any office in the executive branch, and vice versa. However, its system of checks and balances seriously impairs the separation of executive and legislative powers. Thus, the President's power to appoint important officials is subject to the advice and consent of the Senate. It is Congress that creates administrative agencies and in so doing defines their powers. Congress has the power to supervise administrative agencies by its standing committees and often by special investigations. Finally, it can withhold funding for any administrative policy that it finds objectionable. Therefore, Charles O. Jones rejects the common view that the *United States Constitution* has created a government of separated powers: "Based on my understanding of the constitutional structure and how it has evolved, I propose a substitute formulation. The United States has a government of separated institutions *competing for shared powers* (or for shares of shared powers)." (Jones 1997, p. 23) Bruce Ackerman reminds us that this competition can lead to any of three outcomes, especially when the President and Congress are dominated by different parties or different factions within the same party. Although accommodation may be possible it will be very difficult. More often it will result either in a crisis of governability during which each party is disposed to make life miserable for the other or a constitutional breakdown in which urgent problems cannot be resolved. (Ackerman 2000, p. 645) It would seem, then, that our presidential system can provide strong and effective administration only when the legislature and the chief executive agree on basic policies, a situation in which a prime minister can also provide strong leadership.

(6) The chief executive is, or is supposed to be, independent of factions. James Madison insisted that: "Among the numerous advantages promised by a well constructed Union, none deserves to be more accurately developed than its tendency to break and control the violence of factions." (Madison 1961, p. 56) He went on to explain why this is true:

> By a faction I understand a number of citizens, whether amounting to a majority or minority of the whole, who are united and actuated by some common impulse or passion, or of interest, adverse to the rights of other citizens, or to the permanent and aggregate interests of the community. (Madison 1961, p. 57)

Two features of the *United States Constitution* were intended to make the chief executive independent of factions. First, the President is chosen, not directly by a majority of the population as a whole, but by an electoral body consisting of special representatives elected by various segments of the population and supposed to use their best judgment in selecting the most able chief executive. Second, once elected, the President would not be accountable to the people until the end of his or her 4-year term of office. However, the later development of political parties, typically just the sort of factions the founding fathers feared, has greatly reduced, if not eliminated, the independence of the chief executive. Today, the members of the Electoral College are pledged not to vote according to their own best judgment but to vote as their party instructs them. And any President seeking reelection cannot afford to alienate the party to which he owes his or her election. Moreover, the President will need the cooperation of Congress, not always dominated by his or her own party, to carry out his or her policies. Indeed, as we have just seen, divisions between and within political parties often become so fierce that they produce the violent rhetoric and governmental disorder Madison and others were trying to eliminate. This does not imply that one should wish for the elimination of political parties. Granted that political parties are typically factions, they are essential to any democracy. There is no other way in which individual citizens can organize themselves in order to participate effectively in politics. Ideally, it is by the debate between political parties both during an electoral campaign and subsequently in the legislature that their narrow factionalism can be overcome in a resulting majority vote. Still, the danger of factionalism remains and in our presidential system too often leads to either a crisis of governability or a constitutional breakdown.

What are the moral foundations of our presidential system of administration? The authors cited above suggest three of primary importance—democracy, human rights, and the permanent aggregate interests of the community. Precisely how and to what degree these justify retaining this constitutionally established system is a complex and controversial matter.

The constitutional amendments that have extended the suffrage and the party practices that have reduced the role of the Electoral College have transformed the government of the United States from a republic, in which something approaching a majority of the people indirectly elect the President to a democracy in which all citizens may vote for the candidate of their choice. Although many eligible voters choose not to exercise their franchise and some are probably prevented from doing so, today the citizens do choose the President and the President is in turn accountable to them. To be sure, voters can choose only between those candidates nominated by recognized political parties, and only Presidents who run for reelection can be held accountable by the people, but it remains true that our presidential system of administration is by and large democratic and in that respect morally justified.

Any government ought to refrain from violating and to protect the fundamental human rights of its citizens. In this respect, it is the administrative branch of government that presents the greatest danger of violation and the final hope of protection. The constitutional separation of powers and its system of checks and balances together with the Bill of Rights and the Thirteenth, Fourteenth and Fifteenth Amendments are effective in preventing almost any administrative action that would seriously violate human rights and often in requiring administrative action to protect them. However, if there really are positive human rights to social security and an adequate standard of living, these constitutional provisions are not sufficient. On balance, it seems to me that our presidential system of administration does well in respecting human rights.

Its tendency to further the permanent aggregate interests of the community is harder to assess. Alexander Hamilton believed that the proposed constitution would establish a presidential system of administration with the features required to effectively promote the interests if the United States: "The ingredients, which constitute energy in the executive, are first unity, second duration, thirdly an adequate provision for its support, fourthly competent powers." However, although the *Constitution* confers the primary executive power upon a single chief executive, the President, this power is limited by a system of checks and balances that, in effect, means that it is shared with Congress, especially the Senate. And although the President is elected for a fixed term of 4 years, this sometimes ensures only that an impasse with Congress will persist while urgent needs remain unmet. Since Congress controls the purse strings, the President is not assured of adequate support for even the most important administrative agencies. Finally, these agencies may not have powers adequate to fulfill their responsibilities because it is Congress that establishes administrative departments and other agencies and in so doing defines their powers. Therefore, our presidential system of administration can effectively promote the aggregate and permanent interests of the community only when either the political party of the President has the support of a clear majority in both houses of Congress or has the cooperation of the opposition party or parties. Increasingly it seems that neither of these conditions is satisfied in American politics. However, a prime minister could not lead an effective administration without either a supporting majority in parliament or the cooperation of one or more other parties. And although our presidential system fails to fulfill adequately many urgent public interests, it manages to break any impasse between Congress and the administration when disaster threatens. My conclusion is that there is wisdom in the adage "If it ain't broke, don't fix it." In a democracy, it is up to the people to ensure that the political parties they support do not undermine the effective pursuit of the most important interests of the community.

4 A Bicameral Legislature

Article I Section 1 of the *United States Constitution* has two important legal effects. First, it establishes three legislative bodies: the House of Representatives, the Senate, and a Congress consisting of both the House and the Senate. Second, it confers the legislative power-rights specified in the following sections of this article upon these bodies. Leaving the wisdom of establishing a bicameral legislature aside for the moment, let us consider a small sample of the constitutional rights of each legislative body.

Article I, Section 8 specifies the constitutional legislative rights of Congress as a whole. Among the most important of these are the following: (Clause 1) the power-rights to lay and collect taxes and to provide for the common defence and general welfare of the United States; (Clause 3) to regulate commerce with foreign nations and among the several states; (Clause 7) to establish post offices and post roads; (Clause 9) to establish tribunals inferior to the Supreme Court; (Clauses 11–14) to declare war, raise and support armies, provide and maintain a navy, and to make rules governing the land and naval forces; (Clause 15) to provide for calling forth the militia to execute the laws of the union, suppress insurrections and repel invasions; and finally (Clause 18) to make all laws necessary for carrying into execution the foregoing powers and all other powers vested by this Constitution in the government of the United States.

In addition, the House of Representatives has the power-right of impeachment granted by Article I, Section 2, Clause 5 and the power-right to originate all bills for raising revenue specified in Section 7, Clause 1. The Senate has the power-right to try all impeachments conferred by Article I, Section 3, Clause 6 and the power-right to give or withhold its consent to any treaties or nominations to high public offices proposed by the President as specified in Article II, Section 2, Clause 2. The precise content and limitation on each of these constitutional rights has been defined by legislative practice and decisions of the Supreme Court. The justifiability of each of these power-rights is worthy of extensive consideration. However, let us turn our attention to a more basic issue of constitutional design.

Is a bicameral legislature preferable to a unicameral legislature? Very likely there is no answer to this very general question. It may well be that a bicameral legislature would be better than a unicameral one for a nation state extending over several large regions populated by peoples of diverse religious or cultural heritages but a unicameral legislature preferable for a geographically small nation with a relatively homogeneous population. Let us, then, ask whether the bicameral legislature established by the *United States Constitution* is preferable to a unicameral legislature for our country under present circumstances.

An appropriate place to begin our investigation is by considering the arguments given in *The Federalist*. James Madison advances conclusive reasons to institute a legislative body like the House of Representatives. Obviously in a nation as large and populous as the United States it would be impossible for all or even most of the citizens to assemble in any one location and legislate for the entire country. Hence, legislation in the United States must be enacted by representatives of the people. Accordingly, Madison observes that: "The definition of the right of suffrage is justly regarded as a fundamental article of republican government." (Madison 1961, p. 354) Because republicanism requires only that the government represent many of those governed, the *Constitution* originally specified only that qualifications of the electors be the same as those of the most numerous branch of the legislature in their respective states. Today the Fourteenth Amendment specifies that all persons born or naturalized in the United States are citizens of the United States and the Fifteenth Amendment extends the right to vote on all citizens. This definition of the right of suffrage is required by the principle of democracy. Let us postpone the question of why any national government ought to be democratic and tentatively conclude that the United States legislature ought to include a democratic House of Representatives.

However, the question remains whether the members of our House of Representatives genuinely represent the people of the United Sates. Presumably this is ensured by the fact that they are elected by their constituents and subject to reelection or rejection every 2 years. To those who insist that liberty requires annual elections, Madison replies that:

> No man can be a competent legislator who does not add to an upright intention and a sound judgment, a certain degree of knowledge of the subjects on which he is to legislate. A part of this knowledge may be acquired by means of information which lie within the compass of men in private as well as public stations. Another part can only be attained, or at least thoroughly attained, by actual experience in the station which requires the use of it. (Madison 1961, p. 362)

Hence, one needs to balance the frequency of elections necessary to hold legislators responsible to the electorate against the length of time required for them to achieve the information and know how required to perform competently as a legislator. Although one cannot be confident that biennial elections are the best of all possible arrangements, on balance these seem justified for a democratic legislature.

Because the members of the House of Representatives are elected by citizens living in geographically defined districts, it is necessary to apportion the members of the House among the several states. The United States Constitution originally allocated them according to the rule that allocated direct taxes, a rule that counted each slave as only three fifths of a person. Although Madison defended this allocation at length (Madison 1961, pp. 366–372), it became irrelevant after the Thirteenth Amendment abolished slavery. Accordingly, the Fourteenth Amendment now specifies that: "Representatives shall be apportioned among the several States according to their respective numbers…." This is appropriate because democracy presumably requires that those subject to the laws have an equal right to elect the lawmakers. Assuming for the moment that any government ought to be democratic, one should conclude that the legislature of the United States ought to include a House of Representatives in something very like its present form.

Whether its legislature should include a second body, a Senate, is more controversial. Madison advances a number of reasons to explain why the Senate, consisting of two members from each state, is necessary. First, it is required by the fact that the United States has a federal government in which sovereignty is divided between a national government and the several states. "In this spirit it may be remarked, that the equal vote allowed to each state, is at once a constitutional recognition of the portion of sovereignty remaining in the individual states, and an instrument for preserving that sovereignty." This consideration may have had considerable weight when the senators were elected by the state legislatures, but now that they are elected by the residents of each state it is less clear that they represent the states as sovereign bodies.

Second, the Senate provides an impediment, in addition to the separation of executive, legislative and judicial powers, against improper or unwise legislation. Madison argues that: "The necessity of a senate is not less indicated by the propensity of all single and numerous assemblies, to yield to the impulse of sudden and violent passions, and to be seduced by factious leaders, into intemperate and pernicious resolutions." (Madison 1961, p. 417) Because the qualifications for election as a senator require one to be older than and to have been a citizen longer than to be eligible for election to the House of Representatives and because the smaller size of the Senate allows for more thorough debate, the Senate will provide a check to balance any impetuous action by the more populous House. Moreover:

> The objects of government may be divided into two general classes; the one depending on measures which have singly an immediate and sensible operation; the other depending on a succession of well chosen and well connected measures, which have a gradual and perhaps unobserved operation. The importance of the latter description to the collective and permanent welfare of every country needs no explanation. (Madison 1961, p. 424)

Because the members of the House of Representatives are elected biennially, they will be unable to provide for and ought not to be held responsible for enacting complex long-term measures required to promote the vital interests of our country. These considerations suggest, and legislative experience has shown, that the Senate can and often does serve this important purpose. However, this advantage must be balanced against the possibility, too often experienced, of a deadlock between the Senate and the House that prevents any action to resolve urgent national problems. The factor that tips the scales is whether political parties are prepared to make responsible compromises or insist on partisan and self-interested policies.

Third, the Senate will provide the legislative expertise lacking in the members of the House of Representatives.

> Another defect to be supplied by a senate lies in a want of the acquaintance with the objects and principles of legislation. It is not possible that an assembly of men called for the most part from pursuits of a private nature, continued in appointment for a short time, and led by no permanent motive to devote the intervals of public occupation to a study of the laws, the affairs and the comprehensive interests of their country, should, if left wholly to themselves, escape a variety of important errors in the exercise of their legislative trust. (Madison 1961, p. 419)

Although this reasoning probably applied to the state legislatures in Madison's time and might well have been anticipated to apply to the newly-created federal legislature, today most of the members of the House of Representatives are committed to long-term political careers and are reelected for several terms. Hence, this consideration probably has some, but a considerably diminished, force as a justification for our present Senate.

Fourth, the Senate provides a stability lacking in the House of Representatives. Because Representatives are elected for only 2-year terms, the membership of the House will change frequently and therefore future legislative actions of the House will often be unpredictable. But the Senate, whose members serve for 6-year terms, will be a much more stable and reliable legislative body. This will counteract the mischief resulting from mutable government: the lack of confidence and respect of foreign nations, the legal unpredictability that prevents individuals and organizations from planning reliably for ongoing projects, and the diminished attachment of the citizens who find their hopes so often disappointed. (Madison 1961, pp. 419–422) This reasoning also has some, but a diminished, relevance to our government today.

Fifth, a senate is needed to give its advice and consent to treaties proposed by the President. The negotiation of treaties is best conducted by the President in order to ensure dispatch when necessary and the confidentiality of information and opinions exchanged with foreign nations. However, treaties are so important to the continuing welfare of our nation that this power of the President should be supervised by some elected body. The House is too numerous a body to discuss the relevant complications in depth and its members lack the experience of foreign affairs acquired by the members of the Senate who serve for much longer terms. Although this argument may not show that the Senate is absolutely necessary for good government, it does demonstrate its usefulness. (Madison 1961, pp. 433–435) Analogous reasoning applies to the need for the Senate to give its advice and consent to the President's nominations of candidates for the highest public offices.

Sixth, the Senate is needed to serve as a court to try impeached officials. The House is too numerous a body to serve efficiently as a court and its power to impeach should not be combined with a power to convict for impeachable misconduct. The

Supreme Court has too few members to sustain public respect were it to judge such politically controversial issues and it might be swayed by the fact that its members are themselves subject to impeachment. Hence, the Senate is at least a useful, and perhaps a necessary, institution in our government. This reasoning remains relevant under contemporary circumstances.

What developments since the publication of *The Federalist* might add to or modify the force of Madison's arguments? He argued that the Senate was needed to restrain the House from improper or unwise legislation. But the constitution he defended had no Bill of Rights. However, very soon the first ten amendments were ratified and subsequently the Supreme Court's power of judicial review became established. Hence, today the courts provide the primary protection against improper legislation, legislation that infringes the liberties of the people, and the Senate has little if any importance in this respect. Still, it probably continues to restrain the House from unwise legislation.

However, the ability of the Senate to legislate wisely may have been reduced by the gradual admission of new states to the Union. Since each state is represented by two members in the Senate, the number of Senators has increased from the original twenty-six to a hundred. Hence, this body is no longer small enough to enable each member to participate at length in the debate over any serious legislative issue. Nevertheless, it retains some advantage over the House of Representatives in this respect because the membership of the House has grown even more to 435 members.

More significant is the development of welfare state. The members of the House of Representatives pay very close attention to the will of the people because they are subject to election every 2 years. And most of the citizens want generous public benefits but low taxes. Hence, the House tends to support legislation that irresponsibly increases the public debt. Although the Senate is not immune from this temptation, its members are somewhat insulated from popular resentment of fiscal responsibility by their 6-year term of office. Hence, the development of the welfare state now contributes a new dimension to Madison's argument that the Senate is needed to provide a long-term perspective on the public welfare.

The most important change since *The Federalist* was published is doubtless the development of political parties and their domination of political processes. Party discipline has reduced the ability of the members of the Senate to question policies adopted by their respective parties or to vote according to their individual judgments. This might seem to undermine the argument that the Senate provides a legislative wisdom lacking in the House of Representatives, but it probably does not do so because the members of the House, whose terms expire every two rather than 6 years and who also need the support of their party to be reelected, are even more constrained by party discipline.

However, another consequence of the development of political parties does much more to undermine the usefulness of the Senate. Parties are very often factions in the sense defined by James Madison:

> By a faction I understand a number of citizens, whether amounting to a majority or minority of the whole, who are united and actuated by some common impulse of passion, or of interest, adverse to the rights of other citizens, or to the permanent and aggregate interests of the community. (Madison 1961, p. 57)

What distinguishes one party from another is primarily the different interests they promote and that motivate their constituents to vote in their favor. And when parties dominate the legislative process, party discipline will greatly reduce the possibility of individual legislators voting for any measure that would compromise the policies of their parties. Hence, when different parties control the House and the Senate, the result is often a stalemate in which Congress cannot act to resolve urgent national problems. Under such circumstances, the existence of a Senate to check the legislative power of the House is not an advantage but a very serious disadvantage in our government.

How strong, then, are the reason to institute the Senate in the government of the United States? Now that the Constitution contains the Bill of Rights and the Supreme Court has the power of judicial review, the Senate is not needed to protect the partial sovereignty of the states. And for the same reasons, there is much less need for a senate to check the power of the House of Representatives to enact improper legislation. However, the Senate can be and often is useful in preventing unwise legislation by the House. On the other hand, when different parties control the two houses of Congress, the power of the Senate to prevent the House from enacting urgently needed legislation is a serious disadvantage. My guess is that any institutional change should consist in reforming our political parties rather than eliminating the Senate with its power to check unwise legislation by the House. In spite of its greatly increased size resulting from the admission of many new states, the Senate continues to provide greater legislative expertise in our government. The longer term of its members also contributes to the stability of United States statute law. Although not absolutely necessary, the Senate is probably better constituted than the more numerous House to give advice and consent to treaties and nominations to public office or to serve as a court to try impeached officials. On balance, one should conclude that there are reasons sufficient to justify maintaining the Senate in the Congress of the United States.

5 Exclusion

Article I, Section 5 of the United States Constitution reads in part: "Each House shall be the judge of the elections, returns and qualifications of its own members…." Acting on this power-right, the House of Representatives has refused to seat over 30 members certified as duly elected by their respective states. No one questions the propriety of excluding any persons who fail to meet the constitutionally required qualifications of age, citizenship or residence. More controversial have been the refusal to seat B. H. Roberts because he was a Mormon polygamist, Victor L Berger because he had been convicted under the Espionage Act of 1917, and Adam Clayton

Powell, Jr. because of alleged corruption. Ought the House to have the constitutional right to exclude a duly elected member at will?

One reason why the House ought to have a constitutional right to exclude a duly elected member at will is to ensure that no member is unfit to fulfil his or her legislative duties. During the debate about whether Adam Clayton Powell, Jr. ought to be seated, Representative Multer distinguished between the constitutionally required qualifications for election and fitness to serve: "In the Constitution the first reference to the qualification of Members refers, not to fitness, but to qualifications, and they are citizenship, age, not residency, but inhabitancy in the State." Although he was not arguing for a right to exclude duly elected members at will, others could use this distinction to do so. Surely no one who is unfit to perform his or her legislative duties well ought to serve in the House of Representatives. Hence, the House ought to have a constitutional right to exclude duly elected candidates for any reason it considers them unfit.

Another reason why the House ought to have a constitutional right to exclude members at will is to preserve its moral integrity as a legislative institution. Chief Justice Warren, who delivered the opinion of the court in *Powell v. McCormack*, asserted: "Unquestionably, Congress has an interest in preserving its institutional integrity…." (Supreme Court 1969, p. 548) If the moral authority of the legislature is not preserved, then the public respect for the law will be undermined. But Fuller added that "…but, in most cases, that interest can be sufficiently safeguarded by the exercise of its power to punish its members for disorderly behavior and, in extreme cases, to expel a member with the concurrence of two-thirds." (Supreme Court 1969, p. 548) Apparently this was the judgment of the Select Committee appointed to decide whether Adam Clayton Powell, Jr. ought to be seated, for it recommended that he be sworn in and seated, but censured by the House. (Supreme Court 1969, p. 492)

A third reason why the House ought to have a constitutional right to exclude duly elected members at will is to preserve its independence from the other branches of government. As Joseph Story explained:

> It is obvious that a power must be lodged somewhere to judge of the elections, returns, and qualifications of the members of each house comprising the legislature; for otherwise there would be no certainty as to who were legitimately chosen members, and any intruder or usurper might claim a seat, and thus trample upon the rights and privileges and liberties of the people….If lodged in any other, than the legislative body itself, its independence, its purity and even its existence and action may be destroyed, or put into imminent danger…. Accordingly, the power has always been lodged in the legislative body by the uniform practice of England and America. (Story 1994, pp. 604–605)

What is at stake here is the independence of the legislature from the executive and judicial branches of government, the separation of powers fundamental to the United States Constitution.

There are also reasons not to establish any such right. First, there is the danger of abuse. During the debates on the adoption of the federal constitution, James Madison opposed this provision.

> The qualifications of electors and elected were fundamental articles of a republican government, and ought to be fixed by the Constitution. If the legislature could regulate those of either, it can by degrees subvert the Constitution. A republic may be converted into an aristocracy or oligarchy, as well by limiting the number capable of being elected as the number authorized to elect….It has a power, also, which might be made subservient to the views of one faction against another. Qualifications founded on artificial distinctions may be devised by the stronger in order to keep out partisans of a weaker faction. (Madison 1895, pp. 377–378)

Justice Douglas, who joined the opinion of the Court in *Powell v. McCormack*, reminds us that such abuse has in fact occurred:

> But the House is not the sole judge when "qualifications" are added which are not specified in the Constitution. A man is not seated because he is a Socialist or Communist. Another is not seated because, in his district, members of a minority are systematically excludes from voting. Another is not seated because he has spoken out in opposition to the war in Vietnam. The possible list is long. Some cases will have the racist overtones of the present one. Others may reflect religious or ideological clashes. (Supreme Court 1969, pp. 552–553)

Clearly the danger of abuse is very real.

A second reason why the House ought not to have a constitutional right to exclude duly elected members at will is that this violates the democratic principle of equality. Justice Stevens, delivering the opinion of the Supreme Court in *Term Limits*, asserted that the rejection of any such right in *Powell* rested on the fundamental principle that the people should chose whom they please to govern them. He then explained that: "Our opinion made it clear that this broad principle incorporated at least two fundamental ideas. First, we emphasized the egalitarian concept that the opportunity to be elected was open to all. (Supreme Court 1995b, pp. 793–794)" Hence, the House ought not to have the power to effectively deny this opportunity to anyone it disfavored.

Finally, he House ought not to have the constitutional right to exclude duly elected members at will because this would violate the sovereignty of the people. In *Term Limits*, Justice Stevens also explained that:

> Second, we recognized the critical postulate that sovereignty is vested in the people, and that sovereignty confers on the people the right to choose freely their representatives to the National Government. For example, we noted that "Robert Livingston…endorsed the same fundamental principle: 'The people are the best judges who ought to represent them. To dictate and control them, to tell them whom they shall not elect, is to abridge their natural rights.'" (Supreme Court 1995b, p. 794)

And during the House debate about whether to seat Adam Clayton Powell, Jr., Representative Wright argued that: "When we divest a duly elected Member of his right to sit and vote in this Chamber, we disenfranchise the people of an entire congressional district. We rob them of their voice and of their vote." (Weeks 1971, p. 42)

How strong is each of these reasons for or against a constitutional right of the House to exclude duly elected members at will? It is very important to ensure that the members of the House are fit to perform their legislative duties. But it is not clear that the House will be a better judge of this than the electorate, especially because one of these duties is to serve the interests of his or her constituency. Even more important is to preserve the independence of the House from the other branches of government. This is a very strong reason to confer the power to judge the qualifications of each duly elected member upon the House rather than upon some other governmental institution, but not a strong reason to make this power unlimited, to confer a right to exclude at will. The strongest reason to confer upon the House a discretionary right to exclude is to enable it to preserve its moral integrity as a legislative institution. Because of the diversity of actions and character traits that might discredit the House, these could not be specified in the text of the Constitution. Hence, the House will need considerable discretion in preserving its integrity. However, this need not be exercised before a duly elected member is seated. The House could, if it has the will, almost always preserve its moral integrity by exercising its constitutional right to punish its members for disorderly behavior. And in extreme cases, it could expel a member. This power is less subject to abuse because it requires a two-thirds vote, not a simple majority.

On the other side of the issue, the danger that the House will abuse any constitutional right to exclude duly elected members at will has in its practice been proven serious. The principle of equality, especially the equal opportunity to be elected to public office, is basic to any truly democratic government. And excluding any citizen on racial, religious or ideological grounds clearly violates that principle. But there might be reasons to exclude a duly elected member that are not similarly discriminatory. The most fundamental principle of democracy is that the people ought to be sovereign. Excluding a duly elected member does not literally disenfranchise the people of an entire congressional district because the seat becomes vacant and they will have an opportunity to elect a substitute representative. However, it does limit their choice of candidates and to that extent violates their sovereignty. On balance, then, one should conclude that the House ought not to have a constitutional right to exclude duly elecged members at will.

6 Cloture

Article I, Section 5, Clause 2 of the United States Constitution reads in part: "Each House may determine the Rules of its Proceedings…." Acting on this authorization, the Senate has adopted Rule XXII that requires a vote of three-fifths of the Senators duly chosen and sworn to limit debate on any motion under consideration. Many persons, including some members of the Senate, object to this cloture rule because it permits individual Senators to delay or even prevent important legislation favored by the majority of Senators. Ought the Senate to have a constitutional right to require a vote of three-fifths of its members to limit debate?

There are several reasons advanced in favor of this right. First, it is necessary to protect the fundamental moral rights of minorities and the smaller states. When Senator Anderson proposed the consideration of the constitutional option, a controversial procedure that would enable a simple majority of senators to terminate debate, his opponents emphasized the importance of protecting minority and state's rights. (Gold and Gupta 2009, p. 237) In a much earlier debate, Senator Jefferson Davis opposed limiting debate by warning that this would enable a tyrannous majority to trample underfoot a minority. (Binder and Smith 1997, p. 55) Some Senators who regard themselves as primarily representing their states argue that that the constitutional mechanisms for protecting their states' interests are inadequate and need to be supplemented with other measures such as Senate rule XXII. (Binder and Smith 1997, p. 98) Presumably requiring a three-fifths majority could advance these goals, but does it do so in current Senatorial practice?

Another reason why the Senate ought to have a constitutional right to require a three-fifths vote for cloture is to protect important constitutional rights. Years ago Senator Thomas Hart Benton asserted: "With respect to debates, Senators have a constitutional right to speak, and while they speak to the subject before the House, there is no power anywhere to stop them." (Binder and Smith 1997, p. 56) And Chuck Grassley, Senator from Iowa, has recently reminded us that:

> It is important to keep in mind that when senators are blocked from participating in the legislative process, the people they represent are disenfranchised….Forcing a cloture vote before any deliberation prevents even members of the majority party from offering amendments that may be important to the people they represent. (Grassley 2014, Floor Speech)

Although the premature limitation of Senate debate does not literally disenfranchise any citizens, it does devalue the votes of those who elected senators thus denied the opportunity to speak on their behalf.

A third reason why the Senate ought to have a constitutional right to require a three-fifths vote for cloture is to reduce extreme partisanship and facilitate compromise. Michael J Gerhardt insists that the filibuster, permitted by this practice, defines the Senate's uniqueness as a political institution including its historic commitment to encouraging compromise on especially divisive matters. (Gerhardt 2004, p. 449) W. Lee Rawls argues that: "The legislative machinery available for rapid policy change is mostly partisan. Bipartisan change means time-consuming incremental change through hard negotiations by a Senate majority with a Senate minority armed with the filibuster …." (Rawls 2009, p. 103) However, there remains the danger that negotiations are so very hard that the result is gridlock rather than needed change.

A fourth reason why the Senate ought to have a right to require a three-fifths vote for cloture is to promote the stability of governmental policy. Michael J. Gerhardt suggests that the Senate's function as a counter-majoritarian institution has been designed to motivate senators to take the long, rather than the expedient, view. (Gerhardt 2004, p. 471) He argues that by making change difficult, Rule XXII facilitates stability within the system. (Gerhardt 2004, p. 474) And W. Lee Rawls explains that without the filibuster the partisanship inherent in sweeping solutions quickly enacted leaves any such enactment subject to a successful counterattack if the other party gains full control of the federal government. If individuals and private institutions are to plan for their affairs, they need to be able to rely on stable public policies. (Rawls 2009, p. 114)

A fifth reason for the Senate's right to require a three-fifths vote for cloture is to respect the Senate's judgment of its established practices. Michael J. Gerhardt argues as follows:

> Second, the filibuster has been an unbroken practice within the Senate, one that has been ratified expressly and implicitly on a repeated basis since the founding of the republic. While there may be good reason not to defer completely to popular practices, there is good reason to respect an institution's repeated and consistent judgments about its authority in an area of special expertise. (Gerhardt 2004, p.482)

This is quite true, but this respect should be limited by any arguments for institutional change.

There are, as usual, several reasons why the Senate ought not to have a constitutional right to require a three-fifths vote for cloture. First, it undermines the effectiveness of the Senate as a legislative institution. By permitting filibusters it frequently interrupts the legislative process and delays action on bills before the Senate. Near the end of a legislative session this even prevents passage of a measure favored by the majority. Sarah A. Binder and Steven S. Smith report that:

> The Twentieth Amendment did not end general slowdown strategies on the part of Senate minorities. On several occasions since that time, it appears that a minority party has deliberately slowed Senate action throughout a session of Congress in order to reduce the productivity of the majority to contribute to the impression that the majority party cannot govern. (Binder and Smith 1997, p. 147)

Binder and Smith also remind us that: "The filibuster is a tool not only of substantial minorities but also of individual senators. Individual senators cannot prevent cloture from being invoked, but under the Senate's rules a single senator can be heard and delay action. (Binder and Smith 1997, p. 99)" Efficiency is not everything, but surely it is highly important that one of the most important institutions in our government be able to exercise its legislative powers effectively.

Second, the Senate ought not to have the constitutional right to require a three-fifths vote for cloture because this often prevents, or at least weakens, legislation in the national interest. Martin B. Gold and Dimple Gupta report that:

> Among most noteworthy victims of the filibuster was early civil right legislation. By mounting a filibuster, a minority of Senators blocked bills to protect black voters in the South in 1890, anti-lynching bills in 1922, 1935, and 1938, anti-poll tax bills in 1942, 1944, and 1946, and anti-race discrimination bills on eleven occasions between 1946 and 1975. (Gold and Gupta 2009, p. 230)

Sarah A. Binder and Steven S. Smith add that:

> Plainly, filibusters, or the threat thereof, change legislative outcomes in ways beyond the killing of bills, notably through changes in legislation that they stimulate and their influence on the political setting beyond the outcome of the legislation directly affected by them. These political consequences have obvious and significant implications for public policy. (Binder and Smith 1997, p. 143)

However, some supporters of the filibuster reply that use of the filibuster has done little or no harm to the public interest. In 1926 the political scientist Lindsay Rogers proclaimed, "the absence of cloture has been justified by the results; no really meritorious measure has been defeated and some vicious proposals have been killed." (Binder and Smith 1997, p. 127) Thus, one's evaluation of Senate Rule XXII depends upon one's view about that is or is not in the nation's interests.

A third reason why the Senate ought not to have a constitutional right to require a three-fifths vote for cloture is that this often prevents the President from fulfilling his or her constitutional duty to faithfully enforce the laws. Presumably, this duty includes the duty to staff the offices created by congressional legislation. But when this requires that the Senate consent to a presidential nomination, this may be frustrated by a filibuster or even the threat of a filibuster. Even W. Lee Rawls, a defender of the filibuster, admits that: "The filibuster is not an unalloyed good.... Certainly, the nominees of the judicial and executive branches have been harshly and sometimes unfairly treated." (Rawls 2009, p. 113) Still, Michael J. Gerhardt argues that: "It is not bad policy to require supermajority approval of someone who will wield significant power within our system of government long after the dissolution of the majorities which brought into power the President who nominated him and the Senate that confirmed him." (Gerhardt 2004, pp. 483–484)

A fourth reason against the Senate's having a right to require a three-fifth vote for cloture is that this violates majority rule. A democratic government is one in which the people rule. In practice this means that the candidate who receives the majority of votes is elected and that within the legislature the bill approved by the majority of members is passed. However, a Senate majority may be unable to pass a bill under consideration because it cannot muster the three-fifths vote required for cloture. Michael J. Gerhardt argues that Rule XXII leaves majority rule intact: "It does not require 60 votes to adopt a law; it requires at least 60 votes to end debate. Passing a bill, or confirming a nomination, still requires a simple majority." (Gerhardt 2004, pp. 456–457) But it certainly seems that the principle of majority rule is violated whenever the majority is denied the opportunity to vote on a measure because it cannot obtain the supermajority required to end debate.

In my estimation, there are strong arguments both for and against the right of the Senate to require a three-fifths vote to limit debate. By restraining a highly partisan majority, this could facilitate compromise. In practice, however, partisanship is not limited to majorities. Hence, Rule XXII too often results in gridlock. Another reason in favor of this right is that it promotes the stability of governmental policy, both when compromise is achieved and when gridlock occurs. Probably the strongest reason for requiring a three-fifths vote to limit debate is to protect the fundamental rights of minorities. In practice, however, it often today serves the political interests of some individual Senator rather than a minority of the citizens.

A strong reason not to require a three-fifths vote to limit debate is that this too often prevents the passage or results in the weakening of urgently needed legislation in the national interest. It is clearly not true that no meritorious measure has been defeated by Rule XXII, although it may be true that some vicious proposals have been killed by it. For anyone who believes in the value of demo racy, the most fundamental reason not to require a three-fifths vote to limit debate is that this violates the rule of the majority.

Given the existence of such strong reasons both for and against the constitutional right of the Senate to require a three-fifths vote to limit debate, the reasonable conclusion is that some compromise is needed. Sarah A. Binder and Steven S. Smith propose one plausible alternative.

> One possible way to empower a Senate majority is to adopt a sliding scale of votes required to invoke cloture. Most recently, such a ratcheting down of the cloture threshold was proposed by Senators Tom Harkin and Joseph Lieberman, who advocated a sliding scale of sixty, then fifty-seven, then fifty-four, and finally fifty-one votes to end debate. Such a route to majority cloture would slow down the process of limiting debate while ensuring that final action could be taken by the majority.

No doubt other compromise rules are possible. However, the Senate ought not to have a constitutional right to require a three-fifth vote to limit debate.

7 Criminal Legislation

Congress has constitutional rights to enact criminal legislation in a number of limited areas. As Colin V. Ram explains:

> Congress enjoys discrete authority to enact criminal legislation through its Article I, Section 8 enumerated powers. For example, Congress's postal power enables it to criminalize activities affecting the postal system, such as mail fraud. Likewise, under the Counterfeiting Clause, Congress can "provide for the Punishment of counterfeiting the securities and current Coin of the United States." Moreover, the Thirteenth, Fourteenth and Fifteenth Amendments empower Congress to criminalize behavior encroaching on the civil rights of citizens. Congress, however, retains the broadest authority to enact criminal legislation under the Commerce Clause. (Ram 2008, p. 772)

Still, the connection between the crimes Congress attempts to prohibit and interstate commerce is often slight or virtually nonexistent. Therefore, some advocate a general power of Congress to prohibit serious crime. Ought Congress to have a general constitutional right to enact criminal legislation?

One reason why congress ought to have a general right to enact criminal legislation is that all crime affects the national interest. One of the constitutional purposes of establishing our government is to promote the general welfare. Hence, Congress has at least a moral, and perhaps a legally compelling, interest in taking whatever action is necessary to prevent crimes that damage the public welfare. Although there may have been a time when many crimes were merely of local import, Thomas J. Maroney insists that it is no longer possible to draw a bright line between what is truly local and what is truly national because: "The historical record shows a recurrent, periodic, inexorable extension of federal criminal jurisdiction in response to the evolution of the nation from a highly localized level to regional level, to a national level, and eventually to an international level." (Maroney 2000, p. 1350) In *United States v. Lopez*, Justice Breyer, dissenting, explained how what might seem to be a merely local crime of possessing a gun near a public school damages the national interest in high quality education. (Supreme Court 1995a, pp. 618–625)

And in the same case, the United States government argued more generally that crime affects the national interest because it raises the cost of insurance throughout the nation and reduces the willingness of individuals to travel to areas of the country they consider dangerous. (Supreme Court 1995a, pp. 563–564) Arguments such as these imply that Congress ought to have a general constitutional right to enact criminal legislation.

Another reason why Congress ought to have a general constitutional right to enact criminal legislation is that by doing so it can assist the states in reducing crime. Thomas J. Maroney suggests that it is appropriate for Congress to become involved in any criminal area where (1) there is a pressing national concern, (2) state criminal jurisdiction is inadequate to solve this problem and (3) the federal government can make a significant contribution to the solution of this problem. (Maroney 2000, p. 1356) He recognizes that federal intervention can lead to counterproductive competition and friction between federal and state officials, but gives examples to show that cooperation is often possible and highly successful. (Maroney 2000, pp. 1358–1360) But perhaps a better way of assisting the states in fighting crime would be provide financial assistance rather than duplicating their criminal legislation.

A third reason why Congress ought to have a general constitutional right to enact criminal legislation is that this is necessary to preserve the moral legitimacy of the federal government. Federal law imposes serious burdens upon those subject to it, for example the obligations to pay income taxes and even risk life and limb by serving in the armed forces. What gives the federal government the moral right to harm its subjects in these and other ways? It is the fact that such burdens are necessary for the government to protect its subjects from more serious harms and to prevent the violation of their human rights. Another necessary burden is the enactment of criminal legislation that, although restricting the liberty of its subjects, also protects them from the harms and rights violations inflicted by criminal acts. However, some reply that ours is a dual government with national sovereignty divided between the federal government and the states. Hence, the federal government need not, and should not, attempt to serve every legitimate governmental purpose. Justice Kennedy, concurring in *United States v. Lopez*, argued that: “If a State or municipality determines that harsh criminal sanctions are necessary and wise to deter students from carrying guns on school premises, the reserved powers of the **States** are sufficient to enact these measures.” (Supreme Court 1995a, p. 587) If so, then presumably federal intervention is not necessary. However, experience abundantly demonstrates that some states are reluctant to enact harsh legislation and that those who do are often unable to enforce the law they have enacted. As a consequence, Congress ought to have a general constitutional right to enact criminal legislation in order to preserve its moral legitimacy.

There are also reasons why Congress ought not to have any such right. First, it would tempt Congress to misallocate scarce resources. The American Bar Association’s Task Force Report of 1998 asserts that inappropriate federalization scatters, rather than focuses, the resources needed to combat crime. The application of limited federal resources to local problems can deplete their use where they can be better utilized. (Maroney 2000, p. 1338) However, it is not clear that crime is typically a merely local problem or that Congress would enact criminal legislation when to do so would be inappropriate.

Second, Congress ought not to have a general constitutional right to enact criminal legislation because this would increase the danger of tyranny and abuse by the federal government. Chief Justice Rehnquist, delivering the opinion of the Court in *United States v. Lopez*, reminded us that the framers of our Constitution divided the powers of national sovereignty between a federal government with few and defined powers and the states with many and indefinite powers. Their purpose was to reduce the risk of tyranny and abuse, especially by the federal government they considered most dangerous. (Supreme Court 1995a, p. 552) No doubt they were aware of the way in which the English government had misused criminal law to silence and even eliminate its critics. However, some would reply that today in our more democratic government the people could and would hold both state and federal government accountable for their use or misuse of criminal legislation.

At this point, a third consideration becomes relevant. The American Bar Association's Task Force report asserts that federal criminal legislation undermines the accountability of both federal and state governments for combatting crime. Federalization of criminal legislation lessens citizens' perception about their power to have an impact on critical crime issues and diffuses their power to do so. Confusion of state and federal authority can leave citizens uncertain about who bears responsibility for dealing with crime, and it is harder for them to influence federal legislation than for them to influence their state legislatures. (Maroney 2000, pp. 1337–1338) A similar objection was expressed by Representative Michener when Congress considered the 1932 criminal act:

> Congress should be very careful about enacting additional criminal statutes punishing for crimes, when the same result can be obtained through State legislation. Whenever you remove responsibility from the local community to Washington, to that extent you lessen the interest of the local community in the enforcement of the law. (Congressional Record 1932, p. 283)

But if the local community is incapable of or unwilling to enforce adequate criminal law, then perhaps the federal government ought to assume some of this responsibility.

A fourth reason why Congress ought not to have a general constitutional right to enact criminal legislation is that this would sometimes undermine the Double Jeopardy Clause. Often one and the same criminal act would be prohibited by both State and federal legislation. In such cases, the Supreme Court has held that that although the offenses involve the same conduct, they are not the same offense for constitutional purposes. Hence, a criminal may be subject to two disparate sentences. Presumably, such double jeopardy is morally objectionable, but one might wonder precisely why subjecting criminals to double jeopardy is immoral.

A fifth reason why Congress ought not to have a general constitutional right to enact criminal legislation is that such legislation would impose a nationwide criminal law that would prevent the several states from experimenting with alternative ways of combating crime. Justice Kennedy, concurring in *United States v. Lopez*, asserted that: "The statute before us forecloses the **States** from experimenting and exercising their own judgment in an area to which **States** lay claim by right of history and expertise…." Probably the same objection could be made of much, even most, federal criminal legislation. Still, Congress could, although it might not, refrain from enacting criminal law that would prevent experimentation where such experimentation would be useful.

Which set of reasons is more powerful? Although it is probably true that all crime affects the national interest, not all of it does so seriously enough to justify federal intervention. But when crime does pose a serious problem and national criminal legislation would enable the federal government to assist the states in reducing crime, Congress ought to have the right to enact criminal legislation. And in such circumstances, Congress ought also to have a general constitutional right to enact criminal legislation to preserve its moral legitimacy. Hence, two of the three reasons for this right deserve serious consideration.

Although a constitutional right to enact criminal legislation might tempt Congress to misallocate scarce resources, the same is true of every allocation of legislative power to Congress. It is the strength of our democratic institutions, rather than denying the power to criminal legislation, that protects us from tyranny and the abuse of federal power today. And there is little empirical evidence to support the hypothesis that the voters would be less likely to hold the state and federal governments accountable for combating crime were Congress to enact criminal legislation. However, the duplication of state and federal criminal legislation prohibiting the same conduct does impose double jeopardy upon those subject to United States law. And nationwide federal criminal legislation does inhibit useful state experimentation regarding the best way to reduce criminal action. Thus, there are also two strong reasons against establishing a general constitutional right to Congress to enact criminal legislation.

Which pair of reasons ought to prevail? This depends upon how wisely Congress would exercise any general constitutional right to enact criminal legislation and how effectively the voters would hold the members of Congress accountable for any misuse of such a power. If we have faith in our democratic institutions, we ought to confer this power-right on Congress. With much hesitation, I would vote in favor of this general right to enact criminal legislation.

8 Judicial Review

Article III, Section 1 of the *United States Constitution* has two legal effects. First, it establishes the Supreme Court and authorizes Congress to establish inferior courts. In the Judiciary Act of 1789, Congress established a system of district and circuit courts. Second, it confers the judicial power of the United States upon these courts. Hence, federal courts have a constitutional power-right to decide all cases within their jurisdiction as defined by Article III, Section 2. The defining core of this right is the power "to determine actual controversies arising between diverse litigants, duly instituted in courts of proper jurisdiction." (Supreme Court 1911, p. 361)

This very general power-right has subsequently been interpreted to imply at least three ancillary power-rights. (1) The power-right to cite persons or parties for criminal or civil contempt. (Library of Congress 1973, pp. 601–614) (2) The power-right to issue writs, such as *habeas corpus* or *mandamus.* (Library of Congress 1973, pp. 614–625) And (3) The power-right of judicial review. Its defining core is the power to determine whether some administrative or legislative act is or is not authorized by the *United States Constitution*. This right of judicial review, first recognized in *Marbury v. Madison* is highly controversial, and most controversial of all is the power of a court to declare a statute null and void on the ground that it is unconstitutional. (Library of Congress 1973, pp. 669–684) This is what has come to be known as strong judicial review because any decision of the Supreme Court is final; it cannot be nullified or modified by administrative or legislative action.

Accordingly, one might ask: "Ought the United States courts to have the right to strong judicial review under present circumstances?" However, this would commit the fallacy of complex question because the right of strong judicial review presupposes that the Constitution limits the legislative power of Congress. Although United Kingdom courts can declare administrative acts and regulations established by administrative agencies illegal, they cannot declare any statute null and void because a fundamental principle of the United Kingdom constitution is that Parliament is supreme. Hence, one must first ask: "Ought the *United States Constitution* to limit the legislative power of Congress? Only if the answer is in the affirmative, would it be useful to ask whether the United States ought to continue to recognize the right to strong judicial review in its constitutional law."

Ought, then, the *Constitution* to limit the legislative power of Congress? One reason to do so is suggested, although not intended, by James Madison: "The necessity of a Senate is not less indicated by the propensity of all single and numerous assemblies to yield to the impulse of sudden and violent passions, and to be seduced by factious leaders into intemperate and pernicious resolutions." (Madison 1961, p. 418) With the development of political parties and the party discipline that reduces the criticism of proposed measures by individual members of Congress, the danger of legislation that sacrifices long-term interests to short-term considerations and, worse yet, that advances the interests of some limited faction at the expense of the welfare of all the citizens has been greatly increased. Therefore, there is today a need to limit the power of Congress in order to reduce its tendency to enact harmful or unjust legislation. Presumably, this is the purpose of the Presidential veto.

A more important reason to limit the legislative power of Congress is to preserve federalism by protecting the partial sovereignty of the states. As James Madison observes:

> But if the Government be national with regard to the *operation* of its powers, it changes its aspect again when we contemplate it in relation to the *extent* of its powers….In the latter the local or municipal authorities form distinct and independent portions of the supremacy, no more subject within their respective spheres to the general authority, than the general authority is subject to them, within its own sphere. In this relation then the proposed

> Government cannot be deemed a *national* one; since its jurisdiction extends to certain enumerated objects only, and leaves to the several states a residual and inviolable sovereignty over all other objects. (Madison 1961, p. 256)

However, political parties will often attempt to curry favor with the electorate by supporting popular prejudices and sometimes succeed in obtaining national legislation that intrudes into areas best left to state control. One might site federal statutes defining marriage as a union of one man and one woman or criminalizing the provision and possession of marijuana as examples. Therefore, it is necessary to limit the legislative powers of Congress in order to preserve the federalism that I have defended in the first section of this chapter.

A third reason to limit the legislative power of Congress is to preserve the democratic nature of the United States government. It seems at least paradoxical, and perhaps self-contradictory, to attempt to preserve democracy by limiting the legislative power of Congress, for surely Congress is the most democratic of the branches of our national government. However, an unlimited Congress would have the power to disenfranchise unpopular segments of our population, to censor media critical of governmental policies, or even criminalize opposition to controversial administrative actions. Although examples from other nations come readily to mind, it might seem that there is no danger in our country of such undemocratic legislation. Nevertheless, one should not forget the Alien and Sedition Acts of 1798 that criminalized radical criticism of the Adams administration and, much more recently, the Sedition Act of 1918 that criminalized speech and the expression of opinion that cast the government or the war effort in a negative light. And Title 8 Part 313 of the current Code of Federal Regulations, issued pursuant to federal legislation, denies naturalization to any person who is or has been a member of the Communist Party or is or has been a member of any organization that advocates communism. There has been and remains today a need to limit the legislative power of Congress to protect democracy in the United States.

A fourth and most obvious reason to limit the legislative power of Congress is to preserve the liberty of the people, to protect the liberties or moral rights of persons subject to the United States government. James Madison cites Montesquieu's insistence that "there can be no liberty where the legislative and executive powers are united in the same person, or body of magistrates." (Madison 1961, p. 325) And he adds that experience during the Confederation has shown that the separation of powers must be reinforced by a system of checks and balances to limit the legislature.

> If therefore the Legislature assumes executive and judiciary powers, no opposition is likely to be made; nor if made can it be effectual; because in that case, they may put their proceeding into the form of an act of Assembly, which will render them obligatory on the other branches. They have accordingly in many instances *decided rights* which should have been left to judiciary controversy…. (Madison 1961, p. 336)

Hence, Madison argued that the legislature power of Congress needs to be limited in order to protect the liberties of the people. But is this really necessary? Some authorities point out that the government of the United Kingdom, where the legislative power of Parliament is not constitutionally limited, has in the past and still does respect the fundamental rights and freedoms of its subjects. Although this is usually true, there have been some serious deficiencies in this regard.

More to the point is the question of whether the United States Congress has always and still does fully respect the moral rights of its citizens. The Fugitive Slave Law of 1850 illustrates the way in which the absence of morally justified limits on the power of Congress enabled it to deny the moral right to liberty of slaves who had escaped from bondage and fled to another state. Section VI permitted the owner or some legal officer to "pursue and reclaim" a fugitive slave. And it also denied an alleged fugitive's moral right to due process by providing that "In no trial or hearing under this act shall the testimony of such alleged fugitive be admitted in evidence…." And if there is ever a moral right to civil disobedience, Section VII violates this right by imposing a duty upon every individual not to "obstruct, hinder, or prevent" the arrest of a fugitive slave. Today the Thirteenth Amendment would render this act unconstitutional, but Congress still infringes fundamental moral rights in highly questionable ways. Title II of the Patriot Act of 2001, almost entirely reauthorized in 2011, seriously infringes the citizen's right to privacy by permitting wide-sweeping wiretapping and the interception of e-mail and other communications often with a court warrant that does not specify all the common carriers or third parties to be investigated and permits delayed notification of its execution. Title III infringes the property rights of many financial institutions and their clients by the ways in which it restricts the use of funds held in these financial institutions in an effort to prevent money laundering and giving financial aid to terrorists. Finally Title IV infringes the right to liberty by its provisions for mandatory detention. No doubt the United States government is justified in limiting the rights to privacy, property and liberty when this is necessary for a morally compelling reason. But what makes the Patriot Act so very worrisome is that the breadth and vagueness of its provisions enable public officials to infringe these rights when it merely seems convenient and is far from necessary.

There are, then, four reasons to limit the legislative power of Congress—to reduce its tendency to enact harmful or unjust legislation, to preserve federalism, to preserve the democratic nature of our government and to protect the moral rights of the citizens. Together these reasons show that the *United States Constitution* ought to continue to limit the legislative power of Congress. As long as it does so, strong judicial review will be possible. However, there are other ways of preventing *ultra vires* legislation such as self-restraint by the members of Congress and the presidential veto. Thus, one should now ask whether our courts ought to retain the power of strong judicial review.

There is little doubt that the courts ought to have the power of judicial review. Chief Justice Marshall ably defends this power in *Marbury v. Madison*:

> It is emphatically the province and duty of the judicial department to say what the law is. Those who apply the rule to particular cases, must of necessity expound and interpret that rule. If two laws conflict with each other, the courts must decide on the operation of each…. If then the courts are to regard the constitution; and the constitution is superior to any

> ordinary act of the legislature; the constitution, and not such ordinary act, must govern the case to which they both apply. (Supreme Court 1803, pp. 177–178)

And even Lloyd of Hampstead, who defended parliamentary supremacy, asserts that if the United Kingdom were to adopt a bill of rights:

> (a) The code should be given some sort of over-riding authority over other laws.
> (b) Power should be vested in the judiciary (whether generally or by way of a Constitutional or Supreme Court) to interpret the rights set forth in the Bill of Rights and to determine judicially their proper scope, extent and limits, and their relationship *inter se*.... (Lloyd of Hampstead 1976, p. 122)

However, this leaves open the question of whether this power of judicial review ought to be strong or weak.

The paradigm example of the power of strong judicial review is the power conferred upon our courts, especially the Supreme Court, by the *United States Constitution*. It is the power to declare a statute null and void on the ground that it is unconstitutional. It is strong because it is final, well almost final. Although it can be overcome by a constitutional amendment, this requires action by two thirds of both Houses of Congress together with ratification by three fourth of the states. Consequently, this has happened only four times throughout the history of our country. (Ely 1980, p. 46) Otherwise, there is no power of either the legislature or the administration, or both acting together, to reverse a decision of the Supreme Court rendering a statute null and void.

Ought the United States courts to retain this power-right of strong judicial review? There are several reasons that seem to justify this constitutional power-right. (1) The courts are the most independent party to decide disagreements between the legislature and a citizen who claims that some statute violates his or her constitutional right. As Cecile Fabre argues:

> Furthermore, if individuals have rights against the legislature, the latter should not be judge in conflicts it has with rights-bearers, and these conflicts should be settled by an independent party. The courts are such a party and it therefor makes sense to entrust them with this task. (Fabre 2000, p. 89)

It is a fundamental principle of justice that no one ought to be a judge in any dispute to which he or she is a party, and presumably this applies to artificial persons also. Hence, the legislature ought not to have the power to judge that one of its acts is not unconstitutional on the ground that it does not violate any constitutional right of the petitioner. Although the President might seem to be independent of the legislature, he or she will often be of the same party that controls Congress. Therefore, only the courts are really independent parties, and they ought to have the power to judge the constitutionality of any disputed statute. Moreover, this power of judicial review ought to be strong in order that it cannot be reversed by any partisan action of the legislature or the executive or both acting together.

(2) Judges are better qualified than either legislators or administrators to interpret any relevant constitutional right and how it applies to the claim at issue. The legal training of Judges and their rich experience of interpreting legal principles and applying them to past cases prepare them admirably for deciding whether some

statute does or does not violate a constitutional right of the petitioner. Granted that responsible legislators and administrators take care that their actions fall within their constitutional power-rights, this does little to prepare them to undertake the role of interpreting rights and applying them to particular cases, a role primarily reserved to judges. And the courts' power of judicial review ought to be strong in order that it cannot be reversed by some less qualified judgment of the legislature or the administration.

Not everyone accepts this line of reasoning. Lloyd of Hampstead denies that judges are better qualified than legislators to enforce fundamental rights because any bill of rights entrenches specific public policies.

> The judges are not particularly well-equipped to arrive at fundamental policy decisions of this character. Their background and training naturally tend to render them cautious and timid rather than imaginative and even at the present-day they tend to lead rather sheltered lives which do not bring them into close contact with the feelings and attitudes of large segments of our society. (Lloyd of Hampstead 1976, p. 125)

Granted that legislators are better able to choose public policies, once these policies have been enacted into law, especially entrenched in constitutional law, judges may well be more qualified to interpret and apply their legal significance.

W.J. Waluchow echoes a question asked by many. Strong judicial review is called for only when the meaning of some fundamental right, some constitutional norm, is disputed. But "If we cannot agree in advance what these norms mean, then it will be left to the judiciary to assign meanings for us. Does this not leave us prey to elitist judges and their subjective prejudices and agendas?" (Waluchow 2007, p. 217) Waluchow replies that:

> Indeed, I hazard to suggest that a judge's training makes her in many ways an eminently suitable candidate for the job: the test of reflective equilibrium is not far removed from the more traditional task of common law decision making in, for example, tort and contract cases, where precedents and general principles must be reconciled with one another and where processes like drawing analogies, marking distinctions so as to distinguish cases, and so on is commonplace. (Waluchow 2007, pp. 231–232)

How convincing one should take this reply depends upon whether the method of reflective equilibrium overcomes moral prejudices to arrive at some approximation to an objective moral truth. In the end, it remains unclear whether judges are the best qualified officials to interpret and apply constitutional rights when the constitutionality of some statute is at issue.

(3) The courts need a strong power of judicial review in order to check and balance he greater power of the administration and especially Congress. Alexander Hamilton explains why this is true:

> The executive not only dispenses the honors, but holds the sword of the community. The legislature not only commands the purse, but prescribes the rules by which the duties and rights of every citizen are to be regulated. The judiciary on the contrary has no influence over either the sword or the purse, no direction either of strength or of the wealth of the society, and can take no active resolutions whatever. It may be said to have neither Force nor Will, but merely judgment; and must ultimately depend upon the aid of the executive arm even for the efficacy of its judgments. (Hamilton 1961, pp. 522–523)

This assessment of the relative strength of the three branches of government remains true in the United States today.

However, it does not necessarily follow that under present circumstances our courts still need the very strong power-right of judicial review conferred by the *United States Constitution*. It might be that some weaker power of judicial review would be sufficient to protect the rights of those subject to congressional legislation.

Mark Tushnet reminds us of the recent development of alternative forms of judicial review:

> In weak-form systems, judicial interpretation of constitutional provisions can be revised in the relatively short term by a legislature using a decision rule not much different from the one used in the every-day legislative process. I discuss here the design of weak-form review in New Zealand, the United Kingdom, and Canada. I think it worth noting early on that these nations are reasonably well-functioning democracies in which civil liberties and civil rights are reasonably well protected…. (Tushnet 2009, p. 119)

Still, let us not forget the observation of Sir Leslie Scarman that:

> English law sturdily protects the freedom of the individual and respects human personality. But when times are abnormally alive with fear and prejudice, the common law is at a disadvantage. It cannot resist the will, however frightened and prejudiced it may be, of Parliament. (Scarman 1974, p. 15)

Recent counter-terrorism legislation in the United States suggests that we ought not to adopt a weak form of judicial review.

Nevertheless, one ought not to forget that there are degrees of strength and that a less strong power of judicial review might be more justified that the very strong power our courts now possess. For example, the *United States Constitution* might allow an appeal to the people by a more simple and less difficult amendment process. Or it might empower Congress to reverse a Supreme Court decision of unconstitutionality by a two-thirds majority in both houses. It seems to me that some such alternative would provide adequate protection for individual rights and would reduce the force of, but not entirely eliminate, the most serious objection to our present strong form of judicial review, that it is undemocratic.

Any strong form of judicial review certainly seems undemocratic, for it enables judges who are not elected and cannot be held accountable to the people by any need for being reelected to declare null and void legislation enacted by the members of Congress who are the political representatives of the people. Although this would not have worried the founders of our government, for they believed a republican form of government preferable to a democratic one, it seems to undermine the justification of strong judicial review for anyone, like myself, who believes in the value of democracy.

There is a huge literature attempting to meet the charge that strong judicial review is unjustified because it is undemocratic. Steven Holmes argues at length that strong judicial review is not undemocratic because it is a pre-commitment of the American people. (Holmes 1988, pp. 195–240) But it is hard to see how a pre-commitment of our founding fathers can justify the imposition of strong judicial review upon us when it is not our pre-commitment. Samuel Freeman suggests that judicial review can be made consistent with democracy if one rejects a purely procedural definition of democracy and adopts a substantive conception:

> On this conception of democracy, what makes a constitution democratic is not equal consideration of majority procedures, but that it specifies rights and procedures devised to promote the good of each citizen and maintain the equal rights that constitute their democratic sovereignty. (Freeman 1990, p. 350)

But to my mind this evades the force of the objection because that objection rests upon the conviction that democratic procedures, including majority rule, are a necessary feature of any morally justified government. Freeman suggests a much better response to the claim that strong judicial review is undemocratic when he appeals, not to a redefinition of democracy, but to its moral grounds: "My basic claim is that the set of moral principles and ideals that best justify democratic decision-making processes provide a justification for the institution of judicial review under appropriate circumstances." (Freeman 1990, p. 328) However, if one is going to move to the level of justification, as I believe one should, it is simpler and more honest to insist that democratic procedures are only one relevant consideration in the justification of any government and that the promotion of the public welfare and the protection of human rights are also relevant. Therefore, strong, although not unnecessarily strong, judicial review may be justified even though it is undemocratic. Everything considered, I believe that the *United States Constitution* ought to be amended to provide for a strong, but less strong, power-right of judicial review.

9 Conclusions

The conclusions I have reached about our fundamental choices of constitutional institutions are tentative and often speculative. What is important for identifying the moral foundations of constitutional rights is the reasons for and against them. Therefore, let me sum up my reasoning. A federal government is preferable to a confederation because it offers greater military security, economic opportunity and ability to reduce environmental damage. Although a unitary government would protect individual liberties and minority groups as effectively as a federal government, a federal is preferable primarily because it offers more security for regional governments to experiment with solutions to pressing social problems. Although the separation of legislative, executive and judicial powers may enhance the competence of public officials, it does little to protect liberty or democracy and frequently results in harmful deadlocks that prevent action to resolve pressing social problems. Although a parliamentary form of government can avoid deadlocks and may be slightly more democratic than a presidential one, our presidential form of government usually avoids deadlock when disaster threatens, is reasonably democratic and protects individual rights at least as well as a parliamentary one. The House of Representatives is a desirable institution because it is our most democratic legislative body. Although the Senate is no longer needed to protect the partial sovereignty of the states or to prevent unjust legislation by the House of Representatives and it can create harmful legislative deadlocks, it probably does enhance the expertise of our legislators, increase the stability of governmental policies, and provide a competent body to give advice and consent to presidential nominations or proposed treaties. The *United States Constitution* ought to continue to limit the legislative power of Congress in order to reduce its tendency to enact harmful or unjust legislation, to preserve federalism, to preserve the democratic nature of our government and to protect the moral rights of the citizens. Although it is not clear that judges are better qualified than legislators to interpret constitutional provisions, our courts ought to have a strong power-right of judicial review because justice demands an independent party in cases between a right-holder and the legislature that enacted the challenged statute and in order to balance the greater power of the legislature. However, it is not necessary to retain our very strong power of judicial review, and it would be more democratic to amend our *Constitution* to confer a less strong, but not weak, power-right of judicial review.

Some of these morally relevant considerations are more basic than others. Military security and economic opportunity, for example, are among the proper functions of any national government, although why these should have this status calls for explanation. And the competence of public officials or institutional bodies is of importance only because their functions are for some more basic reason important. On the other hand, individual moral rights, minority rights, democracy, justice and avoiding harm to individuals or the general welfare are more fundamental. Perhaps subsequent chapters will reveal more about the moral foundations of constitutional rights and how these support higher-level justifying reasons for them.

References

Ackerman, Bruce (2000). The New Separation of Powers. Harvard Law Review 113:633–729.

Binder, Sarah A. and Smith, Steven S. (1997). Politics or Principle? Filibustering in the United States Senate. Brookings Institution Press. Washington DC.

Briffault, Richard (1994). "What About the 'ism'?" Normative and Formal Concerns in Contemporary Federalism. Vanderbilt Law Review 47:1303–1354.

Choudhry, Sujit and Hume, Nathan (2011). Federalism, Devolution and Secession: from Classical to Post-Conflict Federalism. In Comparative Constitutional Law, Tom Ginsburg and Rosalind Dixon (eds.). E. Eiger. Cheltenham UK and Northampton MA.

Congressional Record (1932). 75 Cong. Rec. 13.

Donahue, John D. and Pollack, Mark A. (2001). Centralism and its Discontents: The Rhythms of Federalism in the United States and the European Union. In The Federal Vision: Legitimacy and Levels of Government in the United States and the European Union, Kalypso Nicolaidis and Robert Howse (eds.). Oxford University Press. Oxford.

Ely, John Hart (1980). Democracy and Distrust: A Theory of Judicial Review. Harvard University Press. Cambridge MA.

Fabre, Cecile (2000). A Philosophical Argument for a Bill of Rights. British Journal of Political Science 30:77–98.

Freeman, Samuel (1990). Constitutional Democracy and the Legitimacy of judicial Review. Law and Democracy 9:327–370.
Gerhardt, Michael J. (2004). The Constitutionality of the Filibuster. William and Mary Law Scholarship Repository 857:445–473.
Gold, Martin B. and Gupta, Dimple (2009). The Constitutional Option to Change Senate Rules and Procedures: A Majoritarian Means to Overcome the Filibuster. Harvard Journal of Law and Public Policy 28:205–272.
Grassley, Chuck (2014). Floor Speech on the Introduction of the Stop Cloture Abuse Resolution to Reform the Senate Cloture Rule. Online.
Hamilton, Alexander (1961). The Federalist, Jacob E. Cooke (ed.). Meridian Books. Cleveland and New York.
Holmes, Steven (1988). Precommitment and the Paradox of Democracy. In Constitutionalism and Democracy, Jon Elster and Rune Slagstad (eds.). Cambridge University Press. Cambridge.
Jones, Charles O. (1997). The American Presidency: A Separationist Perspective. In Presidential Institutions and Democratic Politics: Comparing Regional and National Contexts, Kurt von Mettenhaim (ed.). Johns Hopkins University Press. Baltimore and London.
Library of Congress (1973). The Constitution of the United States of America: Analysis and Interpretation. U. S. Government Printing Office. Washington DC.
Linz, Juan J. (1990). The Perils of Presidentialism. Journal of Democracy 1:51–69.
Linz, Juan J. (1994). Presidential or Parliamentary Democracy: Does it Make a Difference? In the Failure of Presidential Democracy, Juan J. Linz and Arturo Valenzuela (eds.). Johns Hopkins University Press. Baltimore.
Lloyd of Hampstead (1976). Do We Need a Bill of Rights? The Modern Law Review 39:121–129.
Madison, J. (1895) Debates on the Adoption of the Federal Constitution, 2nd edition, J. Eliot (ed.). Printed for the Editor. Washington DC.
Madison, James (1961). The Federalist, Jacob E. Cooke (ed.). Meridian Books. Cleveland and New York.
Maroney, Thomas J. (2000). Fifty Years of Federalization of Criminal Law: Sounding the Alarm or "Crying Wolf." Syracuse Law Review 50: 1317–1378.
Montesquieu, Baron de (1966). The Spirit of the Laws. Hafner Publishing Company. New York and London.
Norman, Wayne J. (1994). Towards a Philosophy of Federalism. In Group Rights, Judith Baker (ed.). University of Toronto Press. Toronto.
Peterson, Paul E. (1995). The Price of Federalism. The Twentieth Century Fund Inc. New York.
Ram, Colin V. (2008). Regulating Interstate Crime: How the Federal Kidnapping Act Blurs the Distinction Between What is Truly National and What is Truly Local. Washington & Lee Law Review 65:767–806.
Rawls, W. Lee (2009). In Praise Deadlock: How Partisan Struggle Makes Better Laws. Woodrow Wilson Center Press. Washington DC.
Riker, William H. (1964). Federalism: Origin, Operation, Significance. Little Brown and Company. Boston and Toronto.
Rockman, Bert S. (1997). The Performance of Presidents and Prime Ministers and of Presidential and Parliamentary Systems. In Presidential Institutions and Democratic Politics: Comparing Regional and National Contexts, Kurt von Mettenheim (ed.). Johns Hopkins University Press. Baltimore and London.
Scarman, Sir Leslie (1974). English Law: The New Dimension. Stevens. London.
Story, Joseph (1994). Commentaries on the Constitution of the United States, Vol. 1. William S, Hein. Buffalo NY.
Supreme Court (1803). Marbury v. Madison, 1 Cr. (5 U.S.) 137.
Supreme Court (1911). Muskrat v. United States, 219 U.S. 346.
Supreme Court (1969). Powell v. McCormack, 395 U.S. 486.
Supreme Court (1995a). United States v. Lopez, 514 U.S. 549.

Supreme Court (1995b). U. S. Term Limits, Inc. v. Thornton, 514 U.S. 779.
Tushnet, Mark (2009). The Supreme Court and Contemporary Constitutionalism: The Implications of the Developement of Alternative Forms of judicial Review. In the Supreme Court and the Idea of Constitutionalism, Steven Kautz et. al. (eds.). University of Pennsylvania Press. Philadelphia PA.
Vile, M. J. C. (1998). Constitutionalism and the Separation of Powers, 2nd edition. Liberty Fund. Indianapolis IN.
Wade, H. W. R. (1982). Administrative Law, 5th edition. Clarendon Press. Oxford.
Waluchow, W. J. (2007). A Common Law Theory of Judicial Review: The Living Tree. Cambridge University Press. Cambridge.
Weeks, Kent M. (1971). Adam Clayton Powell and the Supreme Court. Dunellen. New York.
Wheare, K. C. (1946). Federal Government. Oxford University Press. London.

Chapter 4
Public Officials

Abstract Because the actions of any institution consist in the actions of public officials acting in their institutional roles, the constitutional rights of public officials are essential to any national legal system. This chapter provides a critical examination of the reasons for and against several actual or proposed rights of public officials: the presidential war powers, the presidential power to remove administrative officials, the presidential line-item veto, the speech or debate immunity of congressmen, and the life tenure of federal judges. Finally the moral foundations of such rights are described.

The actions of any institution consist in the actions of one or more human beings acting in their institutional roles. For example, Congress enacts a bill only when a majority of the members of the House and the Senate vote in favor of it, and a federal court decides a case only when one or more judges declare a judgment regarding how the law applies to the facts of the case. Hence, any constitution must confer rights, especially power-rights, upon the officials in whatever institutions it constitutes.

1 The Presidential War Powers

The *United States Constitution* confers a variety of rights upon the President. Among the most important are the following: (1) Article I, Section 7, Clause2 confers the power-right to sign or veto bills passed by both Houses of Congress. (2) Article II, Section 2, Clause 1 confers the power-right to act as Commander-in-Chief of the armed forces of the United States and of the militia of the several states when they are called into the service of the United States. (3) Article II, Section 2, Clause 1 also confers the power-right to grant reprieves and pardons for offences against the United States. (4) Article II, Section 3 confers the power-right to enforce the federal laws, a right implied by the President's constitutional duty to "take Care that the Laws be faithfully executed." (5) Article II, Section 1, Clause 7 confers a claim-right to "a Compensation, which shall neither be increased nor diminished

C. Wellman, *Constitutional Rights -What They Are and What They Ought to Be*,
Law and Philosophy Library 115, DOI 10.1007/978-3-319-31526-3_4

during the Period for which he shall have been elected." And (6) Article II, Section 4 confers an immunity-right against being removed from office except by impeachment.

Of these constitutional rights of the President, the most controversial today is probably the right to act as Commander-in-Chief, the right to exercise what have come to be called the President's "war powers." This right raises two practically important and theoretically difficult questions: What is the scope of the President's war powers? And what ought to be the scope of the President's war powers? Let us consider these in turn.

First, what is the scope of the President's war powers as Commander-in-Chief? In order to answer this question, one needs to understand how these powers are related to the war powers of Congress. Article I, Section 8 of the *United States Constitution* confers a number of war powers upon Congress. Clause 11 confers the power "To declare War." Clause 12 confers the power "To raise and support Armies." Clause 13 confers the power "To provide and maintain a Navy." And Clause 14 confers the power "To makes Rules for the Government and Regulation of the land and naval Forces." These provisions suggest that the President has the constitutional right to act as Commander-in-Chief only when Congress has declared war and that in so acting he or she is limited by the Congressional rules for the government of the armed forces.

The suggestion that the President has the constitutional right to act as Commander-in- Chief only when Congress has declared war is almost certainly false. In the *Prize Cases*, the Supreme Court has decided that:

> If a war be made by invasion of a foreign nation, the President is not only authorized but bound to resist force with force. He does not initiate the war, but is bound to accept the challenge without waiting for any special legislative authority. And whether the hostile party be a foreign invader or States organized in rebellion, it is nonetheless a war although the declaration of it be "unilateral." (Supreme Court 1862, p. 668)

And the Supreme Court refused to consider three cases that challenged the constitutionality of the undeclared war in Vietnam. Moreover, even *The War Powers Resolution of 1973*, in which Congress attempted to limit the President's power as Commander-in-Chief, concedes that the President has the constitutional power to introduce United States forces into hostilities without any declaration of war pursuant to "a national emergency created by an attack upon the United States, its territories or possessions, or its armed forces." (Public Law 1973, p. 1)

However, the suggestion that in acting as Commander-in-Chief the President is limited by Congressional rules for the government of the armed forces remains highly controversial. There are two competing interpretations of the *United States Constitution* aptly named by Stephen I. Vladeck "the disabling theory" and "the overriding theory" of the war powers. (Vladeck 2007, pp. 941 & 950) The disabling theory maintains that the President and Congress share their war powers in such a way that Congress can under many, but not all, circumstances limit the President's power as Commander-in Chief by legislation. The overriding theory insists that the President's power as Commander-in-Chief is separate and independent from the

Congressional war powers so that it renders any legislation that purports to limit it legally ineffective.

The War Powers Resolution of 1973, a joint resolution concerning the war powers of Congress and the President, presupposes the disabling theory. It provides that the President's power as Commander-in Chief may be exercised "only pursuant to (1) a declaration of war, (2) specific statutory authorization, or (3) a national emergency created by an attack upon the United States, its territories or possessions, or its armed forces." It explains its constitutional power to disable the President from exercising any other war power by the following:

> Under article I, section 8, of the Constitution, it is specifically provided that the Congress shall have the power to make all laws necessary and proper for carrying into execution, not only its own powers but also all other powers vested by the Constitution in the Government of the United States, or in any department or officer thereof. (Public Law 1973, p. 1)

Although President Nixon vetoed this joint resolution, Congress overrode his veto and it remains the law of the land.

Advocates of the disabling theory typically appeal to the opinion of Chief Justice Marshall in *Little v. Barreme* holding that the President lacked the power to authorize the seizure of the *Flying Fish* because Congressional legislation had excluded "a seizure of any vessel not bound to a French port." (Supreme Court 1804, p. 178) They can also cite three much more recent opinions. In *Youngstown Sheet & Tube Co. v. Sawyer*, Justice Burton concluded:

> The controlling fact here is that Congress, within its constitutionally delegated power, has prescribed for the President specific procedures, exclusive of seizure, for his use in meeting the present type of emergency. Congress has reserved to itself the right to determine where and when to authorize the seizure of property in meeting such an emergency. Under these circumstances, the President's order of April 2 invaded the jurisdiction of Congress. It violated the essence of the principle of the separation of governmental powers. Accordingly, the injunction against its effectiveness should be sustained. (Supreme Court 1952, pp. 659–660)

In the same case, Justice Clark concluded "that, where Congress has laid down specific procedures to deal with the type of crisis confronting the President, he must follow those procedures in meeting the crisis…." (Supreme Court 1952, p. 662) Finally, in *Hamdi v. Rumsfeld*, Justice Scalia, dissenting, insisted that "Except for the actual command of military forces, all authorization for their maintenance and all explicit authorization for their use is placed in the control of Congress under Article I, rather than the President under Article II." (Supreme Court 2004, p. 569) Accordingly, there are strong grounds to support the disabling theory of the war powers.

There are also strong grounds to support the overriding theory of war powers. The most basic of these are described in the *Memorandum Opinion for the Deputy Counsel to the President* of September 25, 2001. It asserts that:

> Article II, Section 2 states that the "President shall be Commander in Chief of the Army and Navy of the United States and of the Militia of the several States, when called into the actual service of the United States." U.S. Const. art. II, §2, cl. 1. He is further vested with all of "the executive Power" and the duty to execute the laws. U.S. Const. art. II, §1. These powers

> give the President broad constitutional authority to use military force in response to threats to the national security and foreign policy of the United States. (Yoo 2001, p. 4)

and

> Article II, Section 1 provides that "[t]he executive Power shall be vested in a President of the United States." U.S. Const. art. II, § 1. By contrast, Article I's Vesting Clause gives Congress only the powers "herein granted." *Id.* art. I, § 1. This difference in language indicates that Congress's legislative powers are limited to the list enumerated in Article I, Section 8, while the President's powers include inherent executive powers that are unenumerated in the Constitution. (Yoo 2001, p. 4)

The *Memorandum* also notes that the Constitutional Convention amended the working draft of the Constitution that had given Congress the power to "make" war to give it merely the power to "declare" war. (Yoo 2001, p. 3)

The *National Security Agency White Paper* of January 19, 2006 is a more comprehensive justification for the overriding theory of the Presidential war powers. It also begins its constitutional analysis by citing Article II of the *United States Constitution*. It then refers to a wide variety of court cases, of which the following are the most relevant: (1) Justice Grieg in the *Prize Cases* declared that:

> The Constitution confers on the President the whole executive power. He is bound to take care that the laws be faithfully executed. He is Commander-in-Chief of the Army and Navy of the United States....If a war be made by invasion of a foreign nation, the President is not only authorized but bound to resist by force. (Supreme Court 1862, p. 668)

(2) Judge Silberman asserted in *Campbell v. Clinton* that "The Prize Cases stand for the proposition that the President has independent authority to repel aggressive acts by third parties even without specific congressional authorization, and courts may not review the level of force selected." (Court of Appeals 2000, p. 27) (3) In *United States v. Curtis-Wright* Justice Sutherland explained that

> The President is the constitutional representative of the United States with regard to foreign nations....It is important to bear in mind that we are here dealing not alone with an authority vested in the President by an exertion of legislative power, but with such an authority plus the very delicate plenary and exclusive power of the President as the sole organ of the federal government in the field of international relations.... (Supreme Court 1936, pp. 319–320)

Given the strength of the evidence for each of these interpretations of constitutional law, the disabling theory and the overriding theory, it would be rash for me, a philosopher rather than a constitutional lawyer, to decide which is the correct one. Let me instead consider the moral issue raised by the war powers of the President.

Ought the President to have a constitutional right to unlimited war powers? There are several reasons in favor of this right. First, The President is in the best position to know the relevant facts. Justice Sutherland, delivering the opinion of the Supreme Court in *United States v. Curtis-Wright*, described the relative positions of the President and Congress as follows:

> Moreover, he, not Congress, has the better opportunity of knowing the conditions which prevail in foreign countries, and especially is this true in the time of war. He has his confidential sources of information. He has his agents in the form of diplomatic, consular and

> other officials. Secrecy in respect of information gathered by them is highly necessary, and the premature disclosure of it productive of harmful results. (Supreme Court 1936, p. 320)

Obviously uninformed military actions could be disastrous, and sharing sensitive information with the members of Congress would invite disaster. Hence, the President ought to remain free to take or refrain from military action as he sees fit. Second, Complete Presidential discretion is necessary to enable our Commander in Chief to counter unpredictable threats to our national security. Alexander Hamilton argued that:

> The powers essential to the common defence …ought to exist without limitation:
>
> *Because it is impossible to foresee or define the extent and variety of national emergencies, or the corresponding extent & variety of the means that may be necessary to satisfy them….* and for this reason no constitutional shackles can wisely be imposed on the power to which the care of it is committed. (Hamilton 1961, p. 147)

And in *United States v. Curtis-Wright*, Justice Sutherland asserted that:

> It is quite apparent that if, in the maintenance of our international relations, embarrassment—perhaps serious embarrassment—is to be avoided and success for our aims achieved, congressional legislation which is to be made effective through negotiation and inquiry within the international field must often accord to the President a degree of discretion and freedom from statutory restriction which would not be admissible were domestic affairs alone involved. (Supreme Court 1936, p. 320)

Presumably this is especially true when our national security is in danger. Congressional limitations on the Presidential war powers might well prevent or hinder urgently needed action. Third, unified control is essential for the vigorous defense of our national security. Hamilton explained why the war powers ought to be conferred upon one executive official rather than a legislative body:

> That unity is essential to energy will not be disputed. Decision, activity, secrecy, and dispatch will generally characterize the proceedings of one man, in a much more eminent degree, than the proceedings of any greater number; and in proportion as the number is increased, these qualities will be diminished. (Hamilton 1961, p. 472)

This is even more true today when Republican and Democratic members of Congress have very different views of the national interest and are prone to partisan politics. However, Abraham D. Sofaer, legal advisor to the State Department, insisted that:

> This administration recognizes that Congress has a critical role to play in the determination of the circumstances under which the United States should commit its forces to actual or potential hostilities. No Executive policy or activity in this area can have any hope of success in the long term unless Congress and the American people concur in it and are willing to support its execution. (Sofaer 1988, p. 299)

One wonders whether there is any way to combine short term unity of command with long term Congressional limitation.

There are additional reasons against giving the President a constitutional right to unlimited war powers. First, Congressional oversight is necessary to prevent unwise, potentially disastrous, military actions. Louis Fisher reminds us that:

> Truman's sending troops to Korea and Europe finally precipitated a major confrontation with Congress. In an extremely powerful floor statement, Sen. Robert Taft, R-Ohio, delivered a ten-thousand word speech to encourage Congress to defend its prerogatives. He argued that constructive criticism from Congress on foreign policy is essential to the safety of the nation. (Fisher 1991a, p. 204)

Even the most conscientious presidents will be tempted to make dubious decisions such as entering into an unwinnable Vietnam war or invading Iraq on the basis of inaccurate intelligence indicating the possession of weapons of mass destruction. Second, Congressional limitation of the President's war powers is necessary to prevent the violation of the civil rights of United States citizens. This danger is amply demonstrated by the recent Supreme Court cases challenging the President's denial of *habeas corpus* and immunity from unreasonable searches and seizures. Third, the President's war powers ought to be limited in order to prevent the violation of fundamental human rights. Here a wide variety of actions of the administration of George W. Bush are relevant. Targeted killings threatened the human right to life. Indefinite detention threatened the human right to liberty. Coercive interrogation threatened the human right to personal security. The use of military tribunals threatened the human right to due process. And surveillance with inadequate judicial control threatened the human right to privacy. Although these tactics may sometimes be useful, surely they are often morally unjustified.

In my estimation, the reasons against giving the President a constitutional right to unlimited war powers are conclusive. Our presidents have during the past few decades made some very unwise military decisions, violated several civil rights of United States citizens and violated fundamental human rights of both citizens and non-citizens. Although the President is normally in the best position to know the relevant facts, their interpretation is often very controversial. To be sure, highly sensitive information ought not to be communicated to every member of Congress, but it might well be shared with at least some members of its armed services committees. A single commander-in-chief is necessary for strong and effective tactical and even strategic military action and congressional disunity might prevent or postpone taking action in emergency situations. This does not, however, rule out every kind of limitation on the presidential war powers. Any restriction must preserve sufficient presidential discretion to enable the president to act when unpredicted threats to our national security arise. Congress has attempted do precisely this in the *War Powers Resolution* of 1973. Section 2 reads in part:

> The constitutional powers of the President as Commander-in-Chief to introduce United States Armed Forces into hostilities, or into situations where imminent involvement in hostilities is clearly indicated by the circumstances, are exercised only pursuant to (1) a declaration of war, (2) specific statutory authorization, or (3) a national emergency created by an attack upon the United States, its territories or possessions, or its armed forces (Public Law 1973, p. 1).

Unfortunately, national emergencies requiring military action, the deployment of armed forces or even their limited use, are not confined to actual attacks. If the Commander-in-Chief cannot act until after an attack, our national security may already have been severely jeopardized. I suggest that the third clause should be amended to read "(3) a national emergency created by an attack or the imminent threat of an attack upon the United States, its territories or possessions, or its armed forces." Although this is not a fail-safe limitation, it is the kind of limit on the President's war powers that best takes account of the most important relevant considerations.

2 The Removal of Administrative Officials

Article II, Section 4 of the *United States Constitution* reads: "The President, Vice President and all civil Officers of the United States, shall be removed from Office on Impeachment for, and Conviction of, Treason, Bribery, or other high Crimes and Misdemeanors." Presumably civil officers are administrative officials appointed by the President with the advice and consent of the Senate. But the *Constitution* is silent concerning the removal of inferior administrative officials. Arguable, it was originally assumed that the President had the power to remove both civil officers and inferior administrative officials. But from time to time Congress has attempted to restrict the presidential power of removal, and Presidents have typically resisted these attempts. The Supreme Court has struggled to define the limits, if any, on the President's removal power. Ought the President to have a constitutional right to remove administrative officials at will?

One reason why the President ought to have this right is that the power of removal is and ought to be incident on the power of appointment. (Supreme Court 1926, p. 119) The power to appoint is the power to choose who shall occupy an office, and this implies the power to choose who shall not hold this office. Since the President appoints administrative officials, he or she ought to have the power to remove them. But, some remind us, the President cannot appoint the highest officials at will; the President's power of appointment is subject to the advice and consent of the Senate. They infer that the power of removal ought to be similarly limited. However, Chief Justice Taft, delivering the opinion of the Court in *Meyers v. Olson*, argued that the reason for limiting the president's power of appointment, to prevent the appointment of a disproportionate number of officials from the larger states, does not apply to the power of removal. Moreover, to give the Senate the power to limit the President's power of removal is a more serious invasion of the separation of powers than its power to limit the President's power of appointment. (Supreme Court 1926, pp. 120–121)

A second reason why the President ought to have a constitutional right to remove administrative officials at will is that the President is best able to judge the past performance of an administrator. Chief Justice Taft asserted in *Myers* that:

> When a nomination is made, it may be assumed that the Senate is, or may become, as well advised of the fitness of the nominee as the President, but in the nature of things the defects in ability or intelligence or loyalty of one who has served as an officer under the President, are facts as to which the President, or his subordinates, must be better informed than the Senate, and the power to remove him may, therefore, be regarded as confined, for very

> sound and practical reasons, to the governmental authority who has administrative control. (Supreme Court 1926, pp. 121–122)

The same could be argued with even greater force regarding the inability of Congress as a whole to judge the competence of administrative officials. However, those who distrust a powerful Executive might worry that the President could abuse the right to remove in order to fire a competent official merely for insufficient loyalty.

A third reason why the President ought to have the constitutional right to remove administrative officials at will is that this is necessary for the unity of the administration. As Madison argued in the Congressional debate concerning the removal power: "Vest this power in the Senate jointly with the President, and you abolish at once the great principle of unity and responsibility in the Executive department, which was intended for the security of liberty and the public good." (Supreme Court 1926, p. 131) A subordinate officer might often disagree with some policy adopted by the President. In such circumstances, he or she might fail to carry out this policy energetically or even act to frustrate it. Clearly this would impair the efficiency of the Executive department in promoting the public welfare and protecting the rights of the citizens. In addition to efficiency, the unity of the Executive department promotes the rule of law. Justice Scalia, dissenting in *Morrison v. Olson*, asserted that: "It is, in other words, an additional advantage of the unitary Executive that it can achieve a more uniform application of the law." (Supreme Court 1988, p. 732) And only when the law is uniformly applied to all similar cases is there the rule of law rather than the arbitrary rule of men. On the other hand, the efficient promotion of misguided policies or the uniform application of an unjust law would not be desirable.

A fourth reason why the President ought to have the constitutional right to remove administrative officials at will is, as Madison also argued, that this is necessary to preserve the responsibility of the Executive department. In the debate concerning the removal power Mr. Sedgwick of Massachusetts argued similarly against requiring the advice and consent of the Senate:

> Shall a man under these circumstances be saddled upon the President, who has been appointed for no other purpose than to aid the President in performing certain duties? Shall he be continued, I ask again, against the will of the President? If he is, where is the responsibility? Are you to look for it in the President, who has no control over the office, no power to remove him if he acts unfeelingly or unfaithfully? (Supreme Court 1926, p. 132)

Hence, the President must have the right to remove administrative officials at will in order to be held responsible for performing his constitutional duty to take care that the laws be faithfully executed. However, Justice McReynolds in a separate *Meyers v. United States* opinion assuming that Congress has the authority to create officers, prescribe qualifications and set terms, objected that: "The general duty to enforce all laws cannot justify infraction of some of them." (Supreme Court 1926, pp. 186–187)

There are an equal number of reasons against giving the President a constitutional right to remove administrative officials at will. First, this would discourage the most competent candidates from serving in the administration. When the House of Representatives discussed the question of removal, William Smith warned that competent people would be reluctant to accept a position and risk their reputations if the President could remove them at will. (Fisher 2007, p. 49) True enough, but other motives might, and often do, counter this concern.

A second reason why the President ought not to have the constitutional right to remove administrative officials at will is that this would open the door to the reintroduction of the spoils system. This is a system in which a newly elected executive removes large numbers of officials in order to confer these offices upon his or her supporters. This creates an unstable administration with a strong political bias. Congress created the Civil Service, in which the executive can remove civil servants only for cause and pursuant to due process, to end these evils. (Bruff 2006, p. 413) In *Meyers v. United States*, Chief Justice Taft met this argument by noting that this would be limited to inferior offices. (Supreme Court 1926, p. 173) This is small consolation for those who are well aware that the vast majority of administrative officials hold inferior offices.

Third, the President ought not to have the right to remove all administrative officials at will because this would make independent agencies impossible. It is essential that agencies such as the Federal Trade Commission be independent of all executive influence. Justice Sutherland, delivering the opinion of the Supreme Court in *Humphrey's Executor v. United States,* reported that:

> Thus, the language of the act, the legislative reports, and the general purposes of the legislation as reflected by the debates, all combine to demonstrate the Congressional intent to create a body of experts who shall gain experience by length of service—a body which shall be independent of executive authority, *except in its selection*, and free to exercise its judgment without the leave or hindrance of any other official or any department of the government. To the attainment of these purposes, it is clear that Congress was of the opinion that length and certainty of tenure would vitally contribute. (Supreme Court 1935, pp. 625–626)

And presumably the value of these agencies depends upon the fact that the expertise of their members cannot be discounted by any purely political influence. Moreover, the fact that their functions are quasi-legislative and quasi-judicial as well as administrative is another reason why their members ought not to be removable by the President at will. (Supreme Court 1935, p. 628)

A fourth reason why the President ought not to have a constitutional right to remove all administrative officials at will is that this would protect unethical, even illegal, conduct. Chief Justice Rehnquist reported in *Morrison v. Olson* that the Ethics in Government Act allows for the appointment of an independent counsel to investigate, and if necessary, prosecute high governmental officials for violations of federal criminal law. (Supreme Court 1988, p. 660) And to ensure the independence of any such counsel, it provided that:

> An independent counsel appointed under this chapter may be removed from office, other than impeachment and conviction, only by the personal action of the Attorney General and only for good cause, physical disability, mental incapacity, or any other condition that substantially impairs the performance of such independent counsel's duties. (Supreme Court 1988, p. 663)

Obviously, if the President had the power to remove an independent counsel at will, he or she could, and often would, do so in order to protect any official carrying out his or her dubious policies. Justice Scalia, dissenting in *Morrison*, argued than the possibility of being investigated, and even prosecuted, by an independent counsel would intimidate the President's high-level assistants so that they would not provide the President with their honest advice or advocate vigorously his or her policies. (Supreme Court 1988, p. 713) But do we want high-level officials to support any policies that seem to be unethical or illegal? Moreover, if the President had the right to remove all administrative officials at will, this would deter potential whistleblowers from revealing unethical or illegal conduct by their superiors. Here, also, there is a need for independence. (Fisher 1991b, p. 269)

Which set of reasons make the stronger case? It seems to me that the power to appoint and the power to remove are sufficiently different so that the former need not imply the latter. It is probably true that the President is better placed than Congress to judge the performance of the officials serving in his or her administration and that this counts against Congressional limitation of his or her power to remove administrative officials. Although the unity of the executive department contributes to its efficiency, it is unclear whether the unity must be complete or whether a Presidential power to remove administrative officials is necessary for efficiency. The strongest reason to give the President a constitutional right to remove all administrative officials is in order to hold the President responsible for the conduct of his administration.

Although the right to remove all administrative officials at will might discourage some from accepting public office, the President will usually be able to find enough highly qualified candidates willing to serve where needed. I very much doubt that giving the President to remove administrative officials at will would open the door to the reintroduction of the spoils system because this would today outrage public opinion. However, the two remaining reason why the President ought not to have a constitutional right to remove all public officials at will are very strong. This would make truly independent agencies impossible and would too often protect unethical or even illegal administrative action. I conclude that the President ought to have the right to remove many, but not all, administrative officials at will.

3 The Line-Item Veto

Although the governors of 43 states have some form of the line-item veto, this right is denied to the President of the United States. Several Presidents have requested this power and many others have urged that they have either a statutory or constitutional right to veto single items before signing a bill passed by Congress. Others vehemently oppose giving the President any such power. Louis Fisher clarifies what is at issue by reminding us that a line-item veto can take a variety of forms.

> The "item veto" is generally discussed as though it represents a single concept. In fact, it can take a number of forms. The first and most basic form is the authority to veto individual items in appropriation bills, but even this power is controversial when used to strike not merely appropriation [dollar] amounts but substantive law [conditions and qualifications] as well. Second, ten states allow their governors to reduce the level of an item. This is called "item reduction" power. A third type of power is called the "amendatory veto," which allows a governor to condition approval of an enacted bill by returning it to the legislature with suggestions for change. (Fisher 1998, p. 243)

The form with the greatest potential value is the power to veto either single dollar amounts or individual provisions of substantive law. Hence, I will use the expression "line-item veto" to refer to this kind of power-right. Ought the President to have a constitutional right to a line-item veto?

There are several reasons why the President ought to have this right. First, and most obvious, this would enable him or her to reduce wasteful federal spending. Alan J. Dixon describes the present situation as follows:

> By trading support for one another's projects and proposals, Congressmen can pass legislation containing excessive and wasteful spending. Carried to the extreme, pork-barrelling and logrolling can lead to an absurd situation: the more broadly a bill is supported, the more excessive and wasteful it may be. (Dixon 1985, p. 215)

He argues that although there has been no comprehensive study of the economic effects of the line-item veto in the states, there is a fair amount of evidence indicating that the line-item veto will reduce federal spending. (Dixon 1985, p. 213) Mickey Edwards rejects the argument that because governors sometimes use the line-item veto as an effective restraint on state spending, the President ought to have this right.

> Much of the federal budget, including some 100 entitlement programs which account for nearly 50 percent of all federal spending, and the interest payments on the national debt, which account for approximately 12 percent of federal spending, falls outside the scope of the appropriation process. Most federal spending would not be affected in any way by the use of a line-item veto of congressional appropriations. (Edwards 1985, p. 193)

Louis Fisher also argues that:

> The state analogy, in fact, suffers from a number of serious deficiencies. State constitutions differ dramatically from the federal constitution, especially in their distribution of executive and legislative powers….State budget procedures are also substantially different from congressional procedures. Appropriation bills in the states are structured to facilitate item vetoes by governors, whereas appropriation bills passed by Congress contain few items. (Fisher 1998, p. 243)

However, this last difference might not matter much because Fisher also reports that the Line Item Veto Act of 1996 does not limit the president to dollar amounts identified in a bill or joint resolution. (Fisher 1998, p. 249) Hence, it would seem that the line-item veto power would enable the President to reduce wasteful spending in about 30 % of the federal budget.

A second reason why the President ought to have a constitutional right to the line-item veto is that this would shift spending towards national interests. Dr.

William A. Niskanen admits that a line-item veto may not have a substantial effect on the total federal expenditure, but suggests that:

> Another argument for a line-item veto is to change the composition of federal expenditure—from activities preferred by the Congress to activities preferred by the President. A member of Congress is elected by a specific district or state—the President is elected by the nation. As a consequence, a member of Congress has stronger preference for activities that benefit his or her regional constituency, and the President has stronger preferences for activities which benefit the nation. (Niskanen 1988, p. 53)

Hence, he favors a line-item veto because the incentives of the President are somewhat less parochial than those of Congress. (Niskanen 1988, p. 55)

A third reason why the President ought to have a constitutional right to a line-item veto is to increase accountability in the federal government. Under current conditions, members of Congress hide funding for their pet projects in omnibus bill that the President cannot veto without losing essential funding. James C. Miller argues that:

> The exercise of the line-item veto, and any attempt to override a veto, would be committed in broad daylight, before full public scrutiny. There would be no hiding pork barrels in Continuing Resolutions, no games of "chicken" between the President and Congress to see who will yield before the federal government has to close down. If the President had a line-item veto, he would be held accountable for any pork barrels that made it past his desk. If, on the other hand, Congress voted to override the veto and restore the pork, our lawmakers would be held accountable. (Miller 1988, p. 50)

This assumes that the voters are informed, paying attention, and motivated to respond to such irresponsible governmental actions. If not, the consequences might be highly undesirable. Louis Fisher suggests that:

> An item veto could make Congress more irresponsible. To satisfy constituent demands, even of the most indefensible nature, a member need only add extraneous material to a bill with the understanding among colleagues that the President will probably strike the offending amendment. The adoption of an item veto could make the problem of log-rolling worse. (Fisher 1998, p. 246)

It would seem that which of these outcomes is more probable depends upon how well our democratic institutions hold governmental officials accountable for their actions.

There are also plausible reasons why the President ought not to have a constitutional right to the line-item veto. First, there are better alternatives. Recognizing that Congress typically loads appropriation bills with wasteful expenditures, Mickey Edwards argues as follows:

> So the obvious question is whether the granting of more power to the President is the only means of dealing with the problem. It is not. The proper solution is not constitutional, but political.…The term of office for a United States Representative is limited to two years so the voters will have available to them a ready political solution if they are dissatisfied with their representative's performance. (Edwards 1985, p. 194)

But those who vote for or against each Representative are unlikely to disapprove of any item inserted in order to divert federal funds to their district. Justice Stevens, delivering the opinion of the Court in *Clinton v. City of New York*, notes that the President has traditionally had the authority to decline to spend appropriated funds. (Supreme Court 1998, p. 446) However, Congress has at times taken away the President's power to sequester appropriated funds. In any event, it is better to have such presidential action made visible by a line-item veto than hidden from public view by merely refraining to spend appropriated funds.

A second reason why the President ought not to have a constitutional right to the line-item veto is that this would undermine the separation of legislative, executive and judicial powers in the federal government. Mickey Edwards argues that: "Finally, I contend that because the line-item veto effectively transfers control over federal spending, and therefore over domestic policy setting, from the Congress to the President, it would greatly narrow the separation of powers and sharply disturb the balance of powers." (Edwards 1985, p. 203) Justice Kennedy, concurring in *Clinton*, agrees and explains why this would be objectionable.

> Separation of powers was designed to implement a fundamental insight: Concentration of power in the hands of a single branch is a threat to liberty. The Federalist states the axiom in these explicit terms: "The accumulation of all powers, legislative, executive, and judiciary, in the same hands…may justly be pronounced the very definition of tyranny." (Supreme Court 1998, p. 450)

However, some would reply that Congress has final legislative power because it can override any line-item veto with a two-thirds vote.

A third reason why the President ought not to have a constitutional right to the line-item veto is that this would invite Presidential abuse. Justice Kennedy, concurring in *Clinton*, a case concerning a statutory line-item veto, argued that:

> The principal object of the statute, it is true, was not to enhance the President's power to reward one group and punish another, to help one set of taxpayers and hurt another, to favor one State and ignore another. Yet these are its undeniable effects. The law establishes a new mechanism which gives the President the sole ability to hurt a group that is a visible target, in order to disfavor the group or to exact further concessions from Congress. (Supreme Court 1998, p. 457)

By threatening to veto single items dear to particular Congressmen, the President could intimidate them into voting for bills, treaties and appointments they would not otherwise support. Given the realities of practical politics, this is clearly a genuine concern.

Which set of reasons makes the stronger case? Although much of the federal budget would not be vulnerable to a line-item veto, enough remains to enable the President to curtain significant amounts, especially pork barrel items. And it would also enable him or her to eliminate objectionable substantive legal provisions hidden in omnibus appropriation bills. It is unclear that the line-item veto would significantly shift expenditures toward national interests because the President, like Congressmen, is motivated by party politics that is often beholden to special interests. A line-item veto would very probably increase accountability because it would highlight items otherwise hidden in omnibus appropriation bills. It is unlikely that members of Congress would load appropriation bills with very much more wasteful spending than now because any such attempts could be publicized by a presidential veto.

On the other side of the issue, the alternatives proposed are less desirable, not better, than a line-item veto. Although the line-item veto would shift the balance of power slightly from the legislature to the executive branch of government, it would not do so to such a degree as to seriously threaten the separation of powers as long as Congress has the power to override any veto by a two-thirds vote. However, it might be desirable to introduce a constitutional right to the line-item veto that could be overridden by a simple majority vote, as Senator Dixon proposed. (Dixon 1985, p. 208) There remains the danger that the President would abuse his or her line-item veto power to hurt one group and advantage another for partisan political purposes. However, any such abuse would be visible enough so that the electorate could hold him or her accountable for any serious abuse.

On balance, it seems that the prospects of reducing wasteful spending and eliminating objectionable substantive legal provisions together with the increased accountability a line-item would give outweigh the danger of presidential abuse. However, the President probably ought to have a constitutional right to a line-item veto that could be overridden by a simple majority vote in both houses of Congress.

4 The Speech or Debate Immunity

The most important constitutional rights of the members of Congress are the following: (1) Article I, Section 6, Clause 1 together with Amendment XXVII confer a claim-right to Compensation for their services. (2) Article I, Section 6, Clause 1 also confers an immunity-right against arrest during their Attendance at a Session of their respective Houses, and in going to or returning from the same. (3) The same Clause confers the immunity-right against criminal prosecution or civil suit for any speech or debate in either House. (4) Article I, Section 7, Clause 2 together with Article V confer the implied power-right to vote in their respective Houses.

There have been a number of court cases in which the scope of the speech or debate immunity are at issue. The reasoning in these cases raises the question of what the scope of the members' constitutional immunity –right against criminal prosecution or civil suit ought to be. Because there are two dimensions to the scope of this right, one needs to distinguish between two different questions. First, what range of activities ought to constitute speech or debate? Second, what limitations, if any, ought there to be on the immunity provided by this right? Let us consider each of these questions in turn.

First, what range of activities ought to constitute speech or debate? Taken literally, "speech of debate" by a member of Congress would seem to apply only to words spoken in the House or Senate. However, the courts have interpreted them to apply much more broadly. In *Kilbourn v. Thompson*, the leading case concerning the Speech or Debate Clause, Justice Miller in the opinion of the court asserts:

> It would be a narrow view of the constitutional provision to limit it to words spoken in debate. The reason of the rule is as forcible in its application to written reports presented in that body by its committees, to resolutions offered, which, though in writing, must be represented in speech, and to the act of voting, whether it is done vocally or by passing between the tellers. In short, to things generally done in a session of the House by one of its members in relation to the business before it. (Supreme Court 1880, p. 204)

And *Gravel v. United States* even extends the protection of the Speech or Debate Clause beyond members of Congress to Congressional aides when acting as their agents. (Supreme Court 1972b, p. 616)

What could justify applying the Speech or Debate Clause to such a wide range of actions? Presumably "the reason of the rule." But what is this reason? Justice Miller finds it in the case of *Coffin v. Coffin*, a case arising under the *Constitution of Massachusetts*. Here Chief Justice Pearson said:

> These privileges are thus secured not with the intention of protecting the members against prosecution for their own benefit, but to support the rights of the people by enabling their representatives to execute the functions of their office without fear of prosecutions, civil or criminal. (Supreme Court 1880, p. 203)

How is the Speech or Debate Clause supposed to support the rights of the people? Presumably by strengthening the constitutional separation of powers, especially to protect the members of Congress from pressures exerted by the President or other members of the executive branch. Justice Miller reports that the historical source of this clause was the contest between the Tudor and Stuart kings and Parliament settled in the English *Bill of Rights* that declared, among other things, "that the freedom of speech, and debates, and proceedings in Parliament, ought not to be questioned in any court or place out of Parliament." (Supreme Court 1880, pp. 201–202) And it is also generally accepted that those who drafted and argued for the ratification of the original *United States Constitution* took very seriously Montesquieu's assertion that:

> When the legislative and executive powers are united in the same person, or in the same body of magistrates, there can be no liberty; because apprehensions may arise, lest the same monarch or senate shall enact tyrannical laws, to execute them in a tyrannical manner. (Montesquieu 1966, pp. 151–152)

Thus, one might justify interpreting the Speech and Debate Clause as applying to a very broad range of activities by members of Congress and their aides by appealing to the importance of the separation of powers as a protection of the liberties of the people.

A second plausible justification for interpreting the Speech or Debate Clause as applying to a broad range of activities is as a protection for the congressional informing function. In an anonymous petition to the Virginia House of Delegates, Thomas Jefferson explained that:

> [I]n order to give to the will of the people the influence it ought to have, and the information which may enable them to exercise it usefully, it was a part of the common law, adopted as the law of this land, that their representatives, in the discharge of their functions, should be free of cognizance or coercion of the coordinate branches, Judiciary and Executive; and that

> their communications with their constituents should of right, as of duty also, be free, full and unawed by any. (Jefferson 1904, p. 322)

Following Jefferson, one can argue that the Speech and Debate Clause ought to apply to the actions of members of Congress by which they communicate with the members of the public in order to protect the sovereignty of the people. But should it apply equally to other individuals who are not members of Congress? Thus issue was decided by the Supreme Court in the case of *Doe v. McMillan* concerning the publication of a report of a Subcommittee of the Committee on the District of Columbia that petitioners alleged violated their rights to privacy and the privacy rights of their children. (Supreme Court 1973, pp. 308–309) Respondents argued that the publication of this information is protected by the Speech or Debate Clause because public dissemination will serve "the important legislative function of informing the public concerning matters pending before Congress." Justice White in the opinion of the court asserted:

> We do not doubt the importance of informing the public about the business of Congress. However, the question remains whether the act of doing so, simply because authorized by Congress, must always be considered "an integral part of the deliberative and communicative processes by which Members participate in committee and House proceedings" with respect to legislative or other matters before the House. (Supreme Court 1973, p. 314)

The Supreme Court answered this question by deciding that the Speech and Debate Clause did apply to the Congressional Committee members, the Committee staff, the consultant, and the investigator, but not to the Public Printer or the Superintendent of Documents when acting beyond their statutory authority. (Supreme Court 1973, pp. 312 & 324) If this reasoning is sound, the congressional communicative function justifies the application of this clause to a very broad, but still limited, range of activities of both members of Congress and nonmembers cooperating with them in carrying out their legislative duties.

A third justification for applying the Speech or Debate Clause to activities beyond speeches delivered in Congress is to prevent the members of Congress from being distracted from their legislative duties by having to defend themselves from criminal prosecutions or civil suits. In the USSF case, Chief Justice Burger held that this clause applies to the investigative activities of the members of Congress. He explained that:

> Just as a criminal prosecution infringes upon the independence which the Clause is designed to preserve, a private civil action, whether for an injunction or damages, creates a distraction and forces Members to divert their time, energy, and attention from their legislative tasks to defend the litigation. (Supreme Court 1975, p. 503)

Although this consideration carries less weight than the others, it is surely relevant.

Taken together these three considerations justify the conclusion that the Speech or Debate Clause ought not to be read literally and ought to be applied to a wide range of activities of both members of Congress and others who assist them in fulfilling their legislative duties. Whether the Supreme Court has drawn the lines between covered and uncovered activities in precisely the right places is a question best left to future litigation. At least we can be confident that its past decisions have in principle been justified.

Second, what limitations, if any, ought there to be on the protection provided by this immunity-right? This question has been posed most often in the Supreme Court by two sets of cases, those in which a member of Congress has been indicted for alleged bribery and those in which a member of Congress has been sued for alleged defamation. Surely, it would seem, no public official ought to be immune from prosecution for taking a bribe in return for his or her vote in Congress or from being sued for any libelous statement about a colleague or a member of the general public. Presumably the Speech or Debate Clause ought to be limited so that it does not protect these, and perhaps other sorts of serious felonies or torts. However, one must not forget that two very different kinds of protection are possible. Constitutional law might limit the forums in which a member of Congress can be held accountable for misconduct or it might interpret the Speech or Debate Clause as implying specific exceptions to the protection it affords. Each of these calls for consideration.

(1) Ought the protection offered by the Speech or Debate Clause be limited to only some of the available forums? It does in fact do so, for it reads: "and for any Speech or Debate in either House, they shall not be questioned in any other place." Although the words "in any other place" protect members of Congress from criminal indictments or civil suits in the courts, they do not protect them from having their misconduct questioned in Congress. As Justice White observes in *United States v. Brewster*:

> The question presented by this case is not whether bribery or other offensive conduct on the part of Members of Congress must or should go unpunished. No one suggests that the Speech or Debate Clause insulates Senators and Congressmen from accountability for their misdeeds. Indeed the Clause itself is but one of several constitutional provisions that make clear that Congress has broad powers to try and punish its members. (Supreme Court 1972a, p. 557)

Specifically, each House has the power to discipline its own members, and both Houses together have the power in extreme cases to impeach and try a member of Congress. Thus, the question boils down to which forums are preferable for holding members of Congress accountable, the courts or Congress itself.

In delivering the opinion of the Court in *Brewster*, Chief Justice Burger noted several disadvantages of Congress as a forum for holding members of Congress accountable:

> The process of disciplining a Member in the Congress is not without countervailing risks of abuse since it is not surrounded with the panoply of protective shields that are present in a criminal case. An accused Member is judged by no specifically articulated standards and is at the mercy of an almost unbridled discretion of the charging body that functions at once as accuser, prosecutor, judge and jury from whose decision there is no established right of review. (Supreme Court 1972a, p. 579)

And

> Finally, the jurisdiction of Congress to punish its members is not all-embracing. For instance, it is unclear to what extent Congress would have jurisdiction over a case such as this in which the alleged illegal activity occurred outside the chamber, while the appellee

> was a Member, but was undiscovered or not brought before a grand jury until after he left office. (Supreme Court 1972a, p. 520)

At the same time, one should note that Congress might fail to hold its members accountable for their misconduct because colleagues are typically reluctant to discipline fellow members of their groups. More importantly, punishment is not always what justice requires. When Ronald Hutchinson sued Senator Proxmire for defamation he alleged that he had suffered a loss of respect in his profession, injury to his feelings, extreme mental anguish, a loss of income and the ability to earn income in the future. (Supreme Court 1979, p. 118) He was petitioning the court for compensation for these losses. No punishment by Congress would provide Hutchinson with any remedy for what he claimed to have suffered from Proxmire's alleged defamation.

On the other hand, there are serious disadvantages of the courts as forums for holding the members of Congress accountable for their misconduct. To empower public prosecutors to indict members for alleged criminal activity would expose Senators and Congressmen to intimidation by the administration able to threaten them with criminal charges that, even if not well-founded, would seriously damage their reputations. And to permit other officials or private citizens to file civil suits for alleged torts would inevitably distract members of Congress from their legislative duties. As Chief Justice Burger reminds us in his opinion in *Brewster*: "The immunities in the Speech or Debate Clause were not written into the Constitution simply for the personal or private benefit of Members of Congress, but to protect the integrity of the legislative process by insuring the independence of individual legislators." (Supreme Court 1972a, 507) This clause has served this purpose well throughout the history of the United States. Presumably this purpose is important enough to outweigh any deficiencies of Congress as a forum for holding its members accountable. If so, the Speech or Debate Clause is justified in limiting the available forums as it does.

(2) Ought the Speech and Debate Clause to be limited by specific exceptions to the protection it provides for members of Congress? The Supreme Court has not limited it in this respect. Chief Justice Burger, in delivering the opinion of the Court in *Hutchinson v. Proxmire*, explains that although the Speech and Debate Clause creates no "absolute privilege from liability or suit for defamatory statements made outside the Chamber," … "a speech by Proxmire in the Senate would be wholly immune." (Supreme Court 1979, pp. 127 & 130) However, the Supreme Court has interpreted the First Amendment civil right to freedom of speech very differently. In a variety of cases it has held that this constitutional right does not protect, among other forms of speech, sedition, defamation, obscenity or incitement to crime. Ought the Speech or Debate Clause to include explicitly or by implication any exceptions such as these?

Granted that in most cases members of Congress ought to be held accountable by Congress itself rather than the courts, are there not some actions that are so seriously wrong that they ought to be held liable in both forums? Joseph Story, an authority on the *United States Constitution* insisted that "No man ought to have a right to defame others under color of a performance of the duties of his office." (Story 1891, p. 632) And it is surely even more urgent to deter members of Congress from actions, such as accepting a bribe in return for voting as requested, that pervert the legislative process. Notice that the Arrest Clause, also established by Article I, Section 6, Clause 1 of the *Constitution* reads: "They shall in all Cases, except Treason, Felony and Breach of the Peace, be privileged from Arrest during their Attendance at the Session of their respective Houses…." Why not include some such exceptions in the Speech or Debate Clause?

Some would argue that exceptions are not necessary because Congressional discipline is almost always sufficient to deter members of Congress from serious malfeasance. However, the number of recent cases in which they have been sued for alleged torts or indicted for alleged crimes casts doubt upon this argument. At the same time, the number of these cases and the persistence with which unwelcome decisions have been appealed even to the Supreme Court, suggest that it would be dangerous to include exceptions in the Speech of Debate Clause. Each exception would invite additional civil suits or criminal indictments and encourage petitioners or prosecutors to persist to the highest level. Thus, including exceptions would expose the members of Congress to increased intimidation and, at the very least, distraction from their legislative duties. Given the importance of the integrity of the legislative process, it seems to me that on balance the present absence of exceptions in the Speech or Debate Clause is justified. One might add that if it isn't broke, at least not seriously broken, don't fix it. Thus, my overall conclusion regarding the proper scope of the Speech or Debate Clause is that its application ought to be interpreted broadly and that it ought not to include explicitly or implicitly any exceptions.

5 Life Tenure

Article III, Section 1 of the *United States Constitution* confers the following rights upon federal judges: (1) an implied power-right to decide cases within the jurisdiction of the federal courts as defined in Article III, Section 2. (2) An immunity-right against removal from office except for malfeasance. (3) A claim-right to "Compensation, which shall not be diminished during their Continuance in Office." Only the immunity-right against removal from office except for malfeasance, commonly known as life tenure, is controversial. Recently a number of distinguished jurists and even a few judges have argued that the United States ought to replace life tenure with either fixed terms or an age limit to tenure for Justices. Ought the immunity-right against removal from office except for malfeasance be removed from the *Constitution*?

There are several arguments in support of life tenure for Justices. (1) It is necessary to protect the judicial branch of government from interference from the executive or legislative branches. Alexander Hamilton asserts:

> The standard of good behavior for the continuance in office of the judicial magistracy is one of the most valuable of the modern improvements in the practice of government. In a monarchy it is an excellent barrier to the despotism of the prince: In a republic it is a no less excellent barrier to the encroachments and oppressions of the representative body. (Hamilton 1961, p. 522)

And he then explains that:

> The complete independence of the courts of justice is peculiarly essential in a limited constitution. By a limited constitution I understand one which contains certain specified exceptions to the legislative authority....Limitations of this kind can be preserved in practice no other way than through the medium of the courts of justice; whose duty it must be to declare all acts contrary to the manifest tenor of the constitution void. (Hamilton 1961, p. 524)

Therefore, life tenure ought to be established in our constitution in order to preserve the judicial independence of the Supreme Court.

Steven G. Calabresi and James Lindgren agree with Hamilton that judicial independence ought to be preserved, but they believe that life tenure is not necessary to do so. They insist that: "As other have argued, moving from life tenure to a lengthy fixed term—a term longer than the average term of justices who have served on the Court between 1789 and 2005—means that no independence will be lost relative to the other branches or to the public generally." (Calabresi and Lindgren 2006, pp. 67–68)

(2) Life tenure is required in order to protect the justices from political interference by the general public. Hamilton argues that:

> The independence of the judges is equally requisite to guard the constitution and the rights of individuals from the effects of those ill humours which the arts of designing men, or the influence of particular conjunctures, sometimes disseminate among the people themselves, and which, though they speedily give place to better information and more deliberate reflection, have a tendency in the meantime to occasion dangerous innovations in the government, and serious oppressions of the minor party in the community. (Hamilton 1961, p. 527)

Indeed, Hamilton's distrust of the people was so great that he advocates a republican rather than a democratic form of government.

Calabresi and Lindgren, on the other hand, lament the way in which life tenure divorces the Supreme Court from democratic accountability. They assert that: "In sum, judicial independence is not an unqualified good. What we really need is a balance between a substantial measure of judicial independence, combined with some degree of democratic check on the court." (Calabresi and Lindgren 2006, p. 39)

(3) Life tenure is needed to motivate the most qualified persons to serve on the Supreme Court. Hamilton argues that:

> There is yet a further and a weighty reason for the permanency of the judicial office: which is deducible from the nature of the qualifications they require....And making the proper deductions for the ordinary depravity of human nature, the number must be still smaller of those who unite the requisite integrity with the requisite knowledge. These considerations apprise us, that the government can have no great option between fit characters; and that a temporary duration in office, which would naturally discourage such characters from quit-

> ting a lucrative line of practice to accept a seat on the bench, would have a tendency to throw the administration of justice into hands less able, and less qualified to conduct it with utility and dignity. (Hamilton 1961, pp. 529–530)

Given the importance of Supreme Court decisions, this is a serious consideration.

Although Calabresi and Lindgren agree with Hamilton about the importance of appointing persons of high integrity, good judgment and knowledge of the law to the Supreme Court, they argue that life tenure is no longer necessary for this purpose. They assert that: "Life tenure is no longer justified, as Hamilton claimed in Federalist 78, by the need to encourage the best candidates to aspire to be justices. Today, other incentives lure the best candidates to want to be Supreme Court justices." (Calabresi and Lindgren 2006, p. 48)

(4) Life tenure for Justices slows the change in court law. Ward Farnsworth distinguishes between the fast-moving law made by legislators and other officials subject to removal every few years and slow-moving law made by Justices and to a lesser extent judges on the lower courts. He argues that:

> The special value of the Court as a slow lawmaker has to be based on distrust of short-term or even medium-term majoritarian judgments relative to long-term ones. Putting issues on a slower track helps protect them from swifter currents of opinion more likely to produce bad law, perhaps because the swift currents are more likely to have disproportionate force of the kind discussed by public choice theorists, or because they represent views that seem appealing for a while but whose deficiencies become clear with time. (Farnsworth 2005, p. 414)

And life tenure contributes to the slowness of change introduced by the Supreme Court because it reduces the rate at which new Justices replace those who have been making its decisions over the years. Although this might seem to be merely a reformulation of the previous argument, its normative foundation is quite different. While Hamilton defended life tenure as a way to preserve a republic form of government and protect against democracy, Farnsworth advocates slow law as a way to ensure that a democratic government remains true to its own best judgment.

However it can be argued that life tenure slows down legal adjustment to changing circumstances too much. Calabresi and Lindgren respond that:

> The question, however, is just how much conservatism one wants in one's lawmaking processes. Arguably, with separation of powers, checks and balances, federalism, and the Senate filibuster, we do not also need a Supreme Court whose fundamental direction can be reversed only by a sustained twenty-five or thirty year campaign. (Calabresi and Lindgren 2006, p. 69)

Granted the value of slow law, one does not want it to be so slow that urgently needed legal reform becomes impossible.

(5) Life tenure contributes to legal certainty, the high probability that the law will not change unpredictably and without warning. Farnsworth observes that: "It is useful for actors throughout the legal system, as well as the citizenry, to have a reasonably confident sense of what the Court's position on various subjects will be in the near future. A slow turnover creates that confidence." (Farnsworth 2005, p. 442) This is valuable because it enables lawmakers, those who administer the law, and

private individuals subject to the law to plan their future actions on the basis of reasonable expectation of the legal effects of their actions.

Presumably those who propose replacing left tenure with either fixed terms or age limits for Justices can reply that neither reform would greatly reduce legal certainty and that a slight reduction would not seriously undermine the reasonable expectations of anyone.

(6) Life tenure supports the ideal of Justices as neutral, non-political, deciders of disputes between interested parties. Farnsworth believes that: "Indeed, life tenure and the long terms it creates is the regime most consistent with a vision of the Justices as impersonal appliers of interpretive theories." (Farnsworth 2005, pp. 423–424) Introducing fixed terms advocated by those who wish to increase democratic accountability would send just the opposite message to the Justices and to the public. However, the influence of life tenure on anyone's conception of the proper role of Justices is highly speculative.

As one would expect, there are also several arguments for replacing life tenure with either fixed terms or an age limit on tenure for Justices. (1) Term limits encourage hubris in the Justices and the resulting abuse of their judicial power. Paul D. Carrington and Roger C. Cramton argue that:

> Unchecked power, the Founders correctly believed, has a tendency to produce a dangerous hubris and arrogance among those who exercise that power. Many thoughtful citizens are persuaded that even now the Supreme Court's conception and exercise of its power have manifested those traits. And more are likely to reach that conclusion if the trend toward longer periods of service continues. (Carrington and Cramton 2006, p. 469)

And presumably this trend will continue because life expectancy in the United States is steadily increasing.

Ward Farnsworth replies that most of the hubris in Supreme Court opinions is attributable to other sources. Circuit judges write humbler opinions because they are bound by the Supreme Court in a way that Justices are not. Cases before the Supreme Court tend to involve questions to which the legal materials supply no clear answer. And a change to term limits would do little to alter these factors. (Farnsworth 2005, pp. 439–441)

(2) Life tenure raises the stakes of appointing a Justice and therefore places damaging stress on the confirmation process. Calebresi and Lindgren argue that:

> A second cost incurred by the less frequent vacancies and by justices serving for ever longer periods of time is that the process for confirming all federal judges can become so political and contentious as to grind the process itself to a halt. Under the current system, the irregular occurrence of vacancies on the Supreme Court means that when one does arise, the stakes are enormous, for neither the President nor the Senate can know when the next vacancy might arise. Moreover, a successful nominee has the potential to remain on the Court for a very long and uncertain period of time. So much is at stake in appointing a new justice that the President and the Senate (especially when controlled by the party opposite to the President) inevitably get drawn into a political fight that hurts the Court both directly and indirectly—directly, since it is deprived of one of its members, and indirectly, since rancorous confirmation battles lower the prestige of the Court. (Calabresi and Lindgren 2006, p. 39)

And the stress on the confirmation process will probably increase with increased life expectancy in our country.

Ward Farnsworth argues that little if any of this stress is caused by life tenure. He believes that what causes a contentious nomination process is selecting a candidate with less moderate views and refusing to reconsider together with the fact that constitutional issues are often zero-sum games. He adds that it is hard to see how shorter tenure would reduce these factors. (Farnsworth 2005, pp. 432–433)

(3) Life tenure enables Justices who are reluctant to retire to serve even after they become incapacitated with a loss of physical energy or mental ability. Calabresi and Lindgren report that:

> The problem of justices suffering mental or physical health problems while serving on the Court, though occurring throughout American history, has arises more frequently in recent years. This serious and persistent problem has been recognized by many as one that threatens the legitimacy of the Court. (Calabresi and Lindgren 2006, p. 41)

The seriousness of this problem is confirmed by medical statistics that show a greatly increased incidence of Alzheimer's disease and other forms of dementia among our aging population.

Farnsworth insists that this problem is less serious than it sounds because to date it has occurred relatively infrequently and has been mitigated by the presence of eight other Justices with a voice in any decision of the Supreme Court and the possibility of shifting much of the burden of the office to the Justice's law clerks. (Farnsworth 2005, pp. 445–446) However, this problem may become more serious in the future if life expectancy continues to increase.

(4) Life tenure enables justices to engage in strategic retirement. Philip D. Oliver finds this possibility most problematic:

> A Justice considering retirement from the Court at some point within a few years, but not faced with a medical or other personal emergency, might well reflect upon how his successor would affect the future course of decision by the Court. In such a situation, the Justice might attempt to time his retirement so that his successor would be named by a President sympathetic to (or, at least, not unsympathetic to) the retiring Justice's view of the Constitution.… The justification of life tenure relates to the independence of the Justice while he is n the Court. Allowing the Justice a measure of control over the naming of his successor allows him an unchecked power entirely unnecessary to protect his independence of action while on the bench, and in the writer's view cannot be justified. (Oliver 1986, p. 805)

One might add that to enable Justices to engage in politics in this manner undermines the ideal of a judge as an impartial decider of controversial issues.

Although Ward Farnsworth admits that strategic retirement tampers with the separation of powers in our Constitution, he argues that this problem is not in fact very serious. The window of retirement for a Justice tends to be sort enough to make any calculated decision to retire hard to carry out. And most Justices enjoy their position enough to make strategic retirement a low priority. (Farnsworth 2005, pp. 448–449)

(5) Life tenure results in an uneven allocation of opportunities to nominate a Justice by a President. Oliver reports that recently this number has ranged from zero

to six. Given the political importance of selecting a new member of the Supreme Court, this result is unfair and life tenure ought to be replaced with staggered fixed terms to even out the nominations of Justices. (Oliver 1986, pp. 810–811)

Farnsworth recognizes this as a serious problem with life tenure. But he argues that fixed terms will not solve it because Presidential elections also result in an uneven distribution of presidential terms between political parties. And the need for any person nominated by a President to be confirmed by the Senate tends to even out the swings between liberal and conservative candidates appointed to the Supreme Court. (Farnsworth 2005, pp. 435–437)

(6) Life tenure divorces the Supreme Court from democratic accountability. Calabresi and Lindgren point out that checks on the Court by constitutional amendments is so difficult as to be impracticable in most cases and impeachment has proved useless in the past. Hence, the appointment process is the most direct and important formal source of democratic control on the Supreme Court. (Calabresi and Lindgren 2006, pp. 36–37) They ask whether the popular understanding of the Constitution's meaning ought to guide the Supreme Court and reply:

> We believe that it should: The general public is more likely than are nine life-tenured lawyers to interpret the Constitution in a way that is faithful to its text and history, which is how constitutional decision-making ought to proceed. The general public has a great reverence for the constitutional text and for our history, and much of the public intuitively understands that radical departures from text and history are illegitimate. The lawyer class in this country, on the other hand, is still imbued with a legal realist or post-modern cynicism about the constraints imposed by the constitutional text. (Calabresi and Lindgren 2006, p. 59)

Hence, life tenure ought to be replaced with fixed terms for Justices in order that the public can hold them accountable for interpreting the constitutional text properly.

Farnsworth questions the value of replacing life tenure if one's purpose is to hold Justices accountable for their method of interpretation, for interpreting the constitutional faithfully to its text and history.

> The trouble with trying to make the Court more accountable to the public as a matter of method is that there is no evidence that the public understands these issues or is interested in them, nor is there much evidence that the presidents are interested when they pick their nominees. (Farnsworth 2005, p. 421)

Not only would democratic accountability be ineffective for its intended purpose, it would be undesirable: "First, one of the valuable things courts do is to make unpopular decisions that stick: decisions protecting the rights of minorities or preserving structural features of the Constitution that frustrate the majority's will but have long-run benefits." (Farnsworth 2005, p. 419) Thus, if one really wants to be faithful to the Constitution, one ought to retain life tenure not replace it with fixed terms for Justices.

(7) Life tenure undermines the democratic legitimacy of the Supreme Court. Calabresi and Lindgren argue that the legitimacy of the Court and of its decisions rests upon the appointment of judges by elected authorities, the President and the Senate. But for this process to work properly, turnover on the Court must be relatively frequent and regular. (Calabresi and Lindgren 2006, p. 37)

Granting the importance of democratic legitimacy, Farnsworth defends the legitimacy of the Court as follows:

> We have seen that a strong role for the Senate helps mitigate the effects of the arbitrary assignment of nominations to presidents. Now we can also see that it helps tie the Court's membership to a source of political authority more satisfying than the presidency even if every president were to get two appointments. (Farnsworth 2006, p. 259)

Thus, life tenure is not incompatible with the legitimacy of the Supreme Court.

Because each of these pro or con arguments has been challenged, any attempt to weigh them against one another will be complicated and any final evaluation questionable. Nevertheless, the importance of the Supreme Court to our government demands that we attempt to reach some overall conclusion regarding whether the United States ought to retain life tenure for Justices.

Hamilton's argument that life tenure is necessary to motivate enough of the very few qualified persons to serve on the Supreme Court is no longer valid. Today there are many more individuals of moral integrity and with the requisite legal knowledge than in his time, and the opportunity to serve our country in an important way together with the prestige of the Court are sufficient to motivate qualified persons to become candidates for this office.

Although life tenure probably does make some contribution to legal certainty regarding fundamental legal principles and especially constitutional law, this contribution is marginal and it is the predictability of other areas of law that matters more to most individuals planning their future actions. And although life tenure may help a little to sustain the ideal of Justices as neutral and non-political deciders of controversial issues, it is at best only one of many supports for this ideal.

It is the remaining three arguments for life tenure that one should take most seriously. Life tenure does a great deal to protect the judicial independence of Justices from the other branches of government as well as from the people. And it does something to slow changes, especially fundamental changes, to United States law. These are valuable because it is important to prevent the executive and legislative branches of government from exceeding the limited powers specifically granted to them by the *United States Constitution* and to protect these specified limitations together with the rights of minorities from unwise or prejudiced impulses of the majority. Together these three arguments make a very strong case for conferring upon Justices a constitutional immunity-right against removal from office by either another branch of the government or by any popular referendum. However, it is not clear whether this immunity ought to be for life or for some shorter length of time. Either a fixed term of 18 years or a reasonable age limit for holding office would provide almost as much judicial independence as life tenure.

Let us, then, examine the arguments against life tenure. I doubt that that life tenure is a major cause of either judicial hubris or the contemporary stress on the confirmation process. What the opponents of life tenure consider hubris is primarily either a decision they dislike or a non-literal reading of the constitutional text. Because any case accepted by the Supreme Court will be highly controversial, any decision rendered will be disliked by many. And because the language of the constitutional text is typically abstract and its history complex, no literal reading can be decisive. What puts stress on the confirmation process is much less life tenure than the great importance of the decisions of the Supreme Court together with the increasing tendency of both political parties to adopt extreme positions and to refuse to consider any reasonable compromise.

The uneven allocation of opportunities to nominate a new member of the Supreme Court does seem unfair. But as Ward Farnsworth reminds us, the need for confirmation by the Senate tends to limit the partisanship of appointees to the Court, and neither fixed terms nor age limits would eliminate this problem. Hence, this consideration seems to have some, but only a very limited, weight.

Potentially devastating is the double-barreled criticism that life tenure now restricts democratic accountability so much that the Supreme Court lacks democratic legitimacy. First, one should remember that there is a tension between democratic accountability and judicial independence so that a very considerable restriction on the former is needed to protect the latter. More to the point, the legitimacy of the Supreme Court is not determined entirely by its democratic accountability. Granted the importance of democracy, it is only one of the values that justify any governmental institution. Efficiency in promoting the public welfare and the protection of the fundamental rights of those subject to its laws are also relevant. The moral authority of the Supreme Court rests upon all of these and not merely upon its democratic accountability.

To my mind, the two most forceful arguments against life tenure are that it enables Justices to remain on the Court after they have lost full physical stamina and have seriously diminished mental capacities and that it encourages aged Justices to engage in strategic retirement. It may be, as Farnsworth argues, that neither problem is now as serious as it sounds. However, both are already genuine problems and both will become more serious as life expectancy continues to increase in our country. It is they, rather than any lack of democratic accountability, that do the most to cast doubt upon the moral authority of the Supreme Court. If life tenure were really necessary to protect the judicial independence of the Justices, it might be necessary to accept these defects in our Supreme Court. But since either fixed terms or an age limit would provide sufficient judicial independence, the United States ought to replace life tenure with one of these alternatives.

6 Moral Foundations

The President has a power-right to act as Commander-in Chief, that is, to exercise his or her war powers. The foundations of the view that it ought to override Congressional limitation, at least when there is an imminent threat to the United States, are the moral right of a nation to self-defense, that unity and dispatch are necessary for the President to carry out his or her duties as Commander-in-Chief, and that this is necessary to protect the vital interests of the United States.

The members of Congress have an immunity-right against being indicted or sued for any speech or debate in Congress, broadly interpreted. The foundations of this constitutional right are the right of the people that the members of Congress execute their functions as the representatives of the people, that it is required in order to maintain the separation of governmental powers necessary to protect liberty (probably understood as consisting of the fundamental moral rights of persons), and to enable the members of Congress to inform the people of matters concerning legislation (something essential to any genuine democracy).

Justices of the Supreme Court have an immunity-right against removal from office except for malfeasance, commonly known as a constitutional right to life tenure. Its foundations are the necessity to prevent oppression of the people by Congress, to prevent oppression of the minority by the majority of the people, and the demand of justice that the judge in any dispute ought to be neutral between the parties.

The moral relevance and force of some of these, such as the fundamental moral rights of persons or the vital interests of the nation, are obvious. However, the moral value of others, such as executing one's institutional (not necessarily moral) duties or democratic government, calls for further explanation. The moral foundations of democracy, at least, will be considered in the next chapter.

References

Bruff, Harold H. (2006). Balance of Forces: Separation of Powers Law in the Administrative State. Carolina Academic Press. Durham NC.

Calabresi, Steven G. and Lindgren, James (2006). Term Limits for the Supreme Court: Life Tenure Reconsidered. In Reforming the Court, Roger C. Cramton and Paul D. Carrington (eds.). Carolina Academic Press. Durham NC.

Carrington, Paul D. and Cramton, Roger C. (2006). The Supreme Court renewal Act: A return to Basic Principles. In Reforming the Supreme Court: Term Limits for Supreme Court Justices, Roger C. Cramton and Paul D. Carrington (eds.). Carolina Academic Press. Durham NC.

Court of Appeals (2000). Campbell v. Clinton. 203 F.3rd. 19 (D.C.Cir.)

Dixon, Alan J. (1985). The Case for the Line-item Veto. Notre Dame Journal of Law, Ethics & Public Policy 2:207–226.

Edwards, Mickey (1985) The Case Against the Line-item Veto. Notre Dame Journal of Law, Ethics & Public Policy 2:191–206.

Farnsworth, Ward (2005). The Regulation of Turnover on the Supreme Court. University of Illinois Law Review 2005: 407–454.

Farnsworth, Ward (2006). The Case for Life Tenure. In reforming the Court: Term Limits for Supreme Court Justices, Roger C. Cramton and Paul D. Carrington (eds.). Carolina Academic Press. Durham NC.

Fisher, Louis (1991a). War Powers: The Need for Collective Judgment. In Divided Democracy: Cooperation and Conflict Between the resident and Congress, James A. Thurber (ed.). Congressional Quarterly Press. Washington DC.

Fisher, Louis (1991b). Congress and the Removal Power. In Divided Democracy: Cooperation and conflict Between the President and Congress, James A. Thurber (ed.). Congressional Quarterly Press. Washington DC.

Fisher, Louis (1998). The Politics of Shared Power: Congress and the Executive, 4th edition. Texas A&M University Press. College Station TX.
Fisher, Louis (2007). Constitutional Conflict between Congress and the President, 5th edition. University Press of Kansas. Lawrence KS.
Hamilton, Alexander (1961). The Federalist, Jacob E. Cooke (ed.). Meridian Books. Cleveland and New York.
Jefferson, Thomas (1904). Petition to the Virginia House of Delegates. In the Works of Thomas Jefferson, vol. 8, Paul Leicester Ford (ed.). G. P. Putnam's Sons. New York and London.
Miller, James C. (1988). An Expanded Veto Power and the Budget. In Pork Barrels and Principles: The Politics of the residential Veto, Charles J. Cooper et. al (eds). National Legal Center for the Public Interest. Washington DC.
Montesquieu, Baron de (1966). The Spirit of the Laws. Hafner Publishing Company. New York and London.
Niskanen, Dr. William A. (1988). The Line-item Veto: A Weak Instrument for Controlling Federal Spending. In Pork Barrels and Principles: the Politics of the Presidential Veto, Charles J. Cooper et al. (eds). National Legal Center for the Public Interest. Washington DC.
Oliver, Philip D. (1986). Systematic Justice: A Proposed Constitutional Amendment to Establish Fixed, Staggered Terms for Members of the United States Supreme Court. Ohio State Law Journal 47:799–834.
Public Law (1973). 93–148.
Sofaer, Abraham D. (1988). Senate Committee on Foreign Relations. The War Power after 200 Years: Congress and the resident at a Constitutional Impasse. 100th Congress, 2nd Session.
Story, Joseph (1891). Commentaries on the Constitution of the United States, vol. 1, Melville M. Bigelow (ed.). Little Brown. Boston.
Supreme Court (1804). Little v. Barreme. 6 U.S. 170.
Supreme Court (1862). Prize Cases. 67 U.S. 2 Black 635.
Supreme Court (1880). Kilbourn v. Thompson. 103 U.S. 168.
Supreme Court (1926). Myers v. United States. 272 U.S. 52.
Supreme Court (1935). Humphrey's Executor v. United States. 295 U.S. 602.
Supreme Court (1936). United States v. Curtis-Wright Export Corporation. 299 U.S. 304.
Supreme Court (1952). Youngstown Sheet & Tube Co. v. Sawyer. 343 U.S. 579.
Supreme Court (1972a). United States v. Brewster. 408 U.S. 501.
Supreme Court (1972b). Grovel v. United States. 408 U.S. 606.
Supreme Court (1973). Doe v. Macmillan. 412 U.S. 306.
Supreme Court (1975). Eastland v. United States Servicemen's Fund. 421 U.S. 491.
Supreme Court (1979) Hutchinson v. Proxmire. 443 U.S. 111.
Supreme Court (1988). Morrison v. Olson. 487 U.S. 654.
Supreme Court (1998). Clinton v. City of New York. 524 U.S. 417.
Supreme Court (2004) Hamdi v. Rumsfeld. 542 U.S. 507.
Vladeck, Stephen I. (2007). National Security: Detention, War Powers and Anti-Proliferation. Transnational Law 7 Contemporary Problems 16:933–964.
Yoo, John C. (2001). The President's Constitutional Authority to Conduct Military Operations Against Terrorists and nations Supporting Them. Memorandum Opinion for the Deputy Counsel to the President. Available online at http:www.justice.gov/olc/warpowers925.Htm.

Chapter 5
Private Persons

Abstract The constitutional rights that first come to mind are rights of private persons. This chapter provides a critical examination of the reasons for or against the actual or proposed constitutional rights to life of the unborn child, to vote of resident aliens, to public education of illegal aliens, to habeas corpus of enemy combatants, to marriage of same-sex couples, to equal opportunity of disabled persons, to freedom of hate speech, to keep and carry assault weapons, and against the death penalty. Finally it explains different ways in which such reasons are relevant to constitutional rights.

The majority of constitutional rights, and those that receive by far the most attention in discussions of civil rights, are rights of private persons. Therefore, any attempt to discover the moral foundations of constitutional rights must consider this category of rights with care. And because the moral considerations that are relevant to any right become most prominent when that right becomes controversial, I will focus in this chapter on disagreements about the constitutional rights of private persons, both concerning what they are and what they ought to be. Some of these will be enumerated rights, such as the right to life or the right to vote, others will be unenumerated rights established by decisions of the Supreme Court, such as the right to privacy, and some will be advocated rights not yet recognized, such as the right to education.

1 Life

The right to life is usually believed to be the most fundamental of all human rights because no human being can exercise or enjoy any other right unless he or she is alive. Nevertheless, the right to life was first established in the *United States Constitution* by the Fourteenth Amendment that reads in part:"nor shall any State deprive any person of life, liberty, or property without due process of law." The right to life is relevant to a number of controversial issues such as the permissibility of physician-assisted suicide, capital. punishment and abortion. Although the ongoing debates about abortion raise a wide variety of legal and moral questions, let us

C. Wellman, *Constitutional Rights -What They Are and What They Ought to Be*, Law and Philosophy Library 115, DOI 10.1007/978-3-319-31526-3_5 consider here only two of these. Does the unborn child have a constitutional right to life? And should the unborn child have a constitutional right to life?

Does the unborn child have a constitutional right to life? Almost certainly not. In *Roe v. Wade*, after examining all the uses of the word "person" in the *Constitution* and finding that none indicates any possible prenatal application, the Supreme Court concluded that: "All this, together with our observation, supra, that throughout the major portion of the nineteenth century prevailing legal abortion practices were far freer than they are today, persuades us that the word "person" as used in the Fourteenth Amendment does not include the unborn." (Supreme Court 1973a, p. 153) Accordingly, the unborn child does not possess any constitutional right to life. Years later, Justice Stevens observed that "From this holding, there was no dissent…; indeed, no Member of the Court has ever questioned this fundamental proposition." (Supreme Court 1992b, p. 913) And it is highly significant that none of the four Justices that argued for overruling *Roe v. Wade* in their dissenting opinions challenged this part of its reasoning. (Supreme Court 1992b, pp. 939–1002) Therefore, until the *Constitution* is amended or the Supreme Court rules otherwise, the unborn child does not have any constitutional right to life.

Ought the unborn child to have a constitutional right to life? It is probably no accident that the Fourteenth Amendment gives constitutional protection to the three natural rights central to John Locke's political philosophy—life, liberty and property. This suggests that the moral foundation of the constitutional right to life is the moral human right to life. Thus, if the unborn child possesses the moral human right to life, presumably the constitutional right to life ought to apply to the unborn also. However, I have argued and still believe that only beings with the capacity for moral agency can possess any moral right and that fetuses do not possess this capacity in any relevant sense. (Wellman 1995, pp. 107–113 and 136–145) This is because on my adversarial conception of rights, a right confers dominion (freedom and control) over some core legal or moral position upon the right-holder in face of some second party who might interfere with the exercise or enjoyment of that position. Hence, every real right must include some liberty, power or claim, and typically all three. Since only agents can exercise liberties or powers or make claims, only agents can meaningfully be said to possess rights. If this is correct, then the moral human right to life does not justify the recognition of any constitutional right to life.

But perhaps the grounds of the moral human right to life of normal adult persons would justify a constitutional right to life of the unborn child. Although what is called the moral right to life is really a rights-package, a cluster of moral rights concerning the life of a person, what is relevant here is the claim-right not to be killed. I have argued elsewhere that its primary ground is the serious harm done to the life of the person killed and its secondary ground is the serious harms done to others who love or are dependent upon that person. (Wellman 2011), pp. 42–43) This primary ground does not exist in the case of the unborn child. Although the fetus is a living organism, and in some sense a human being, it does not yet have a life. As Justice Stevens explained in another context:

> Life, particularly human life, is not commonly thought of as a merely physiological condition or function. Its sanctity is often thought to derive from the impossibility of any such reduction. When people speak of life, they often mean to describe the experiences that comprise a person's history, as when it is said that somebody "led a good life." (Supreme Court 1990, p. 346)

The great intrinsic value of the normal human life consists in the rewarding personal relationships and ongoing projects of the person experiencing that life. But the unborn child is not yet interacting with other persons or pursuing any ongoing projects. Hence, although killing the fetus clearly harms it as a biological organism, it does not damage or destroy its life. Admittedly, the secondary ground of the moral human claim-right not to be killed may, and often does, exist. Other persons who have already become emotionally attached to the unborn child may suffer loss. However, this harm is typically much less than in the death of a living human being. Because the harms inflicted by killing an unborn child are so much less than those inflicted by killing a normal adult person or even a young child, the grounds of the moral human right to life are not sufficient to justify the recognition of any constitutional right to life of the unborn child.

The right to life is also recognized in international human rights law, most notably in Article 6.1 of the *International Covenant on Civil and Political Rights*, Article 2 of the *European Convention for the Protection of Human Rights and Fundamental Freedoms*, and Article 4 of the *American Convention on Human Rights*. Do any of these international treaties confer the right to life upon the unborn child? And if so, is this any reason for the United States to establish a constitutional right to life of the unborn child? There is no evidence as to whether the right to life recognized in the first of these treaties is applicable to the unborn child. However, the European Court of Human Rights has explicitly held that it is neither desirable nor possible to answer the question of whether the unborn is a person for the purposes of Article 2 of the *European Convention*. (European Court of Human Rights 2004, pp. 3–4) Most relevant is Article 4.1 of the *American Convention* that reads in part: "Every person has the right to have his life respected. This right shall be protected by law, and in general, from the moment of conception…." Although the United States has signed this convention, it has never ratified it. Accordingly under the international law of treaties, it has no legal obligation to observe its provisions. Whether it has any moral obligation to do so in order to strengthen international human rights law is unclear. Everything considered, I do not believe that the human right to life as recognized in international law provides any serious justification for the United States to establish a constitutional right to life of the unborn child.

Although the Supreme Court in *Roe v. Wade* denied that the unborn child is a person with a constitutional right to life, it did recognize "the State's important and legitimate interest in potential life." (Supreme Court 1973a, pp. 158 & 163) Is this State interest important enough to justify establishing a constitutional right to life of the unborn child? Well, why might the State have an interest in potential human life or lives? Unborn children will normally be born and grow into adult human beings. Given the chance to develop their potentialities they will become contributing members of society. They will become workers in its economy, taxpayers, scientists or teachers or artists or public officials, mothers and fathers giving birth to the next generation that will enable the society to continue to exist into the indefinite future. Surely the State has a legitimate and important interest in its continuing well-being and existence.

Notice also a subsequent paragraph in which the Supreme Court suggests that this State interest might even be a State duty: "The Third reason [to explain historically the enactment of criminal abortion laws] is the State's interest—some phrase it in terms of duty—in protecting prenatal life. (Supreme Court 1973a, p. 150) Why might the state have a duty to protect prenatal life or lives? Probably this is because in most cases their parents care deeply about them and their future lives. These unborn children will normally be born and become members of families in which they will enter into personally enriching relationships with their parents and grandparents and family friends. Their death would constitute a severe loss to these living members of society. And the State has a duty to protect its members from serious harms. This is because by claiming a monopoly on the authorization of the use of force, the State limits the right of its members to protect themselves from harm and from the violation of their moral rights. Hence, the legitimacy of the State's enacting and enforcing its laws requires it to do its best to protect the interests and rights of its members. Although this duty is owed to persons who are already born, not to the unborn, it does ground an indirect interest in protecting the prenatal lives of unborn children. Therefore, the State has both a direct and an indirect interest in potential human life. Together these interests might well be important enough to justify establishing a constitutional right to life of unborn children.

However, these important State interests seem reasonably well served by our existing law that does not confer any constitutional right to life upon unborn children. And any incremental advancement of these interests in potential human life that would result from recognizing unborn children as persons with a constitutional right to life would have to be weighed against the resulting social and personal costs. David Westfall examines several proposed constitutional amendments and the Helms-Hyde bill that would make the unborn child a person with a constitutional right to life from the moment of fertilization or conception. (Westfall 1982, pp. 99–101) He describes the potential substantive effects, often harmful, to United States law concerning legislative apportionment, distribution of governmental fiscal benefits, civil liberties, federal income tax, criminal law, torts, health care and medical malpractice, laboratory research and in-vitro fertilization, gender-based employment discrimination and finally estates, property and trusts. (Westfall 1982, pp. 110–130) His conclusion regarding a human rights amendment is that:

> The substantive effects of an HLA in areas other than abortion could be severely limited by judicial decisions. If that happens, the problems posed in Part II will be resolved in due course. Bur the years required to complete this process may stretch into a decade or more. The social costs of chaos and confusion in the legal system while this process is taking place would be very high....The potentially heavy cost of finding out what an HLA means will be felt by the courts, Congress, state legislatures, administrative agencies, and private sector. (Westfall 1982, p. 130)

And the courts might not eliminate all the potentially harmful legal consequences of any amendment that would make unborn children persons with a constitutional right to life. I would add only that if a human right amendment were to severely restrict legal abortions, as it is intended to do, then there would also be severe personal costs for many pregnant women. There would be the moral injustice of forcing victims of rape or incest to bear and often raise children conceived by criminal acts for which they are not responsible. Other results would be the felt shame of those resorting to illegal abortions together with the many cases of infection, infertility and even death of the sorts common before *Roe v. Wade* provided a legal alternative for women unwilling to give birth to an unwanted child. On balance, the State interest in potential human life is not sufficient to justify establishing a constitutional right to life of unborn children. Nor do any other plausible justifications spring to mind. Therefore, I conclude that unborn children ought not to have any constitutional right to life.

2 The Vote

The constitutional right to vote is a paradigm example of a rights-package, a cluster of rights concerning eligibility to vote in elections to federal offices. Article I, Section 2, Clause 1 of the *United States Constitution* reads: "The House of Representatives shall be composed of Members chosen every second Year by the People of the several States, and the Electors in each State shall have the Qualifications requisite for Electors of the most numerous Branch of the State Legislature." The founding fathers probably assumed that this right to vote would be limited to male owners of property in amounts to be specified by each state. However, the discretion of the states to exclude citizens from the right to vote in federal elections has been limited by the Fifteenth Amendment that specifies that the right of citizens to vote shall not be denied or abridged on account of race, color or previous condition of servitude, by the Nineteenth Amendment on account of sex, by the Twenty-fourth Amendment by reason of failure to pay any poll tax or other tax, and by the Twenty-sixth Amendment on account of age after the age of 18 years. Article I, Section 3, Clause 1 provided that the Members of the Senate shall be chosen by the State legislatures. But the Seventeenth Amendment now confers the right to vote for the two Senators from each State upon those citizens qualified to vote for the members of the most numerous branch of the State legislature. Article II, Section 1, Clauses 2 and 3 establishes a body of Electors appointed by the several States with the power to choose the President according to their best judgment. Although this Electoral College has never been eliminated or modified by any subsequent constitutional amendment, there is now a constitutional convention that these Electors shall be elected by the citizens of the several States and that they will vote for the presidential candidate to whom they are pledged. In effect, the *Constitution* now confers the right to vote for the President upon the qualified citizens of the United States. Unlike the constitutional right to life that is held by private persons as persons, each of these constitutional rights to vote in elections to federal office is held by private persons as citizens.

Aliens, even resident aliens, are not citizens. Hence, resident aliens do not have any constitutional right to vote. Ought resident aliens to have the constitutional right to vote in federal elections? Although strictly speaking there are several categories of resident aliens, I will simplify my exposition and argument by using the expression "resident aliens" to refer only to those aliens granted permission to reside in the United States permanently. If the moral grounds of the right to vote apply to resident aliens as well as to citizens, then presumably they ought also to have this right. What, then, are the moral reasons that justify the right to vote in the *United States Constitution*? James Madison suggests one relevant consideration when he defends the provisions for the House of Representatives in the proposed constitution:

> As it is essential to liberty that the government in general, should have a common interest with the people; so it is particularly essential that the branch of it under consideration, should have an immediate dependence on, & an intimate sympathy with the people. Frequent elections are unquestionably the only policy by which this dependence and sympathy can be effectively secured. (Madison 1961, p. 366)

The people, the persons subject to a government, ought to have the right to vote for representatives in order to select officials who will promote their personal interests and to remove from public office those who fail to do so. Hence, one moral ground for the constitutional right to vote is that it is necessary to protect the interests of those governed.

The word "liberty" in the above passage suggests another moral ground for the right to vote, a ground presupposed when Madison defends the apportionment of members of the House to the several States.

> It is not contended that the number of people in each State ought to be the standard for regulating the proportion of those who are to represent the people of each State. The establishment of the same rule for the apportionment of taxes, will probably be as little contested, though the rule itself in this case, is by no means founded on the same principle. In the former case, the rule is understood to refer to the personal rights of the people, with which it has a natural and universal connection. (Madison 1961, p. 366)

The implicit reasoning here is that the persons subject to a government ought to have the right to vote for or against candidates for public office in order to protect themselves from the violation of their fundamental moral rights by unjust legislation.

The slogan "No taxation without representation" points to a third moral ground of the constitutional right to vote. Although the American colonists used this slogan to claim what they believed was a traditional right of Englishmen, a resident alien could today use it to refer to a special case of a moral principle of social fairness. Some moral philosophers justify political obligation, the obligation to obey the laws of one's society, by appealing to the principle that one who accepts, or even receives, the benefits of social institutions has a moral obligation to accept his or her fair share of its burdens, including obeying its institutional rules. (Rawls 1971, pp. 111–114) Conversely, one can argue that when social institutions impose serious burdens upon someone, then he or she has a moral right to his or her fair share of the advantages conferred by these institutions. One of these advantages is the right to have a say in what these burdens should be and how they should be distributed. Since resident aliens are subject to taxation in the United States, surely a serious burden, they have a right to vote in elections that affect this and other legally imposed burdens.

Thus there are at least three moral grounds of the present constitutional right of citizens to vote: their personal interests, their fundamental moral rights, and a principle of social fairness. Each of these grounds applies to resident aliens in precisely the same way that it applies to citizens. Therefore, presumably resident aliens should also have the constitutional right to vote in federal elections. There is also another, and less speculative, reason to extend the constitutional right to vote to resident aliens. The Supreme Court has recognized in *Graham v. Richardson* that the Equal Protection Clause applies to resident aliens. (Supreme Court 1971, p. 372) Although the *United States Constitution* explicitly grants the right to vote to citizens, the Equal Protection Clause reads: "[No State shall]…nor deny to any person within its jurisdiction the equal protection of the laws." Since resident aliens are similarly persons within the jurisdiction of the United States, presumably they also have a constitutional right to equal protection from federal law. One of the most important protections federal law confers on citizens is the legal power to protect their interests and rights by voting. Therefore, to provide equal protection to all those within its jurisdiction it ought to confer this right upon resident aliens also.

The moral foundation of the constitutional right to equal protection is the moral human right to equitable treatment. This is a moral right not to be treated worse than others who are similarly situated without a just-making or justicizing reason. (Wellman 2011, pp. 62–63) For example, each student enrolled in one of my classes has a moral right that I not give him or her a lower grade than I give to anyone else who is similarly enrolled in that class without a justicizing reason. I might give a student a lower grade because he seems to be a smart aleck who needs to be shown that his action s are counterproductive. Although this is a genuine reason to give him a lower grade, it is a paternalistic rather than a reason concerning fairness or justice. However, giving him a lower grade because his assigned papers were less well researched or more badly reasoned than another student to whom I gave a higher grade is a just-making reason. Analogously, all persons, resident aliens as well as full citizens, within the jurisdiction of the United States are similarly situated as persons subject to its law. Therefore, resident aliens have the moral human right that United States law not provide less protection to them than it provides to its citizens. Therefore, United States law ought to give resident aliens the constitutional right to vote.

Unless, of course, there are more important reasons not to confer the right to vote on resident aliens. Although the Supreme Court has not overruled *Graham*, it has carved out a political function exception to its holding that any discrimination against resident aliens must survive strict scrutiny. The relevant passage in *Sugarman v. Dougall* reads: "We recognize a State's interest in establishing its own form of government, and in limiting participation in that government to those who are within 'the basic conception of a political community.'" (Supreme Court 1973c, p. 642)

This principle would permit a State to deny the right to vote or to serve in public State offices to resident aliens provided it has merely some rational purpose in doing so. Presumably the federal government has a similar interest as one aspect of its sovereignty. The moral grounds for this political function exception are that internal sovereignty, the right to impose coercive legislation upon those resident within its territory, is justified when it protects them from serious harms and the violation of their moral rights together with the fact that different forms of government are best suited to provide these protections under different circumstances. However, the moral liberty of a sovereign state to choose its form of government is not unlimited. In particular, it must not seriously violate the moral human right to equitable treatment. Therefore, this political function exception would justify denying the right to vote to resident aliens only if the state provides them with some other form of protection, perhaps a special right against discrimination, that is equally effective. Since the *United States Constitution* includes no such special protection, the political function exception offers no justification for denying the right to vote to resident aliens.

A second plausible reason for denying the right to vote to resident aliens is that they lack the knowledge required to exercise this right responsibly. Justice Rehnquist suggests this argument in his dissenting opinion in Sugarman. After noting that the appellees "took no steps to obtain citizenship or indicate any affirmative desires to become citizens," (Supreme Court 1973c, p. 650) he observes that: "The process of naturalization was specifically designed by Congress to require a foreign national to demonstrate that he or she is familiar with the history, traditions, and institutions of our society in a way that the native-born citizen would learn from formal education and basic social contact." (Supreme Court 1973c, p. 659) Therefore, resident aliens may not be as well qualified to vote as citizens are. True enough, but those who have chosen to become resident aliens will probably have a desire to learn about their new country of residence, and those who have resided in the United States for any significant time will have acquired significant knowledge of our history, traditions and institutions. And one may well doubt that most native-born citizens have significantly greater knowledge in this regard. Moreover, citizens are not required to demonstrate any such basic knowledge or to become informed regarding the candidates or the issues at stake in order to exercise their constitutional right to vote. Therefore, this consideration provides at best a weak justification for denying the right to vote to resident aliens.

Another consideration often advanced against giving resident aliens the right to vote is that they have divided loyalties, loyalties to both their original nation within which they have retained their citizenship and to the nation that has granted them permanent residency. (Hayduk 2005, pp. 77–78) At the very least, they will be less committed to the institutions and welfare of the United States because they can always return to their home countries; at worst they might betray the interests of the United States when these conflict with those of their native land. However, the fact that they have chosen to leave their native land to become residents of the United States indicates a very serious commitment to our country, and conferring the right to vote upon them would integrate them more fully into our institutions and deepen that commitment. And although the fact that they have retained citizenship in their native land might be a reason to deny them access to highly sensitive information or the highest governmental offices, it does not seem relevant to the power to vote in federal elections. Moreover, those who apply for permanent residency are required to undergo careful screening to eliminate those who might constitute a danger to the United States. Hence, their divided loyalty is not a serious reason to deny them the constitutional right to vote.

Finally, some argue that granting the right to vote to resident aliens would be unfair to citizens of the United States. After reminding the reader that the principle of fairness requires that the balance between the enjoyment of benefits of social cooperation and its burdens be preserved, Ruth Rubio-Marin explains this argument as follows:

> Now the reason why the full inclusion of resident aliens could break the delicate equilibrium has to do with the fact that they supposedly belong to the political community of their country of nationality. Agreeing to aliens' political inclusion would imply that they are allowed to determine the political destiny of the state while at the same time they are both able to evade their political responsibility by returning to their state of origin, and exonerated from the burden to defend the state from inimical forces risking their lives when this is required by a state of war. In other words, the link between resident aliens and their country of nationality prevents the state from possibly accommodating, on the side of burdens, the expansion that full political inclusion would entail on the side of benefits. (Rubio-Marin 2000, p. 45)

This objection to granting resident aliens full citizenship has less force regarding the present proposal that would grant them only the right to vote but not to hold positions in the federal government. Also one might well doubt how valuable the benefits of their original citizenship are while they are residing in another country. And whatever benefits resident aliens enjoy from citizenship in their native counties will normally be balanced by associated burdens, such a being required to pay taxes there and serve in their armed forces. In short, it is far from clear that granting the right to vote to resident aliens would be unfair to the citizens of the United States. What does seem clear is that the reasons to confer the constitutional right to vote on resident aliens are far stronger than those against doing so. However, what gives force to these pros and undermines the cons is not merely their legal status as resident aliens, but the fact of their ongoing residency together with the fact that this renders them subject to United States law. Hence, their right to vote might well be contingent on a reasonable period of past residency together with a statement that they intend to continue living in the United States for the indefinite future. Some such right to vote ought to be introduced into the *United States Constitution*.

3 Public Education

The Supreme Court has declared that the right to education is neither enumerated in nor implied by the *United States Constitution.* (Supreme Court 1973b, p. 35) However, no one denies the tremendous importance of education, both for the welfare of the individual and for our society as a whole. Therefore, it would seem that the United States ought to establish a constitutional right to education. And some would argue that it ought to be broad enough to ensure adequate education for all residents and their children, even illegal aliens who are residents of any state. Ought there to be a federal constitutional right to public education of all residents in the United States?

One reason to recognize a federal constitutional right to public education is that considerable education is required in order for one to be a responsible citizen and to exercise effectively enumerated rights, such as the right to free speech and the right to vote, essential to the democratic governance of the United States. As Chief Justice Warren explained in *Brown v. Board of Education*:

> Compulsory school attendance laws and the great expenditures for education both demonstrate our recognition of the importance of education to our democratic society. It is required in the performance of our most basic public responsibilities, even service in the armed forces. It is the very foundation of good citizenship. (Supreme Court 1954, p. 493)

Justice Marshall explained this reason more fully in his dissenting opinion in *San Antonio Independent School District v. Rogriguez*:

> Of particular importance is the relationship between education and the political process. "Americans regard the public schools as a most vital civic institution for the preservation of a democratic system of government." Education serves the essential function of instilling in our young an understanding of and appreciation for the principles and operation of our governmental processes. Education may instill the interest and provide the tools necessary for political discourse and debate.... But of most immediate and direct concern must be the demonstrated effect of education on the franchise by the electorate. The right to vote in federal elections is conferred by Art. I.2, and the Seventeenth Amendment of the Constitution, and access to the state franchise has been afforded special protection because it is "preservative of other basic civil and political rights." (Supreme Court 1973b, pp. 113–114)

Anyone who takes democratic institutions and the constitutional rights that sustain them seriously must recognize the force of this reason to establish a federal constitutional right to public education.

A second reason to establish a federal constitutional right to public education is to remedy the unjust inequality of educational opportunity of residents in different states. Goodwin Liu reminds us of this grave injustice:

> For disadvantaged children in substandard schools, the recent success of educational adequacy lawsuits in state courts is a welcome development. But the potential of this legal strategy to advance a national goal of equal educational opportunity is limited by a sobering and largely neglected fact: the most significant component of educational inequality across the nation is not within states but between states. Despite the persistence of this inequality

> and its disparate impact on poor and minority students, the problem draws little policy attention and has evaded our constitutional radar. (Goodwin 2006, p. 330)

A constitutional right to public education is required to remedy this violation of the moral right to equitable treatment because the constitutional right to equal protection of the law conferred by the Fourteenth Amendment is limited to inequalities within each state. It reads:" nor [shall any State] deny to any person within its jurisdiction the equal protection of the laws" (emphasis added). This limitation of the reach of the Equal Protection Clause has been clearly recognized by the Supreme Court.

> Manifestly, the obligation of the State to give the protection of equal laws can be performed only where its laws operate, that is, within its own jurisdiction. It is there that the equality of legal right must be maintained. That obligation is imposed by the Constitution upon the States severally as governmental entities, each responsible for its own laws establishing the rights and duties of persons within its borders. (Supreme Court 1938, p. 350)

And that inadequate educational opportunity is a federal problem is made clear by the constitutional right to interstate travel.

A third reason to recognize a federal constitutional right to public education is that this is necessary in order to require the federal government to ensure adequate funding for the education of all the residents of our country. Central to the right to public education of the residents is the legal claim that the government provide effective public educational facilities available to them and their children. This requires considerable expenditure of public funds. Because primary and secondary education is financed primarily by real estate taxes, school districts with a low tax base lack the ability to provide quality education to their residents. Although most state provide some additional funding, this is very seldom sufficient to provide an adequate standard of education. Hence, there is an urgent need for the federal government, that has a greater ability to raise funds than many state governments, to provide financial assistance to the poorer school districts. Although the Interstate Commerce Clause now permits federal aid to education, it does not require adequate funding and the political will to increase federal aid to education is weak. Therefore, a federal constitutional right to public education is needed to require the federal government to do its share in financing adequate education for all of its residents.

One might grant the case for establishing a federal constitutional right to public education but deny that it ought to be possessed by all residents, even those who entered the United States illegally or who entered legally but have remained here illegally after their visas have expired. What reasons might there be to extend any federal constitutional right to education to illegal aliens and their children? The most obvious reason to do so is that this is necessary to protect the human right to education of illegal aliens and their children. Article 26.1 of the *Universal Declaration of Human Rights* asserts that:

> Everyone has the right to education. Education shall be free, at least in the elementary and fundamental stages. Elementary education shall be compulsory. Technical and professional

> education shall be made generally available and higher education shall be equally accessible to all on the basis of merit.

And Article 13 of the *International Covenant on Economic, Social, and Cultural Rights* establishes this human right in international law. Although the United States is not a party to this treaty, presumably it reflects an analogous moral human right. Because illegal aliens and their children are human beings in the same sense and to the same extent as citizens of the United States, any constitutional right to education ught to apply to them in order to give equal protection to their human right to education.

A second reason to extend any constitutional right to education to illegal aliens and their children is to enable them to become contributing members of our society and to prevent the social costs they would impose were they denied an adequate education. In its 1954 *Brown v. Board of Education* decision the Supreme Court asserted that: "In these days, it is doubtful that any child may reasonably be expected to succeed in life if he is denied the opportunity of an education. Such an opportunity, where the state has undertaken to provide it, is a right which must be made available to all on equal terms." (Supreme Court 1954, p. 493) This is much more true today when technology is rapidly decreasing the need for unskilled and undereducated labor. If the constitutional right to education is made available to illegal aliens and their children then they can succeed in life and utilize their developed talents to benefit our society and as income earners pay taxes to support public programs. If, on the other hand, they are denied the right to equal education, they will impose tremendous costs upon our society. Halle I. Butler argues that:

> Moreover, one cannot simply ignore the societal costs that will result if illegal immigrant children are denied an education. Law enforcement costs will increase to ensure these children do not get into trouble, as statistics indicate that more than forty percent of juvenile arrests occur during school hours. When juveniles do get into trouble, it costs an estimated $24,000 a year to keep the child in juvenile custody, and an estimated $33,000 per year to run youth offender facilities in the state of California alone, regardless of the offender's immigrant status. (Butler 1997, p. 1492)

Hence, any constitutional right to education ought to be extended to illegal aliens and their children in order that the United States can profit from their potential contributions to our society and avoid the inevitable costs if they are denied an adequate education.

The third reason to extend the constitutional right to illegal aliens is to ensure that they receive their fair share of the benefits of a social institution for which they shoulder the same burdens as citizens of the United States. In our country, public education is funded primarily by real estate taxes. As residents, illegal aliens pay directly or indirectly through their landlords these taxes just as do citizens. A principle of social justice is that those who bear the burdens of a cooperative social institution ought to receive their fair share of its benefits. Hence, the constitutional right to education ought to be extended to illegal aliens and their children in order to guarantee to them their fair share of the educational benefits of a social institution supported primarily by the taxes they pay on equal terms with others in our society.

As one would expect, there are also reasons not to establish any federal constitutional right to education. Some could argue that this would be redundant because a constitutional right to education is already conferred by the constitutions of the several states. However the number of cases in the federal courts claiming greater educational rights suggests that this is not entirely true.

A second, and more plausible reason, not to establish any federal constitutional right to education is that this would empower the courts to interfere in decisions that ought to be decided democratically by the people rather than a few judges with life tenure. Jeannie Oakes reports the testimony of education experts for the state in *Williams v. California* as follows:

> **Objecting to Current Policies Subverts Democratic Processes.** Finally, the State's experts assert that the plaintiffs, by bringing the case, seek to violate "democratic" processes of education policy making. They argue that legislation, administrative regulation setting,, local school boards, etc., are the means by which California should (and do) establish the educational policies they prefer. (Oakes 2010, p. 61)

However, this argument seems to prove too much. If the most important governmental decisions, such as those concerning education, ought always to be decided by the normal democratic processes, then there ought to be no constitutional rights of any kind that would authorize the courts to protect the fundamental moral rights of those subject to the jurisdiction of state or federal government.

A third and by far the strongest reason not to establish any federal constitutional right to education is that this would authorize the federal government, both Congress and the federal courts, to impose nationwide standards and policies that would be inappropriate for the local conditions. When the issue of local control arose on the more modest state level in *Williams v. California*, Jeannie Oakes reports the testimony of expert witnesses argued as follows:

> They claim that, if the state held all schools to standards regarding teachers, instructional materials, and facilities, it would undermine local control. That would frustrate good managers and discourage parent involvement, which in turn, would depress achievement and provide destructive excuses for students' test scores. (Oakes 2010, p. 59)

This argument is much more powerful when directed against federal control of educational policies. In *Rodriguez* the Supreme Court opined that:

> The persistence of attachment to government at the lowest level where education is concerned reflects the depth of commitment of its supporters. In part, local control means, as Professor Coleman suggests, the freedom to devote more money to the education of one's children. Equally important, however, is the opportunity it offers for participation in the decision making process that determines how those local tax dollars will be spent. Each locality is free to tailor local programs to meet local needs. Pluralism also affords some opportunity for experimentation, innovation, and a healthy competition for educational excellence….No area of social concern stands to profit more from a multiplicity of viewpoints and from a diversity of approaches than does public education. (Supreme Court 1973b, pp. 49–50)

There can be no doubt that a considerable measure of local control is essential to any effective system of public education. Whether this is sufficient to exclude any federal constitutional right to education depends upon the strength of the countervailing reasons.

Even if one were to advocate a federal constitutional right to education, one might well argue that it ought not to be broad enough to apply to illegal immigrants and their children. One reason to deny any right to education to illegal aliens and their children is that they deserve punishment, or at least deportation, rather than reward for entering or remaining in the United States against the law. Jennifer L. Maki argues that:

> Providing undocumented aliens with these privileges incorrectly rewards their illegal status as compared to the legal status held by nonimmigrant foreign students….Undocumented aliens should be required to correct their illegal status before a state institution recognizes their right to receive benefits accorded to U.S. citizens and visa-holding students in the United States. (Maki 2005, p. 1345)

However, the Supreme Court in *Plyle*r suggests that although this sort of argument applies to adult illegal aliens, it does not apply to their children who "can affect neither their parents' conduct nor their own status." (Supreme Court 1982, p. 220) Hence, Maki's argument is probably irrelevant to primary and secondary education. Moreover, if there is a human right to education, then education is not a mere privilege that may be withheld at the discretion of the state.

A second plausible reason not to confer any constitutional right to education on illegal aliens and their children is that this would encourage more foreigners to enter the United States illegally and discourage illegal aliens who are here from returning home. However, the Supreme Court asserted in Plyler that: "The dominant incentive for illegal entry into the State of Texas is the availability of employment; few if any illegal immigrants come to this country, or presumably to the State of Texas, in order to avail themselves of the free education." (Supreme Court 1982, p. 228) And a later Jordan Commission report did not advocate denying free public education to illegal immigrant children because "illegal immigrants do not come here to get their kids in school; they come here to get a job." (Butler 1997, p. 1488)

A third, and much more cogent, reason not to extend any federal constitutional right to education to illegal aliens and their children is that this would require states to use their limited financial resources needed for more urgent state interests. Lora L. Grandrath asserts that:

> Because of the 1982 United States Supreme Court decision of Plyler v. Doe, states are required to provide illegal immigrant students with a free public education. Thirteen years after this Court decision, public school systems in states with large illegal immigrant populations are going bankrupt. These states have stretched finite education resources beyond the limit. (Grandrath 1996, pp. 750–751)

If several states really are going bankrupt because of their attempts to educate illegal aliens and their children, then they ought not to be required by the federal government to give public education to such persons. It is true that the resources available to any state are not unlimited, and presumably any state ought to enjoy considerable discretion as to how it allocates its resources in meeting its obligations to its residents. But is it really true that even those states with large immigrant populations are unable to devote more resources to education? And might not a federal constitutional right to education require the federal government to assist these states in meeting their obligation to educate all their residents, even illegal aliens and their children?

A fourth reason not to extend any federal constitutional right to education to illegal aliens and their children is that this would reduce the quality of public education in many states. Lora L. Grandrath argues that:

> First, the states have a greater obligation to provide their own citizens and lawful resident students with a public education than they do to provide illegal immigrants with such a benefit. Second, the children of the taxpayers are unfairly affected because the quality of their education decreases. With more students, a state must hire additional teachers, particularly bilingual ones, because many illegal immigrant students speak little or no English. School districts must also buy more textbooks, and pay for more school lunches. However, with limited state budgets, many school districts are forced to sacrifice these essential items.....Thus, less funds spent per student generally leads to a lower quality of education. (Grandrath 1996, pp. 796–797)

It is probably true that the states do have a greater obligation to provide their own citizens and lawful resident students with public education than to provide public education to illegal aliens and their children. However, one should not forget that illegal aliens are also taxpayers and contribute to the support of the public school systems. Still, there is considerable force to this argument against extending any federal constitutional right to education to illegal aliens and their children.

Clearly there are two serious issues facing our nation. The first question before the nation is whether there ought to be a federal constitutional right to public education. One reason to establish this right is that considerable education is required in order for one to be a responsible citizen and to exercise effectively rights, such as the rights to free speech and to vote, enumerated in the federal constitution. Another reason to establish a federal constitutional right to education is to remedy the unjust inequality to educational opportunity of the residents in different states. A third and less urgent reason is that this is necessary to require the federal government to ensure adequate funding for the education of all residents in the United States. Although some might allege that any federal constitutional right to education would be redundant, given that state constitutions normally include a right to public education, I doubt that this is true. A more plausible reason is that this would authorize the courts to interfere in decisions that ought to be decided democratically by legislatures and the people. However, this falsely implies that there ought to be no constitutional rights at all. A third and very strong reason not to establish any federal right to public education is that this would authorize the federal government to impose nationwide policies and standards that would be inappropriate for the local conditions. Effective public education requires that local school districts, perhaps with some state assistance, have wide discretion regarding educational policies and practices. However, although a federal right to public education would authorize the national government to exercise some control over the several states and their local school districts, it could do so in ways that would retain a considerable measure of local authority. Therefore, I believe that on balance the reasons in favor of establishing a federal constitutional right to education outweigh those against such a right.

A second and more difficult question is whether any federal constitutional right to public education ought to extend to all residents of the United States, even illegal aliens and their children. One reason to extend any federal constitutional right to public education to illegal aliens and their children is that this is necessary to protect their human right to education. A second and more pragmatic reason is that this is necessary in order to enable illegal aliens and their children to become contributing members of our society and to prevent the social costs they would impose were they denied adequate education. A third reason to extend any federal constitutional right to education to illegal aliens and their children is to ensure that they receive their fair share of the benefits of a social institution for which they shoulder the same burdens of paying local and state taxes as citizens. On the other hand, many argue that illegal aliens deserve punishment or deportation rather than the reward of free public education because they have broken the law either by entering the United States illegally or by remaining here after their visas have expired. Although some argue that extending the right to public education to illegal aliens would encourage more foreigners to enter the United States illegally and discourage illegal aliens who are here from returning home, it is doubtful that any such incentives are very powerful. A more plausible reason not to extend any federal constitutional right to public education to illegal aliens and their children is that this would force the states to exhaust their limited financial resources needed for more important state purposes. A final reason not to extend any federal constitutional right to public education to illegal aliens and their children is that this would reduce the quality of public education in many states. Although I consider the increased costs imposed on school systems by the influx of illegal students and the special burdens they impose on efforts to maintain high-quality education serious, I discount them somewhat because they could be reduced to a considerable extent by the additional funding from the national government that would be required by any federal constitutional right to public education. However, I can think of no alternative measures that would satisfy the reasons in favor of extending the federal constitutional right to public education to illegal aliens and their children. Therefore, my conclusion is that the United States ought to establish a federal constitutional right to public education of all residents, even illegal aliens and their children.

It is interesting to observe that the moral foundations of the pro and con reasons in this debate are very similar. Both those who appeal to the need to educate residents in order to enable them to become responsible citizens and to exercise their rights to free speech and to vote and those who insist that decisions regarding public education ought to be made by legislatures and the people rather than the courts presuppose the moral value of democracy. Again, both those who argue that illegal aliens ought to receive their fair share of the public education they support with their tax dollars and those who reply that they deserve punishment or deportation rather than the reward of free public education for breaking the law presuppose the moral principles of justice. Everyone agrees that one of the most important moral obligations of state governments is to provide high quality public education and that state and federal governments ought to allocate their limited resources in proportion to the urgency of the needs of the public. And there is no reason to assume that those who oppose extending public education to illegal aliens deny the existence or importance of their human right to education. They may well assume that the obligation to satisfy this human right is their native countries, not the United States.

4 Habeas Corpus

One of the most important constitutional rights of private persons is the right of habeas corpus, the right of a detained individual to petition a court to ascertain whether his or her detention is lawful. Article I, Section 9, Clause 2 of the *United States Constitution* reads: "The Privilege of the Writ of Habeas Corpus shall not be suspended, unless when in Cases of Rebellion or Invasion the public Safety may require it." This clearly incorporates the common law writ of habeas corpus into our constitutional law and places very strict limits on its suspension. However after 9/11 the Bush administration first insisted that enemy combatants do not have any constitutional right of habeas corpus and later that they have it only to a very limited degree. A series of Supreme Court cases have challenged the arguments of the United States government attempting to detain suspected terrorists indefinitely without trial and to deny them the right to petition a court for their release. Whatever the final decision may be regarding what our constitutional law is, the moral question remains: Ought enemy combatants to have the constitutional right of habeas corpus?

One reason for applying the constitutional right of habeas corpus to enemy combatants is that this is necessary to comply with Common Article 3 of all four of the Geneva Conventions. The United States should comply with this article both because it has ratified these conventions and because these conventions serve the moral purpose of making warfare less inhumane. Relying on Part IC of the Memorandum of January 22, 2002, the Bush administration argued that Common Article 3 is inapplicable to enemy combatants. However, the Supreme Court rejected this argument in *Hamdan* and asserted that: Common Article 3, then, is applicable here and, as indicated above, requires that Hamdan be tried by a "regularly constituted court affording all the judicial guarantees which are recognized as indispensable by civilized peoples." (Supreme Court 2006, pp. 631–632) Denied the right of habeas corpus, enemy combatants would be subject to indefinite detention without any power to petition a court to determine whether they are being lawfully detained, much less to have any charges against them tried by a legally constituted court. This clearly violates Common Article 3 and ought not to be permitted by our constitutional law.

Another reason to extend the constitutional right to habeas corpus to enemy combatants is to protect their human right to liberty, one of the most fundamental of all moral rights and one firmly established in international human rights law. Article

9.4 of the *International Covenant on Civil and Political Rights* reads: "Anyone who is deprived of his liberty by arrest or detention shall be entitled to take proceedings before a court in order that that court may decide without delay on the lawfulness of his detention and order his release if the detention is not lawful." In Ex Parte Milligan, the Supreme Court has recognized the importance of the legal protection of human rights as follows: "By the protection of the law, human rights are secured; withdraw that protection and they are at the mercy of wicked rulers or the clamor of an excited people." (Supreme Court 1866, p. 119) Whatever their legal status may be, enemy combatants are human beings and as such possess every human right. And the United States ought to secure their human rights both because it has ratified the *International Covenant on Civil and Political Rights* and because of the grave harm inflicted upon any human being when one of his or her human rights is violated.

A third reason to confer the constitutional right of habeas corpus on enemy combatants is to preserve the constitutional checks and balances necessary to maintain our democratic form of government. The Bush administration justified its denial of this right to enemy combatants detained at Guantanamo Bay by the fact that it lacked sovereignty over this part of Cuba. The Supreme Court responded that:

> The Government's formal sovereignty-based test raises troubling separation-of-powers concerns as well….The necessary implication of the argument is that by surrendering formal sovereignty over any unincorporated territory to a third party, while at the same time entering into a lease that grants total control over the territory back to the United States, it would be possible for the political branches to govern without legal constraint. (Supreme Court 2008a, pp. 34–35)

Alexander Hamilton explained the importance of these concerns in *The Federalist*:

> The establishment of the writ of *habeas corpus*, the prohibition of *ex post facto* laws, and of TITLES OF NOBILITY, *to which we have no corresponding provisions in our constitution*, are perhaps greater securities to liberty and republicanism than any it contains. For the creation of crimes after the commission of the fact, or in other words, the subjecting men to punishment for things which, when they were done, were breaches of no law, and the practice of arbitrary imprisonments have been in all ages the favorite and most formidable instruments of tyranny. (Hamilton 1961, p. 577)

Thus, the right of habeas corpus ought to be conferred on all of those subject to detainment by the United States government, including enemy combatants, in order to preserve the democratic structure of the *United States Constitution*, the separation of powers that enables the judiciary to check any executive branch intent on maintaining its despotic rule by the unlawful imprisonment of its opponents.

The fourth and most important reason to confer the constitutional right of habeas corpus upon all those subject to the jurisdiction of the United States, even enemy combatants, is to secure the liberty, indeed all the liberties, of private persons threatened with unlawful indefinite detention. In response to the government's argument that habeas corpus is inapplicable to enemy combatants imprisoned at Guantanamo Bay because it lay outside the sovereign territory of the United States, the Supreme Court reasoned that:

> By the express terms of the agreement with Cuba, the United States exercises "complete jurisdiction and control" over Guantanamo Bay Naval Base, and may continue to exercise such control permanently if it so chooses....Application of the habeas corpus statute to persons detained at the base is consistent with the historical reach of the writ of habeas corpus. (Supreme Court 2004a, pp. 480–481)

Justice Scalia, dissenting, complained that the Court does not explain how complete jurisdiction and control without sovereignty justifies the application of the domestic law of the United States. (Supreme Court 2004a, p. 501) But the opinion of the Court attempted to do so by referring to "the historic purpose of the writ." (Supreme Court 2004a, p. 481) Blackstone explains this purpose with admirable clarity:

> **Suspension of writ of habeas corpus**--Of great importance to the public is the preservation of this personal liberty, for if it were left to the power of any, the highest, magistrate to imprison arbitrarily whomever he or his officers thought proper (as in France it is daily practiced by the crown) there would soon be an end to all other rights and immunities. (Blackstone 1902, p. 124)

Therefore, the United States Constitution ought to confer the right of habeas on all persons, including enemy combatants, who could be arbitrarily detained because only in this way could their personal liberties of all those subject to our government be completely and firmly protected.

There are, of course, reasons not to extend the constitutional right of habeas corpus to enemy combatants. One reason is that this would empower the courts to intrude into military decisions best left to those responsible for our national security. As Jonathan Hafetz notes: "Habeas review during wartime risks injecting judges and lawyers into matters beyond their expertise...." (Hafetz 2011, p. 178) This is especially true of the war on terror conducted in large part by agencies such as the CIA using sophisticated technologies to discover strictly classified information. But judges often decide cases concerning matters beyond their expertise. And typically they decide these cases well by relying upon the testimony of expert witnesses.

A second and much more plausible reason not to confer the right of habeas corpus upon enemy combatants is that this would hamper the conduct of the war on terror. In *Eisentrager*, a case concerning enemy aliens captured during the Second World War, the Supreme Court explained this reason as follows:

> A basic consideration in habeas corpus practice is that the prisoner will be produced before the court....To grant the writ to these prisoners might mean that our army must transport them across the seas for hearing. This would require allocation of shipping space, guarding personnel, billeting and rations. It might also require transportation for whatever witnesses the prisoners desired to call as well as transportation for those necessary to defend legality of the sentence. The writ since it is held to be a matter of right, would be equally available to enemies during active hostilities as in the present twilight between war and peace. Such trials would hamper the war effort and bring aid and comfort to the enemy. (Supreme Court 1950, pp. 778–779)

However in *Rasul v. Bush*, a case concerning alleged enemy combatants held at Guantanamo Bay, Justice Kennedy, concurring, argued that: "The facts here are distinguishable from those in *Eisentrager* in two critical ways, leading to the conclusion that a federal court may entertain the petitions. First, Guantanamo Bay is in every practical respect a United States territory, and it is far removed from any hostilities." (Supreme Court 2004a, p. 487) Although one might argue that no place on earth is far removed from the hostile threats presented by terrorists, it remains true that producing enemy combatants in the war on terror before a court would be much less disruptive than doing so during conventional warfare.

A third reason not to extend the right of habeas corpus to enemy combatants in the war on terror is the urgent need to protect classified information. Were an enemy combatant entitled to petition a court to require the United States government to establish that detaining him or her is not unlawful, this would require the administration either to release a detainee who could then resume terrorist activities or justify continued detainment by producing classified information that would be very useful to our terrorist enemies. In *Boumediene*, the Supreme Court considered but rejected this reason as follows:

> We make no attempt to anticipate all of the evidentiary and access-to-counsel issues that will arise during the review of the detainees' habeas corpus proceedings. We recognize, however, that the Government has a legitimate interest in protecting sources and methods of intelligence gathering; and we expect that the District Court will use its discretion to accommodate this interest to the greatest extent possible. (Supreme Court 2008a, pp. 67–68 slip opinion)

Jonathan Hafetz suggests that the Classified Information Procedures Act addresses this concern adequately. (Hafetz 2011, p. 223) But one may wonder whether in practice it is really possible both to fully protect sensitive intelligence of value to terrorist enemies of the United States and to enable a detained enemy combatant to robustly challenge the government's evidence against him or her.

A fourth reason not to confer the constitutional right of habeas corpus on enemy combatants is that the procedural rules of federal courts are too restrictive to enable the government to continue to detain terrorists or supporters of terrorism who pose a serious threat to national security. For example the government responded to Hamdan's habeas corpus petition as follows:

> Finally, the President's determination that "the danger to the safety of the United States and the nature of international terrorism" renders it impracticable "to apply in military commissions…the principles of law and rules of evidence generally recognized in the trial of criminal cases in the United States district courts." (Supreme Court 2006, p. 622)

However, the Supreme Court had in large measure undermined this response with the following concession:

> We therefore hold that a citizen-detainee seeking to challenge his classification as an enemy combatant must receive notice of the factual basis for his classification, and a fair opportunity to rebut the Government's factual assertions before a neutral decisionmaker….At the same time, the exigencies of the circumstances may demand that, aside from these core elements, enemy-combatant proceedings may be tailored to alleviate their uncommon potential to burden the Executive at a time of ongoing military conflict. (Supreme Court 2004b, p. 533)

Precisely how such proceedings ought to be tailored remains controversial.

How should one balance these pro and con reasons against each other? National security is a morally as well as a legally compelling state interest. This is true even though what is threatened by international terrorism is not the continued existence of the United States, as might be the case in a conventional war against one or more foreign nation states, but the liberty of United States citizens who might be taken as hostages or the life and limb of those who might be victims of terrorist violence. Still, granting habeas corpus to enemy combatants would not seriously burden the administration in its war on terror. More serious are the dangers of revealing classified information useful to terrorists and the inability to submit reliable information to justify the continued detainment of enemy combatants because it would be inadmissible under the restrictive procedural rules of federal courts. However, both of these concerns could, and probably should, be significantly reduced by introducing a special court to hear cases concerning terrorism or modifying the procedural rules of federal courts when they hear habeas corpus petitions by enemy combatants.

Two significant, but not in themselves conclusive, reasons to extend the constitutional right of habeas corpus to enemy combatants are to respect Common Article 3 of the Geneva Conventions and to maintain the constitutional checks and balances that enable the courts to restrain any administration tempted to abuse its power of imprisonment. What does matter to a much higher degree is the need to secure the liberty, indeed all the fundamental rights, of innocent individuals who are mistakenly or maliciously detained as enemy combatants. This is a very serious concern because the government and the public almost inevitably vastly overestimate the threat to national security posed by terrorists. Therefore, I believe that the reasons to confer the constitutional right of habeas corpus on enemy combatants considerably outweigh the reasons against doing so.

The underlying moral values are obvious. They include the importance of maintaining the democratic structure of the United States Constitution, the prevention of serious harm to individuals by terrorist actions or unlawful detainment, securing the constitutional rights of all those subject to the de facto jurisdiction of the United States and protecting the human rights of private persons.

5 Same-Sex Marriage

One of the most fiercely contested issues during the past few years is whether United States law ought to recognize same-sex marriages and give them constitutional protection. This has been debated in Congress and in state legislatures, in popular referenda, and in both state and federal courts. The Supreme Court has recently decided two landmark cases concerning same-sex marriage. *United States v. Windsor* struck down provisions of the federal Defense of Marriage Act that deny to same-sex couples legally married according to state law all the federal benefits provided to heterosexual married couples. (Supreme Court 2013, pp. 25–26 slip opinion) And in *Obergefell v. Hodges* it has recognized a constitutional right of same-sex couples to marry. (Supreme Court 2015, p. 28) However, many insist that this decision is both legally mistaken and morally objectionable while some predict that an increasingly conservative Supreme Court will soon reverse this decision.

Ought persons subject to United States law to have a constitutional right to marry another person of the same sex? The most obvious reason why the United States ought to establish this right is that this is required by the international human right to marry. Article 16 of the *Universal Declaration of Human Rights* reads as follows:

1. Men and women of full age, without any limitation due to race, nationality or religion, have the right to marry and to found a family. They are entitled to equal rights as to marriage, during marriage and at its dissolution.
2. Marriage shall be entered into only with the free and full consent of the intending spouses.
3. The family is the natural and fundamental group unit of society and is entitled to protection by society and the State.

Article 23 of the *International Covenant on Civil and Political Rights* establishes this right in international law. Presumably this implies that each State Party has an obligation to establish a right to marry analogous to the human right to marry. And the strongest protection of the human right to marry would be provided by an analogous constitutional right.

However, opponents of same-sex marriage can reply that the United States has established a constitutional right to marry. Although no such right is mentioned in the text of the *Constitution*, the Supreme Court has recognized the right to marry in a number of its decisions, most notably in *Meyer v. Nebraska* and *Skinner v. Oklahoma*. And they argue that the scope of this right is appropriately limited to heterosexual couples. The crucial question thus become whether the international human right to marry is thus limited. The fact that the *Universal Declaration* links the right to marry with the right to found a family and that it does not mention sex in specifying impermissible limitations strongly suggests that it declares a right to marry only of heterosexual couples. On the other hand, its recognition of the importance of choice when it insists that marriage shall be entered into only with full and free consent might imply that the choices of whether to marry and if so, whom to marry ought not to be denied. Hence, the relevance of the international right to marry to United States law is unclear.

But probably there is a more fundamental moral human right to marry that would be relevant. A human life is not merely a series of momentary perceptions and feelings together with isolated actions and reactions. It is a continuing flow of experience influenced by one's activities and the environment. The value of a human life depends very little on moments or short periods of pleasure and pain but very much upon the meaning of each experience in the history of one's life. In this respect, what matters most is the success or failure of one's main projects and how rewarding or frustrating are one's personal relationships. This is why the choice of whether to marry and found a family or to remain single and devote one's energies primarily to some career or vocation is truly momentous. If one chooses to marry, the choice of one's partner is crucial to the value of the family the couple founds. Therefore, to deny or limit these choices does immeasurable and irremediable harm to any normal human being. This potential harm grounds a moral duty of one's society that it not completely deny or significantly hinder these two marriage choices and that its legal system protect their exercise. It also grounds the moral power of each human being to claim performance of these duties in the event that one's society fails to do so. Together this moral duty and moral power to claim constitute the core of a moral claim-right of each human being that his or her society permit and protect full and free marital choice.. The most secure protection would be a constitutional right of persons to marry ensuring both the full and free choice of whether to marry and, if so, whom to marry. Since some persons intensely desire to marry another person of the same sex and whether they are free to do so will determine in large measure the value of their lives, the constitutional right ought to be broad enough to permit same-sex marriage.

Another reason to extend the constitutional right to marry in United States law to permit same-sex marriage may be that this is required by the constitutional right to liberty of homosexuals and lesbians. The Fifth and Fourteenth Amendments specify that no person shall be deprived of life, liberty or property without due process of law. Although this does not ground any unlimited right of personal liberty, it does require that any legal limitation be justified. The degree of justification required differs between fundamental liberties that require that the limitation be necessary for some compelling state interest and other liberties that require only some permissible reason. In *Obergefell v. Hodges,* Justice Kennedy *has recently asserted that:*

> This analysis compels the conclusion that same-sex couples may exercise the right to marry….A first premise of the Court's relevant precedents is that the right to personal choice regarding marriage is inherent in the concept of personal autonomy. This abiding connection between marriage and liberty is why *Loving* invalidated interracial marriage bans under the Due Process Clause. (Supreme Court 2015, p. 12 slip opinion) His reasoning is surely plausible and seems valid.

There is also a fundamental moral human right to liberty. Its defining core is not the moral liberty to do anything one wishes, but the moral liberty to act or refrain from acting in any way that is not contrary to any moral duty. This bilateral liberty is protected by a moral duty of others not to obstruct or hinder one in exercising this core liberty. This moral duty is a special case of the moral duty to respect the rationality of any normal human being. This duty is grounded on the fact that each rational individual is more likely to know what he ir she ought to do, in the light of self-interest and moral considerations, than others together with the ways in which interference with one's freedom breeds frustration and resentment damaging to both self-respect and social interaction. However, this moral duty to refrain from interference with the freedom of others is not unlimited. Others may, sometimes even ought, to prevent persons from acting in exceptionally harmful ways. Once more a tentative conclusion is in order. The United States constitutional law ought to permit persons to may someone of the same sex unless doing so would cause morally excessive harm to themselves or others.

A third reason why the United States ought to establish a constitutional right to same-sex marriage may be that this is required by the right to privacy of homosexuals and lesbians. Although the right to privacy is not enumerated in the *United States Constitution*, the Supreme Court recognized this right in *Griswold v. Connecticut (Supreme Court 1965)*. It clearly indicated the relevance of the right to privacy to marriage in the following passage: "Would we allow the police to search the sacred precincts of marital bedrooms for telltale signs of the use of contraceptives? The very idea is repulsive to the notions of privacy surrounding the marriage relationship." Most recently in *Lawrence v. Texas* the Supreme Court has confirmed the relevance of the constitutional right to privacy to both marriage and same-sex couples.

In the reasoning by which it overruled *Bowers v. Hardwick*, a decision that upheld the criminalization of sexual acts between homosexuals, it asserted:

> The *Casey* decision again confirmed that our laws and traditions afford constitutional protection to personal decisions relating to marriage, procreation, contraception, family relationships, child rearing, and education….Persons in a homosexual relationship may seek autonomy for these purposes, just as heterosexual persons do.

Justice Kennedy presumably appeals to the right to privacy when he asserts:

> A second principle in this Court's jurisprudence is that the right to marry is fundamental because it supports a two-person union unlike any other in its importance to the committed individuals. This point was central to *Griswold v. Connecticut*, which held the Constitution protects the rights of married couples to use contraception. (Supreme Court 2015, p. 13 slip opinion)

This reasoning seems legally compelling.

One might argue that it is also morally compelling because this constitutional right to privacy protects the human right to privacy. Article 12 of the *Universal Declaration of Human Rights* affirms a right to privacy, a right later introduced into international law by Article 17 of the *International Covenant on Civil and Political Rights*. But because neither document gives any definition or criterion to determine what constitutes privacy, one has no way of knowing whether this human right is relevant to marriage, and if so, in what manner. Therefore, let us turn our attention to the moral human right to privacy. I believe that there is some such right, the moral right of any human being to make and act on private decisions. It is best understood as a specific human right derived from the more general human right to liberty. Presumably it is grounded on much the same moral considerations that ground the more fundamental human right to liberty. More controversial is the scope of this human right. What constitutes a private decision? I suggest that it is a decision that fundamentally affects the right-holder for better or worse and that does not seriously harm any public interest, any important interest of the general public. Surely, the decision of whether to marry and the choice of whom to marry fundamentally affect the value of the life of any normal human being. But whether some marital decisions seriously harm any important public interest remains in doubt. Thus whether the moral human right to privacy would justify the introduction of a constitutional right to same-sex marriage into United States law depends upon the reasons against establishing this right. Tentatively, one should conclude that the moral human right to privacy may well be a reason for a constitutional right to same-sex marriage.

Probably the strongest reason to establish a constitutional right of persons to marry someone of the same sex is that this is required by the right of homosexuals and lesbians to the equal protection of the law. Although the power to regulate marriage lies primarily within the jurisdiction of the several states, it is limited by the *Constitution of the United States*. The Fourteenth Amendment reads in part: "nor [shall any State] deny to any person within its jurisdiction the equal protection of the law." In *Windsor v. United States* the Supreme Court held that the Defense of Marriage Act is unconstitutional insofar as it denies same-sex couples residing in states that recognize their marriage the many federal benefits available to heterosexual couples. And in Obergefell v. Hodges it similarly held that:

> Under the Constitution, same-sex couples seek in marriage the same legal treatment as opposite-sex couples, and it would disparage their choices and diminish their personhood to deny them this right. The right of same-sex couples to marry that is part of the liberty promised by the Fourteenth Amendment is derived, too, from the Amendment's guarantee of the equal protection of the laws. (Supreme Court 2015, p. 19 slip opinion)

Surely this conclusion is legally sound.

It could be similarly justified by an appeal to the international human right to equal protection of the laws. Article 7 of the *Universal Declaration of Human Rights* asserts a human right to equal protection of the law, a right later established in international law by Article 26 of the *International Covenant on Civil and Political Rights*. Both explain that this requires protection against discrimination, and the *International Covenant* includes sex as one of the grounds for prohibited discrimination. However this international human right to equal protection may not be applicable to same-sex marriage because sex is not the same as sexual orientation. Moreover, the *Convention On the Elimination of All Forms of Discrimination Against Women* of 1979 asserts that "…the States Parties to the International Covenants on Human Rights have the obligation to ensure the equal rights of men and women…." This strongly suggests that the international human right to equal protection does not apply to any legal distinctions based upon sexual orientation rather than biological sex.

Is there a more fundamental moral human right to equal protection of the law and, if so, does it apply to the constitutional right to same-sex marriage? I have argued previously in my discussion of the right of resident aliens to vote that there is such a right and that it is grounded on the moral human right to equitable treatment. Because the scope of the moral human right to equal treatment of the law is determined by its grounds, the remaining question is whether the moral human right to equitable treatment, the right not to be treated worse than others who are similarly situated without a just-making reason, applies to same-sex marriage. Surely to deny the right to marry the person of one's choice to homosexuals and lesbians is to treat them worse than to provide constitutional protection to the right of heterosexuals to marry the person of their choice. Although this denial might be legally justified by some compelling state interest, most state interests appeal to the general welfare rather than to any principle of justice. Therefore very probably the moral right to equitable treatment and the derivative moral human right to equal protection of the law do require that the United States establish a constitutional right to same-sex marriage.

Some opponents of same-sex marriage will reply that the previous constitutional law that lacks any right to same-sex marriage really does not treat homosexuals and lesbians worse than it treats heterosexual persons. After all, homosexuals and lesbians already have the constitutional right to marry and many of them in fact marry persons of the opposite sex. Although not all of these marriages are successful, the same is true of marriages of heterosexual couples. However, the present constitutional right to marry continues to deny homosexuals and lesbians the opportunity to marry the person of their choice, an opportunity to gives to heterosexual persons. Given the importance of free choice of one's spouse, this is a serious deprivation. An opponent of same-sex marriage might grant this but reply that the introduction of a constitutional right to same-sex marriage is not necessary because domestic partnerships can provide all the benefits of heterosexual marriages. At this point, the reasoning of *Brown v. Board of Education* becomes relevant. In overruling the separate but equal doctrine of *Plessy v. Ferguson* it reasoned as follows:

> To separate them [black pupils] from others of similar age and qualifications solely because of their race generates a feeling of inferiority as to their status in the community that may affect their hearts and minds in a way unlikely ever to be undone….We conclude that in the field of public education the doctrine of "separate but equal" has no place. Separate educational facilities are inherently unequal.

The same reasoning applies to any legal system that provides a constitutional right to heterosexual marriage but only domestic partnerships for same-sex couples. This treatment is inherently unequal because it stigmatizes same-sex couples and threats them as second-class members of society. Therefore, the United States ought to establish a constitutional right to same-sex marriage unless there is some morally, not merely legally, compelling reason not to do so.

What, then, are the reasons most often advanced not to establish a constitution right of persons to marry someone of the same sex? The reason given by state courts when petitioners first sought the right to same-sex marriage was that this is impossible. "Same-sex marriage" is by definition a contradiction in terms because marriage is by definition the union of one man and one woman as husband and wife. Now it is true that state courts and more recently legislatures have adopted this definition of marriage. However, what is at stake here is marriage as a legal status. And because this legal status has been created by state courts and legislatures, they could just as easily change it. The fact that this is by no means impossible is clearly shown by the fact that several states have already legalized same-sex marriages.

A second reason often given not to establish a constitutional right to marry someone of the same sex is that this is the first step on a slippery slope that would lead to the legalization of polygamy, incest and prostitution. If the several states can change the legal definition at will, then they could change it to permit all of these pernicious institutions. It is true that the states could do so; these next steps are not logically impossible. But if these deviant marital institutions really are pernicious, then the state courts and state legislatures would probably be wise enough not to recognize them in their marriage regulations. Moreover, legalizing some of these institutions might violate be unconstitutional. For example, polygamy might violate the right to equal protection because it gives one male power over several females. Similarly, incest, that is typically the act of a more powerful parent or other relative over some weaker victim, would thus equal protection. Hence, this objection has only slight moral force at best.

A third reason advanced against establishing any constitutional right to same-sex marriage is that this would give society's stamp of approval to the gay lifestyle. Homosexuals, and to a lesser extend lesbians, typically engage in promiscuous short-term sexual relationships with a variety pf partners and even impersonal sexual encounters with complete strangers. This lifestyle sets a very bad example to impressionable members of society and degrades the quality of their own lives. However, legalizing same-sex marriages does not constitute approval of this sort of extra-marital behavior. And it might well encourage many homosexuals and lesbians to give up promiscuous sexual activity in favor of long-term commitment to one same-sex spouse. Again, this reason seems to have very little, if any, force.

A more common reason not to establish a constitutional right to same-sex marriage is that this would damage our traditional social institution of marriage. It is true that in the United States marriage as a social institution has normally instituted a family consisting of a husband and a wife, typically with one or more children. Notice, however, that traditionally the roles of husband and wife have been clearly defined. The husband is the bread-winner and the wife performs the household chores and cares for the children before they leave home. It is not clear that this sexist institution ought to be protected by the law. In any event, it is disappearing from the scene. Women are increasingly working outside the home, either for financial reasons or for personal satisfaction, and single-parent families are becoming more common. Moreover, Caucasian, African-American and Hispanic families tend to be structured differently. More to the point, it is hard to see how legalizing same-sex marriage would damage or even weaken any of these social institutions of marriage, for they would remain fully available to heterosexual couples. Hence, one should not take this reason against establishing a constitutional right of persons to marry someone of the same sex very seriously.

A more plausible reason not to establish any constitutional right to marry someone of the same sex is that procreation is the essential purpose of marriage and same-sex couples are biologically incapable of procreation. Rather than arguing that marriage ought to be limited to heterosexual couples because that is traditional, the way we have always instituted families, this argument appeals to the defining value of heterosexual marriage, having children. However, this reasoning seems to prove too much. If the legal status of marriage really ought to be limited to couples capable of, and presumably intending to, procreate, then the law ought not to permit sterile or infertile heterosexuals to marry and perhaps ought to require a couple to certify that they intend to have children before issuing a marriage license. And it is surely a mistake to insist that marriage has one and only one essential function. Marriage as a social institution founds a family, and families perform many valuable functions. In addition to producing and rearing the next generation, they serve as the basic economic unit in a society by which goods and services are distributed to its members and the primary institution to provide social security as it cares for its members when they become ill or lose their income. Finally, homosexuals can procreate with the cooperation of surrogate mothers and lesbians can have children by in vitro fertilization with donated or purchased sperm. Although plausible, this reason against same-sex marriage does not survive critical examination.

Granted that same-sex couples are capable of procreation or alternatively adopting children, a sixth reason not to establish a constitutional right to same-sex marriage is that same-sex couples are incapable of providing healthy/good parenting for their children. In defending itself against the claim of same-sex petitioners to a constitutional right to marriage in *Baehr vs. Miike*, the State of Hawaii asserted that all things being equal, it is best for a child that it be raised in a single home by its parents, or at least by a married male and female. It is true that every state, and the United States as a whole, has a strong, perhaps compelling, interest in the psychological well-being of their future citizens. However, after hearing the testimony of the expert witnesses for the defense and another four for the Plaintiffs, the Court concluded that the sexual orientation of parents is not in and of itself an indicator of parental fitness. This conclusion is confirmed by almost all of the published studies by child psychologists and social psychologists. And Justice Kennedy has even suggested that because same-sex couples are often permitted to have children, their children need the benefits that marriage provides.

> Under the laws of the several States, some of the protections for children and families are material. But marriage also confers more profound benefits. By giving legal recognition and legal structure to their parent's relationship, marriage allows children "to understand the integrity and closeness of their own family and its concord with other families in their community and in their daily lives." (Supreme Court 2015, p. 15 slip opinion)

Therefore, this asserted reason not to establish a constitutional right of persons to marry someone of the same sex carries no significant weight.

Although other objections to same-sex marriages are sometimes alleged, the ones described above are the most plausible to those who do not have access to the word of God. Since none of these objections survives critical examination, there is no strong reason not to establish a constitutional right of persons to marry someone of the same sex. Moreover, the moral human rights to liberty and to privacy are reasons of moderate weight to do so. And the moral human rights to marry and especially to equal protection of the law are strong reasons for extending the constitutional right to marry to same-sex couples. Therefore our constitutional law ought to be modified to include a right of persons to marry someone of their own sex.

6 Equal Opportunity

Equal opportunity is a political ideal accepted by most Americans, and many persons here and abroad believe that there is a human right to equal opportunity. This suggests that there ought to be a constitutional right to equal opportunity possessed at least by all citizens of the United States. No doubt our society denies equal opportunity to many of its members, especially African-Americans, the undereducated and those living in poverty. However, there is considerable disagreement about what the content of this right might be and whether in fact establishing any such right would be justified. Because the relevant moral and legal literature is voluminous, it is impossible to assess it briefly. In order to limit our consideration to manageable proportions, I shall examine only the reasons for and against establishing a constitutional right to equal opportunity broad enough to apply to disabled person. That there ought to be such a right seems to be assumed by Chapter 126 of the *Americans with Disabilities Act* entitled "EQUAL OPPORTUNITY FOR INDIVIDUALS WITH DISABILITIES" and by the *Standard Rules on the Equalization of Opportunities for Persons with Disabilities* issued by the United Nations General Assembly.

What should be the content of any such right? Obviously any right to equal opportunity must be a right to opportunity. The *Oxford English Dictionary* defines opportunity "As a mass noun: a time, condition, or set of circumstances permitting or favourable to a particular action or purpose." It then defines opportunity "As a count noun: an instance of this." Thus it distinguishes between overall opportunity and an opportunity. Presumably, then, a right to opportunity must be a right to overall opportunity consisting of a large variety of more specific opportunities. Opportunity is not merely negative, not merely the absence of obstructions or limitations, although it may require this also. It consists of positive conditions or circumstances that enable a person to engage in or refrain from action to achieve his or her purposes.

Who might possess any constitutional right to equal opportunity? Some constitutional rights, such as the rights to life or liberty, are rights of all persons; others, such as the right to vote, are rights of only citizens. Because any constitutional right to equal opportunity would sometimes, perhaps often, require the state to provide conditions or circumstances favorable for its possessors to pursue their purposes, a right limited to citizens would be less expensive and thus easier to justify than one possessed more widely by persons. Hence, I will consider only a constitutional right of citizens to equal opportunity.

But opportunity to do what? If there is any reason sufficiently strong to justify establishing a constitutional right to equal opportunity, it must be an opportunity to achieve something of great value. Since this right is to be possessed by all citizens, it must be something very valuable for all of them. And because it would be a right to some sort of overall opportunity, it must be opportunity to achieve something more general than the opportunity to get a job or inherit wealth, to marry or remain single. This suggests that the constitutional right to equal opportunity ought to be the right to achieve one's well-being. If so, then the right to equal opportunity is a contemporary version of the traditional natural right to the pursuit of happiness. However, it is very doubtful that the state ought to provide all citizens with the opportunity to achieve the greatest possible well-being, to live lives of luxury, especially since this would often have to be subsidized by taxes paid by one's fellow citizens. Therefore, I believe that the most plausible candidate for any constitutional right to equal opportunity is the right to opportunity to satisfy one's basic human needs, not to satisfy all of one's desires.

Finally, this should be a constitutional right to equal opportunity, equal on two dimensions. First, it must be the right to achieve equal goals. Presumably all citizens have the same basic human needs and to the same degree. Therefore, the content of the constitutional right I have described would confer equality regarding its content. Second, equal opportunity must provide conditions or circumstances for its possessor equally favorable for achieving this purpose as the opportunity available to every other citizen. Probably this implies an equal probability of satisfying one's basic human needs if, but only if, one chooses reasonable means and does one's best to achieve this purpose.

Most Americans, including myself, probably believe that equal opportunity is morally required in order that individuals are able to achieve what they deserve. This is probably presupposed by Robert M. Veatch (1986) when he writes:" A first stab at figuring out the principle of equal opportunity might lead to a formula like the following: if people are competing for a scarce resource not available to all, their chance of success should not be influenced by extraneous social, psychological, or biological factors." This is an application of the principle of retributive justice to competitive situations such as applications for a job or requests for a heart transplant. However, the principle of retributive justice is a principle applicable only to rewards and punishments because it is the requirement that individuals receive what they deserve for their past actions. Retributive justice is relevant to punishments because punishment is a response to wrongful action. And it is relevant to competitions such as sports or games because the purpose of these competitions is to reward competitors according to their merit. But it is not clear that it is relevant to the lack of opportunity for a job because of lack of education or to receive a heart transplant because of inadequate medical insurance. These lacks are not punishments for misconduct, nor are competitions for jobs or transplantable hearts sports or games intended to reward one for one's effort or skill. Hence, this justification for equal opportunity is probably not a reason to institute any constitutional right to equal opportunity to satisfy one's basic human needs.

More relevant is the second principle of social justice advocated by John Rawls (1993). As reformulated in *Political Liberalism*, it reads: "Social and economic inequalities are to satisfy two conditions: first, they are to be attached to positions and offices open to all under conditions of fair equality of opportunity, and second, they are to be to the greatest benefit of the least advantaged members of society." Although this principle of social justice would require that the social institutions of our society respect fair equality of opportunity, it would not justify the constitutional right to equal opportunity I have suggested. For one thing, it concerns opportunity to achieve social positions and offices, not to satisfy one's basic human needs. For another, it would permit unequal opportunity when this would be to the greatest benefit of the least advantaged members of our society. Finally, it would not justify a constitutional right of the physically and mentally disadvantages because Rawls explains that their special needs should be dealt with at the less fundamental legislative stage in constituting the institutions of a just society.

A third plausible reason to establish a constitutional right of equal opportunity to satisfy one's basic human needs is to enforce the right to equal protection of the law. This is an essentially negative right. It imposes upon the government the duty not to discriminate when conferring benefits or imposing burdens upon those subject to the law. Accordingly, the *Americans with Disabilities Act of 1990* defines its purpose to be "to provide a clear and comprehensive national mandate for the elimination of discrimination against individuals with disabilities." However, any real right to equal opportunity requires more than this. It requires that the government not only refrain from discrimination regarding opportunity, but that it also enact positive measures to equalize opportunity for the disadvantaged. As Richard J. Arneson (2000) reminds us when arguing that the norm of nondiscrimination is not enough to provide equal opportunity:

> The Americans with Disabilities Act requires more of employers than that they do not discriminate against the handicapped. It requires that if one can do a job if one's handicap is given a reasonable accommodation by the employer, and if one would be best qualified among the applicants if that reasonable accommodation was made, one must be hired.... Examples of reasonable accommodation would be adjustments in break times, hours, or equipment.

Although nondiscrimination is a necessary condition for equal opportunity, it is not a sufficient condition. Therefore, the right to equal protection of the law is an incomplete justification for establishing a constitutional right to equal opportunity.

A more positive justification for establishing a constitutional right to equal opportunity combines two moral duties of any legitimate government, the duty to promote the well-being of its subjects and the duty to respect their moral agency. Any viable government must impose serious burdens upon its subjects such as the duty to pay taxes, jury duty, perhaps military service and certainly the duty to obey all legal restrictions on their conduct. And it must enforce the laws that impose these burdens, typically with coercive measures. It would be unjust for a government to impose these burdens were it not also to provide compensatory benefits for its subjects. However, its duty to respect the moral agency of its subjects limits its right to promote their welfare by paternalistic measures. Its most appropriate role is to provide them with the opportunity to advance their own well-being, especially to satisfy their basic human needs. And to respect their equal status as moral agents, it must provide equal opportunity. Although the premises of this reasoning are not self-evident, it is at least a very plausible justification for a constitutional right to equal opportunity.

A fifth argument for establishing a constitutional right to equal opportunity suggested by the reasoning of many advocates of equal rights for the disabled is that this is necessary to remedy the disadvantages imposed by society upon its members.

They reject the medical model of disability that reduces it to the underlying physical or mental states of the person and adopt a social model of disability. Jerome E. Bickenbach (2000) explains that:

> Most modest and defensible versions of the social model of disability argue that while having a disability means being limited in the range of activities one can perform, what accounts for this limitation is often if not always a matter of the environmental context in which human action occurs. In particular, physical and socially created or tolerated barriers limit when they do not prevent the performance of human activities, roles or behaviors which, in composite, account for the sum total of human life in all its social dimensions…. The social world that produces barriers or fails to remove them creates much of the disadvantage of having a disability.

Thus, because society causes much of the lack of opportunity available to the disabled, and presumably to many others, it has a moral obligation to remedy this lack of opportunity by providing equal opportunity for those it has wrongfully harmed in this way. And the best way to remedy this wrong is by means of a constitutional right to equal opportunity. Although this is a very strong argument for social action to increase the opportunity of the disabled and others, it is also limited in it reach. Defensible social models of disability assert only that much, not all, of the limitations on the opportunity of the disadvantaged are caused by society. Therefore, its moral obligation is presumably limited to remedying that part of their lack of opportunity for which it is responsible. This will usually not require it to provide full equality of opportunity to the disabled or others similarly situated.

A strong reason to establish a constitutional right to equal opportunity is that this is the most effective way to protect the moral human right to equal opportunity. To lack the opportunity to satisfy one's basic human needs is to be threatened with very serious harms. Any individual or institution that is in a position to prevent serious harms presumably has a moral duty to do so. Hence, persons and institutions capable of providing the opportunity to satisfy their basic human needs to those who lack it have a moral duty to do so. Also those in need have the moral power to claim performance of this duty because the act of claiming changes the relation between claimant and duty-bearer from one in which the duty-bearer merely neglects the basic human needs of a fellow human being to one in which he or she deliberately disregards and disrespects them. And because the basic human needs of all persons are the same, the claim right to the opportunity to meet one's basic human needs is a right to equal opportunity, opportunity equal to that of all other human beings. Finally, one's own government is in the best position to provide equal opportunity to any human being, ideally by adopting and implementing a constitutional right to equal opportunity. However, any moral human right is prima facie. Hence, it can be overridden by more urgent moral considerations. Hence, we should consider any important reasons not to establish a constitutional right to equal opportunity.

One reason not to establish a constitutional right to equal opportunity might be that this is unnecessary because any such right would be redundant. The existing constitutional right to equal protection is sufficient to guarantee equal opportunity to all those who are subject to United States law. However, this is not entirely true. The right to equal protection does prohibit unequal opportunity arising from discrimination against individuals, but providing equal opportunity requires more than refraining from discrimination. As we have seen previously in this section, it often requires positive measures to increase the opportunity of the disadvantaged, including disabled persons.

This suggests a second reason not to establish a constitutional right to equal opportunity; it would often require positive measures that would be unreasonably expensive. For example, it would require extensive and expensive rehabilitation of persons seriously injured in accidents or who have suffered debilitating medical events such as heart attacks or strokes. It would probably require providing organs such as hearts, kidneys or even lungs to many medical patients and then providing the long-term medical care needed by those who have undergone organ transplantation. Because many persons are seriously handicapped by psychosis or neurosis, it would require providing psychoanalysis or comparable treatment, typically for very long periods of time. Together these measures to equalize opportunity for the disadvantaged would be unreasonably expensive because they would consume scarce funds needed for more urgent public purposes such as preserving the social security and Medicare programs, maintaining our national transportation and communication systems, and national defense. Although this is a relevant and significant consideration, I do not believe that it is conclusive. No constitutional right is absolute. The courts often recognize exceptions when they are necessary for some compelling state interest. Therefore, it might be justifiable to establish a constitutional right to equal protection if, but only if, there were strong reasons to do so.

Another reason not to establish a constitutional right to equal opportunity is that this might require leveling down. It would often be much less expensive to reduce the opportunity of advantaged citizens than to increase the opportunity of the disadvantaged, and some kinds of physical or mental disability are so implanted that there are no practicable measures that would eradicate them. Under such circumstances, any constitutional right to equal opportunity would seem to require Congress and the courts to equalize the opportunity of all citizens by leveling down rather than leveling up. However, if the language of the constitutional provision establishing a right to equal opportunity were interpreted in the light of its purposes, as is customary, this harmful and unjust consequence would not follow; for these include promoting the well-being of all citizens, respecting their moral agency and protecting the moral human right to equal opportunity grounded on the great harm suffered by anyone incapable of satisfying his or her basic human need.

A fourth reason not to establish a constitutional right to equal opportunity is that this would be formulated in very abstract generic language that would fail to distinguish between the various species of opportunity individuals too often lack and the very different measures required to equalize these different kinds of opportunity. This is why Rawls proposed providing fair equality of opportunity at the legislative rather than the constitutional level. And John E. Roemer (2003) responds to the proposal of Richard Arneson to equalize the all-round welfare in the whole population as follows:

> This is surely correct, as ideal theory. But, donning now the hat of a practical social scientist, I demur. For I believe that, if equality-of-opportunity is to become influential in social policy, it will surely be on a piecemeal basis, in one and then another sphere of social life. It is therefore incumbent upon a policy-oriented advocate to define the appropriate limits of EOp policy, that is, to provide some rules of thumb for its scope.

If it were necessary to choose between establishing a general constitutional right to equal opportunity and conferring a variety of statutory rights to equal opportunity of specific kinds, this reason against a constitutional right would be very strong indeed. However the United States could, and perhaps should, both establish a constitutional right to equal opportunity and, as is usual for other civil rights, authorize Congress to implement this right.

Finally, the United States ought not to establish a constitutional right of all citizens to equal opportunity to satisfy their basic human needs because any such opportunity would be of no value, and might even be harmful, to some citizens. Individuals who are severely mentally retarded lack the practical rationality required to choose the means to advance their basic human needs and will often choose to act in disastrously counterproductive ways. And some persons may be so seriously impaired physically that they are incapable of doing what would be necessary to take advantage of the opportunities available to them. What such citizens need is not to be provided with greater opportunity but to receive the care that would, as far as practicable, satisfy their basic human needs. Hence, any constitutional right to equal opportunity of all citizens would be unjustifiably broad.

As we have seen, not all the pro and con arguments survive critical examination. However, there remain two very strong reasons to establish some sort of a constitutional right to equal opportunity. This would promote the well-being of those subject to the law in a way that respects their moral agency and it would protect the moral human right to equal opportunity. On the other hand, a constitutional right of all citizens to equal opportunity to satisfy their basic human needs would often require measures that would be unreasonably expensive and greater opportunity would be of no value, and might sometimes be harmful, to some citizens who are severely mentally or physically disabled. To my mind, it is this last consideration that is decisive. Notice that it impossible to respect the moral agency of those who lack the mental capacities required for moral choice and that, as I have argued elsewhere, only individuals with the capacity for moral agency can possess moral rights. Therefore, on balance I conclude that the United States ought not to establish a constitutional to satisfy their basic human needs of all citizens.

7 Freedom of Speech

The draft additions July 2002 of the *Oxford English Dictionary* define hate speech as "speech expressing hatred or intolerance of other social groups, esp. on the basis of race or sexuality; hostile verbal abuse (though the term is sometimes understood to encompass written and non-verbal forms of expression." The legal systems of most democratic nations prohibit hate speech. But in a recent decision, The Supreme Court of the United States declared a Saint Paul ordinance that made placing a burning cross or Nazi swastika on public or private property a misdemeanor an unconstitutional violation of the First Amendment right to freedom of speech. The legal reasoning in its decision is highly controversial. Even more controversial is the moral issue concerning what our constitutional law ought to be. Ought our constitutional right to freedom of speech to protect hate speech?

There are a number of reasons why the right to freedom of speech ought not to protect hate speech. One such reason is that international human rights law requires that nation states prohibit hate speech. Article 19 of the *International Covenant on Civil and Political Rights* of 1966 establishes a human right to freedom of expression. However Article 20.2 reads: "Any advocacy of national, racial or religious hatred that constitutes incitement to discrimination, hostility or violence shall be prohibited by law." The reasoning behind this requirement seems to be that hate speech leads to the violation of several fundamental human rights, especially the rights to the equal protection of the law and to security of one's person. Some might argue that although the United States has ratified this treaty, it is not bound by it because in doing so it entered the reservation that none of its article should restrict the right of free speech and assembly. Others might respond that the United States is legally bound by this provision because the in the *Barcelona Traction Case* the International Court of Justice held that human rights law imposes obligations *erga omnes*. However one should decide concerning this technical legal issue if hate speech does indeed lead to the violation of fundamental human rights, then morally it would seem that the United States ought to prohibit it.

Another reason why the right to free speech ought not to protect hate speech is that hate speech damages fraternity in any society. Bhikhu Parekh asserts that:

> Hate speech…lowers the tone of public debate, coarsens the community's moral sensibility, and weakens the culture of mutual respect that lies at the heart of a good society. It views members of the target group as an enemy within, refuses to accept them as legitimate and equal members of society, lowers their social standing, and in these and other ways subverts the very basis of a shared life. It creates barriers of mistrust and hostility between individuals and groups, plants fears, obstructs normal relations between them, and in general exercises a corrosive influence on the conduct of collective life.

What is at stake here is one of the three goals of the French Revolution, fraternity in the sense of brotherliness, friendship or good-will. This is a moral value in any society and a practical value because it enhances the cooperation needed to achieve public goods. It is especially important in any multicultural or multiracial society in which the majority is suspicious of one or more minority groups. But one may well wonder whether prohibiting hate speech would make any significant contribution to the level of fraternity in our society. If not, then this is not a sufficient reason to sacrifice the value of free speech.

A third reason why the right to freedom of speech ought not to protect hate speech is that hate speech undermines the equal dignity of members of the targeted group. While fraternity is a matter of subjective feeling and attitudes, dignity concerns the objective status of citizens. As Jeremy Waldron explains:

> I have said several times in this book that laws restricting hate speech should aim to protect people's dignity against assault. I am referring to their status as anyone's equal in the community they inhabit, to their entitlement to basic justice, and to the fundamentals of their reputation. Dignity in that sense may need protection against attack, particularly against group-directed attacks which proclaim that all or most members of a given group are, by virtue of their race or some other ascriptive characteristic, not worthy of being treated as members of the society in good standing. (Waldron 2012, pp. 105–106)

He asserts that: "A democratic society cannot work, socially or politically, unless its members are respected in their character as equals, and accorded the authority associated with their vote and their basis rights." (Waldron 2012, pp. 108–109) Although the words "cannot work" suggest that this is a merely pragmatic argument about the good consequences of protecting dignity, the reference to "their basic rights" points to a more fundamental moral reason. This reason become explicit when Waldron explains that the international law against degrading treatment "is designed to protect people against being treated in ways that diminish their elementary status as persons." (Waldron 2012, p. 109) Thus, the social and legal status of equal dignity of all citizens ought to be protected in order to protect their more fundamental status as persons of equal moral worth. However, even granted that the equal dignity of citizens ought to be protected because it is grounded on their equal moral worth as persons, one would like empirical evidence that hate speech does in fact significantly undermine dignity and that legal restrictions on hate speech would be effective in protecting dignity.

A fourth reason why the right to free speech ought not to protect hate speech is that hate speech encourages violence against its target groups and by outraged members of these groups against the majority.

> Consider this scenario. You witness someone giving a public speech in which your nation is vilified and ridiculed. The speech is deeply offensive to you, and you try to shout the speaker down. Someone in the audience, a supporter of the speaker, tries to carry you out of the hall, and you struggle to remain. A brawl follows.
>
> Now consider another scenario. A delivers a speech in which he violently accuses members of an ethnic minority of his country of a high tendency to commit crimes, to lie, and to engage in bizarre religious practices. B, having heard the speech, becomes so enraged against the minority vilified by A that, the following day, he violently beats up C, a member of that minority. (Sadurski 1991, pp. 196 & 200)

Clearly the law ought to prevent violence whenever possible.

A fifth reason why the right to free speech ought not to protect hate speech is that hate speech supports wrongful discrimination. Bikhu Parekh asserts that:

> Hate speech is also unacceptable because of its long-term consequences. It encourages a climate in which, over time, some groups come to be demonized and that discriminatory treatment becomes accepted as normal….It legitimizes and generates pressure for discrimination against the target group and provides moral support and encouragement to those inclined to discriminate. (Parekh 2012, p. 45)

On the other hand, James Weinstein suggests that a possible cost of any ban Is that the prosecution of those who engage in hate speech will publicize racists and the virulent ideas they espouse. (Weinstein 1999, p. 150)

Finally, the constitutional right to freedom of speech ought not to protect hate speech because hate speech inflicts serious psychic injury upon its targets. Wojciech Sadurski writes:

> Now consider a third scenario. Imagine that you are a recently naturalized resident and, since you want to be an active and loyal citizen of your new country, you go to a meeting of the town council in your suburb. At the first meeting, quite unexpectedly, a speaker rises and makes a fiery speech in which she proposes a zoning ordinance which will make it more difficult for new immigrants, especially from your home country, to settle in the suburb.... Nothing in particular happens after the incident; no one assaults you in any perceptible physical way. Yet, since the day you heard the speech, your life has clearly been transformed for the worse. Whenever you meet your neighbors or co-workers or salespersons in shops, you search for expressions of dislike or contempt in their eyes. When they are rude, you attribute it to their hatred of your ethnic group. When they are polite, you treat it as a symptom of their patronizing attitude, or their attempts to protect you from further distress. (Sadurski 1991, p. 206)

However, Nicholas Wolfson writes: "I personally believe that racist and sexist insults and epithets harm the listener, but I confess that I do not know the amount or permanence of the alleged harm with scientific certitude." (Wolfson 1997, p. 56) Hence, it might be unwise to limit free speech on the basis of subjective judgments of the degree of psychic harm hate speech inflicts upon its victims. Although none of these six reasons is compelling, together they make a strong case against protecting hate speech from criminal and civil penalties.

Not everyone is convinced by these arguments. They insist that the constitutional right to freedom of speech is so important to our society that it ought to protect almost all speech, even speech as odious as hate speech. Some argue that prohibitions on hate speech are no longer needed. Granted that the Puritans who first settled in New England were intolerant of other religions, African slaves made the southern plantations profitable, and unjust sex roles once were traditional, moral reforms have over time greatly reduced, although not completely eliminated, religious intolerance, racism and sexism to a tolerable level. Jeremy Waldron responds:

> But the position of minority groups as equal members of a multiracial, multiethnic, or religiously pluralistic society is not something that anyone can take for granted. It is a recent and fragile achievement in the United States, and the idea that law can be indifferent to published assaults upon this principle seems to me a quite unwarranted extrapolation from what we have found ourselves able to tolerate in the way of political and religious dissent. (Waldron 2012, p. 21)

And contemporary research by social scientists clearly demonstrates that religious intolerance, racism and sexism remain strong forces in our society.

Another reason advanced to show that the right to freedom of speech ought to protect hate speech is that there are better alternatives than prohibition to deal with the social problems it reflects and exacerbates. Bhikhu Parekh reports: "Second, it is argued that evil ideas are best defeated not by banning them but by subjecting them to critical scrutiny and confronting them with better ideas. The answer to hate speech is not less but more speech." (Parekh 2012, p. 45) And C. Edwin Baker writes:

> As an empirical hypothesis, I suggest that more active (and thus more effective) opposition to racist views is likely to come from social practices of not tolerating racist expression than from laws making it illegal....Legal prosecutions focus on the wrong issues—legal requirements, legal line drawing, propriety of prosecution of this rather than other cases. In any minimally decent society that legally permits hate speech, such expression of the reflexively creates, for those who object to racism, a platform to explain and justify their objections. This expressive activity may provide the greatest safeguard racist cultures and politics. (Baker 2009, p. 131)

However, society's choice of how to deal with hate speech is not a simple either prohibition or better alternatives. Probably both are needed in the United States today.

A third reason why the right to freedom of speech ought to protect hate speech is that any prohibition would almost certainly be overbroad. If the law prohibited hate speech as such, it would apply to every expression of racial, ethnic religious or sexual hatred, even those uttered at a cocktail party or in the family dining room. Hence, it would violate the fundamental moral right to privacy of the speaker. Even if restricted to public discourse, it would punish much relatively harmless, although objectionable, hate speech. An observation of Justice Stevens in *R. A. V. v. ST. PAUL* is relevant here.

> Unlike the Court, I do not believe that all content-based regulations are equally infirm and presumptively invalid;...To the contrary, I believe our decisions establish a more complex and subtle analysis, one that considers the content and context of the regulated speech, and the nature and scope of the restriction on speech. (Supreme Court 1992a, p. 428)

If the constitutionality of any prohibition of speech depends upon content and context, this is even more true morally than legally. And because the law must be formulated in general terms, this suggests that any prohibition of hate speech will be morally overbroad. Notice, however, that Justice Stevens refers to "our decisions." In practice, the courts can usually take account of content and context when applying general legislation to particular cases.

A fourth reason why the right to freedom of speech ought to protect hate speech is that any prohibition would inevitably be misapplied by a government intent on censoring its opposition or even becoming an undemocratic regime. Bhikhu Parekh writes:

> Third, it is argued that a ban on hate speech inhibits and has a chilling effect on public discussion and debate, and that once we go down this road, we open the floodgates to all kinds of restrictions. This argument makes an important point. As the experiences of societies with a ban on hate speech show, people do sometimes feel inhibited and hold themselves back from making robust criticisms of and even expressing their views on the beliefs and practices of different groups....Furthermore, the argument relies on the misleading metaphor of the slippery slope and the implied fear that once we go down a particular road, we would not know where to stop. If this were true, we would not be able to make any exception to any principle or value lest it should open the floodgates to others. We make such exceptions all the time; indeed human life, which is not a slope at all, let alone a slippery one, would be impossible unless we did so. (Parekh 2012, p. 49)

This is a reasonable assessment of the danger of governmental abuse of any ban on hate speech. James Weinstein argues similarly.

> Most democracies in the world today have some sort of ban on racist speech, including the United Kingdom, Denmark, France, Germany, the Netherlands, Canada, Israel, Italy and Sweden. …Yet none of these countries is sliding down the slope to totalitarianism….A more realistic fear is that law enforcement officials will misapply these laws to punish expression that is unpopular or offensive but neither racist nor pornographic….Such misuse will also likely cause would-be speakers to censor themselves for fear that what they want to express, although neither racist nor pornographic, might be mistaken for such. This chilling effect could occur even if law officials would not in fact misapply the statute to innocent speech. (Weinstein 1999, pp. 142–143)

Hence, the possible misuse of any prohibition of hate speech constitutes a genuine, but limited, reason why the right to freedom of speech ought to protect hate speech.

A fifth reason why the right to freedom of speech ought to protect hate speech is that any restriction on hate speech will inevitably be viewpoint-based. Any law that prohibits hate speech will violate the principle of social justice that a liberal state must be neutral between competing moral viewpoints. In *R. A. V. v. ST. PAUL* Justice Scalia, delivering the opinion of the Court, asserted:

> Applying these principles to the St. Paul ordinance, we conclude that, even as narrowly construed by the Minnesota Supreme Court, the ordinance is facially unconstitutional…. Displays containing abusive invective, no matter how vicious or severe, are permissible unless they are addressed to one of the specified disfavored topics. …St. Paul has no such authority to license one side of a debate to fight freestyle, while requiring the other side to follow Marquis of Queensberry rules. (Supreme Court 1992a, pp. 391–392)

However Justice Stevens concurring in judgment, rejected this analysis: "Significantly, the St. Paul ordinance regulates speech, not on the basis of its subject matter or the viewpoint expressed, but rather on the basis of the harm the speech causes. In this regard, the Court fundamentally misreads the St. Paul ordinance." (Supreme Court 1992a, p. 433) Nevertheless, Wojciech Sadurski suggests that this is not the end of the matter.

> Suppressing an expression based on an alleged resulting harm reflects a viewpoint that the expression is indeed harmful. Since the characterization of a given effect as "harmful" is morally laden and thus necessarily controversial, it reflects a viewpoint which may not be, and usually is not, shared by all. A harm discourse, when applied to expressions, may therefore collapse into a viewpoint discourse. (Sadurski 1991, p. 68)

Nevertheless, Bhikhu Parekh argues that:

> Beyond a certain point, the moral neutrality of the state is itself problematic. A liberal state should not enforce a particular view of the good life on its citizens and should allow a free flow of ideas, but some values are so central to its moral authority that it cannot remain neutral regarding them. A state committed to human dignity, gender and race equality, or the spirit of free inquiry cannot be neutral between forms of speech or behavior that uphold or undermine these values. (Parekh 2012, p. 50)

Thus, whether liberalism, even if one accepts it as a valid political theory, rules out laws that prohibit hate speech remains controversial.

A sixth reason why the right to freedom of speech ought to protect hate speech is that any ban on hate speech would impoverish political discourse. This is a very important consideration because uninhibited political debate is essential to democracy. Cass R. Sunstein asserts that:

> The placement of sovereignty in "We the People," rather than the government, may well have been the most important American contribution to the theory of politics….It created an ambitious system of "government by discussion," in which outcomes would be reached through broad public deliberation. It put a premium not on authority or privilege, but on the arguments set out in and resolved through general discussion. (Sunstein 1999, p. xvi)

Hence, if the prohibition of hate speech would in fact limit the arguments citizens could use in public debate, then this would undermine our democratic system of government. However, one might cite *Chaplinsky v. New Hampshire* to show that this would not happen.

> There are certain well defined and narrowly limited classes of speech, the prevention and punishment of which have never been thought to raise any Constitutional problem. These include the lewd and obscene, the profane, the libelous, and the inciting or "fighting" words—those which, by their very utterance, inflict injury or tend to incite an immediate breach of the peace. It has been well observed that such utterances are no essential part of any exposition of ideas, and are of such slight social value as a step to truth that any benefit that may be derived from them is clearly outweighed by the social interest in order and morality. (Supreme Court 1942, pp. 571–572)

But is it so clear that hate speech has little or no social value or that its prohibition would not impoverish political debate? Much intellectual debate is vitriolic and derisive. Any cursory reading of book reviews or commentaries upon other thinkers will reveal the biting, often vicious, cut and parry of the members of the academy. Hence, one should not be too quick to conclude that hate speech has no intellectual or political content. Nevertheless, Jeremy Waldron argues that this fact does not preclude the prohibition of hate speech.

> And the racist doesn't *need* to use the sort of vicious hate propaganda that the law punishes in order to explain his opposition to laws about discrimination and so on. Most racial and religious hatred laws that exist in the world define a legitimate mode or legitimate forum for roughly equivalent expression that will not incur legal sanctions. (Waldron 2012, p. 183)

Others insist that merely roughly equivalent expression lacks the robustness of hate speech and therefore something is lost from political debate when hate speech is prohibited. But even granted that something is lost, is this something essential to full democratic deliberation?

Finally some argue that the right to freedom of speech ought to protect hate speech because any prohibition would undermine the legitimacy of some or all laws. For example, C. Edwin Baker explains:

> My remises are: (i) that the legitimacy of the state depends on its respect for people's equality and autonomy and (ii) that as a purely formal matter, the state only respects people's autonomy if it allows people in their speech to express their own values—no matter what these values are and irrespective of how this expressive content harms other people or makes government processes or achieving government aims difficult….A state cannot coherently ask a person to obey its laws unless it treats the person as capable of making choices for herself, for example, the choice to obey the law.(Baker 2009, p. 142)

But Wojciech Sadurski suggests that although hate speech may be important to autonomy, there are other ways of fulfilling hateful autonomy that is part of one's identity. (Sadurski 1991, p. 18)

Ronald Dworkin also presents an argument for the conclusion that any prohibition of hate speech would undermine the legitimacy of at least some laws.

> People who believe in democracy think that it is fair to use the police power to enforce the law if the law has been adopted through democratic political procedures that express the majority's will. But though majoritarian procedures may be a necessary condition of political legitimacy, they are not a sufficient condition. Fair democracy requires what we might call a democratic background: it requires, for example, that every competent adult have a vote in deciding what the majority's will is. And it requires further, that each citizen have not just a vote but a voice: a majority decision is not fair unless everyone has had a fair opportunity to express his or her attitudes or opinions or fears or tastes or presuppositions or prejudices of ideals, not just in the hope of influencing others (though this hope is crucially important), but also just to confirm his or her standing as a responsible agent in, rather than a passive victim of, collective action. The majority has no right to impose its will on anyone who is forbidden to raise a voice in protest or argument or objection before the decision is taken. (Dworkin 2009, p. vii)

He concludes that: "We might have the power to silence those we despise, but it would be at the cost of political legitimacy…." Jeremy Waldron responds that it will be hard to keep Dworkin's argument under control because it will apply to every exception to the free speech principle, even fighting words, obscenity and libel. My concern is that neither Baker nor Dworkin has provided a moral theory of political legitimacy to explain why the conditions they require are really necessary conditions for legitimacy.

When I began thinking about the problem of hate speech in our society, I firmly believed that the constitutional right to freedom of speech ought not to protect it from abridgement. Now I am not so sure. It is probably true that hate speech causes five kinds of harm. It damages fraternity, undermines dignity, encourages violence, supports discrimination, and inflicts psychic injury. However, there is not enough reliable scientific evidence to show to what degree these harms come from hate speech rather than other influences in our society, and one cannot be sure how effective legislation would be in reducing these harms. On the other hand, given the ambiguity and imprecision in the concept of hate speech, it is very likely that any prohibition would be overbroad. However, the experience of other democratic nations should enable the Congress or the state legislatures to draft workable legislation. Our democratic institutions are strong enough to prevent any long slide down the slippery slope, but there would probably be a chilling effect of any prohibition of hate speech. If this were to moderate the tone of public speech, this would be an advantage; but if it were to eliminate political and social beliefs, this would impoverish political debate and thus damage our democracy. The experience of other democracies with hate speech bans suggests that this would happen, but only to a limited extent. On balance, and with hesitation, I conclude that because hate speech probably does result in serious harms our constitutional right to freedom of speech ought not to protect it.

8 Firearms

One of the fiercest political debates is between advocates of gun control and defenders of gun rights. Recently, these have alternated between periods of relative quiet followed by a burst of antagonistic rhetoric occasioned by some mass shooting. After Patrick Purdy used an AK-style firearm to mow down children on the playground of the Stockton, California, elementary school, Congress passed the Assault Weapons Ban of 1994. However, it expired 10 years later and subsequent efforts to renew it have so far failed. Its effectiveness was very limited, in part because it excluded previously owned assault weapons from its provisions. This suggests that some more extensive regulation is needed. Hence, let us ask: Should the constitutional right to keep and bear arms permit a ban on the ownership of assault weapons by private persons. This would require all residents of the United States, other than members of the police or military, to give up any assault weapons they now own and prohibit them from acquiring any other such weapons.

Before we attempt to answer this question, a word of caution is in order. The term "assault weapons" has various uses in ordinary language and even in federal and state legislation is ambiguous. I shall adopt the definition advocated by Senator Dianne Feinstein when she proposed the Assault Weapons Ban of 2013. By "assault weapons" I shall mean semi-automatic rifles or pistols that can accept a detachable magazine and have at least one military feature.

One reason why the constitutional right to keep and bear arm ought to permit a ban on the possession of assault weapons by private persons is to prevent mass shootings. When Senator Dianne Feinstein proposed the Assault Weapons Ban of 2013, she asserted that the mass shootings in Newtown, Aurora, and Tucson have demonstrated all too clearly the need to regulate military-style assault weapons and high capacity ammunition magazines. Although mass shootings are rare, they do happen. Christopher S. Koper reports that:

> Since 2007, for example, there have been at least 11 incidents in which offenders using assault weapons or other semi-automatics with magazines larger than 10 rounds have wounded or killed eight or more people. Some of the most notorious of these incidents have been a 2007 shooting on the college campus of Virginia Tech that left 33 dead and 17 wounded; a 2011 shooting in an Arizona parking lot that killed 6 and wounded 13, including Congresswoman Gabrielle Gifford; a 2012 shooting in an Aurora, Colorado, movie theater that left 12 dead and 58 wounded; and, most recently, a shooting in a Newtown, Connecticut, elementary school that left 26 victims dead, 20 of whom were children (an additional victim was killed elsewhere).(Koper 2013, pp. 157–158)

And preventing them is a morally compelling state interest because the legitimacy of any government depends upon its protecting its subjects from the violation of their fundamental moral rights and from other serious harms. Mass shootings violate the right to life of those killed, the right to personal security of those injured, and harms third parties who depend upon or care about its victims.

A second reason why the right to keep and bear arms ought to permit a ban on the possession of assault weapons by private persons is to reduce other armed crimes such as robbery or rape. But Gary Kleck reports that:

> Contrary to widespread claims, these semiautomatic "military Style" weapons are rarely used by criminals in general or by drug dealers or juvenile gang members in particular. While both legitimate ownership and involvement of semiautomatic pistols in violence has been common in the United States since the 1920s, probably fewer than 2 percent of gun crimes involve these models of semiautomatic weapons which are commonly labelled "assault weapons". (Kleck 2001, p. 278)

Nevertheless, even a modest reduction in armed crime is desirable. Hence, this purpose constitutes a modest reason for prohibiting the possession of assault weapons by private persons.

A third reason why the right to keep and bear arms ought to permit a ban on the private possession of assault weapons is to weaken resistance to the police. The ability of a government to fulfill its duty to protect its subjects from the violation of their fundamental moral rights and from other serious harms depends upon its police power. A ban on the possession of assault weapons by private persons, including criminals, but exempting the police would improve the balance of power between the police and armed criminals. William J. Vizzard asserts that: "…the compact size of assault rifles, particularly those with folding stocks, and their popularity with young urban males greatly increases the potential for their use against police." (Vizzard 2000, p. 143) And Christopher S. Koper reports that "A Ws and other guns equipped with LCMs tend to account for a higher share of guns used in murders of police and mass public shootings, though such incidents are very rare." (Koper 2004, p. 2) Although rare, such incidents urgently require that the police have the ability to enforce the criminal law effectively.

Finally, the constitutional right to keep and bear arms ought to permit a ban on the private possession of assault weapons in order to reduce the attractiveness of violence. Although rare, perhaps because they are rare, mass shootings are portrayed on television and reported in other media repeatedly and vividly. Most of us respond to the deaths, injuries and intense sufferings of third parties with horror and revulsion. But to some who feel aggrieved and vengeful or who feel alienated and insignificant mass shootings show the possibility of power and recognition. Hence, in addition to its direct effect of preventing mass shootings, a ban on the private possession of assault weapons would have the indirect effect of eliminating media coverage that renders criminal violence attractive to some members of our society.

As usual, there are plausible arguments on the other side of the debate. One reason not to permit a ban on the private ownership of assault weapons is that there are better alternatives, measures that would not undermine the constitutional right to keep and bear arms. Constance Emerson Crooker reports that:"A repeated theme of gun rights groups is that we have enough laws on the books and that we should focus on enforcing the ones we have." (Crooker 2003, p. 9) Gary Kleck argues:

> That is, opponents recommend "criminal control" as an alternative to gun control. However, proponents point out that to regard these as forced choice alternatives is an error, since there is nothing to prevent governments from doing both….A long series of "get tough" strategies have been tried carefully evaluated, and found to be either ineffective in producing significant crime reduction or hopelessly expensive. (Kleck 2001, p. 83)

Crooker also reports that: "Next on the list, and possibly fueling much of the debate, is the economic value of the gun industry itself. The manufacture and sale of guns creates jobs and contributes to commerce, and the taxable proceeds go toward the common good." (Crooker 2003, p. 8) However a ban on the private possession of only assault weapons would leave most of the gun industry intact, including the manufacture and sale of assault weapons to the police and the military. Some argue that any ban on the possession of guns will be counterproductive because responsible citizens will obey the law while criminals will evade it. "When guns are outlawed, only outlaws will have guns." (Doherty 2008, p. 93) Granted that the Assault Weapons Ban of 1994 could not keep assault weapons out of the hands of criminals because it did not regulate or limit those already in private hands, a ban on the ownership of assault weapons by any private person could, if enforced, eliminate the main source of these weapons available to criminals. Some argue that the best alternative is to eliminate the causes of gun violence, especially mass shootings. These causes include urban poverty, inadequate education, and mental illness. The government ought to take all feasible measures to eliminate these social problems. But this is a long-term project that can never be completed and ought to be accompanied with immediate steps, such as a ban on the private possession of assault weapons narrowly tailored to eliminate mass shootings.

A second reason why the constitutional right to keep and bear arms ought not to permit a ban on the private ownership of assault weapons is that this would undermine one of the central purposes of the Second Amendment, to prevent tyranny. The Second Amendment reads: "A well regulated Militia, being necessary to the security of a free State, the right of the people to keep and bear Arms shall not be infringed." In *District of Columbia v. Heller*, Justice Scalia, delivering the opinion of the Court, explained that: "There are many reasons why the militia was thought to be "necessary to the security of a free state."…Third, when the able-bodied men of a nation are trained in arms and organized, they are better able to resist tyranny." (Supreme Court 2008b, pp. 24–25 slip opinion) More generally, the widespread possession of arms by the members of a society enables the citizens to resist any attempt by their government to violate their human rights or fundamental freedoms. As Raymond G. Kessler explains, the argument is that gun control helps prevent opposition to and facilitates repressive action by government. (Kessler 1984, pp. 462–464) Samuel C. Wheeler argues that the empirical evidence is that governments are more violent and dangerous than citizens and that they have a tendency to go bad. Although institutions such as written constitutions and courts can often restrain arbitrary and unjust executive and legislative actions, in the end these institutions can be defended only by force requiring an armed citizenry. (Wheeler 2001, p. 23) However, a ban on the private ownership of assault weapons would still enable citizens to own rifles, shotguns and pistols. And several recent of popular uprisings by citizens armed with little more than rocks and home-made Molotov cocktails provide empirical evidence that assault weapons are not needed to resist tyrannical or repressive governments.

A third reason why the right to keep and bear arm ought not to permit a ban on the private possession of assault weapons is that this might undermine another central purpose of this right, to enable individual citizens to defend themselves against violent attacks. In Heller, Justice Scalia traces the origin and justification of the Second Amendment to the English Bill of Rights and Blackstone's commentaries on its common law. A provision of the former is "That the subjects that are Protestants may have arms for their defense suitable to their conditions and as allowed by law." And Blackstone interpreted this right as "the right of having and using arms for self-preservation and defence." (Supreme Court 2008b, p. 20 slip opinion) Justice Scalia concludes: "As the quotations earlier in this opinion demonstrate, the inherent right of self-defense has been central to the Second Amendment right. The handgun ban amounts to a prohibition of an entire class of "arms" that is overwhelmingly chosen by American society for that lawful purpose." (Supreme Court 2008b, p. 56 slip opinion) However, assault weapons are chosen by only a minority of American citizens to use for self-defense, in part because hand guns are more useful for this purpose. And as Samuel C. Wheeler argues, assault weapons are not needed for self-defense in our contemporary society.

> There are some kinds of reasonable expected assaults where a high capacity semi-automatic shotgun would be appropriate. If I am a Russian Jew in the 18th century, I can expect that, several times during my lifetime, I and my family will be attacked by angry mobs, with the tacit approval of the authorities....In our current situation, there are negligible chances of assaults where such weapons as a 20 mm cannon or high magazine-capacity 12-gauge shotguns are appropriate. (Wheeler 1997, pp. 438–439)

In the United States, an assault weapon might have been useful for self-defense in the past. An African-American might have needed such a weapon to defend against a Ku-Klux-Klan mob or in the Wild West period someone suspected but not convicted of a crime might have needed a semi-automatic high-capacity weapon to defend himself against a posse of vigilantes determined to hang him. However, a ban on the private ownership of assault weapons would not today undermine anyone's fundamental moral right of self-defense.

A fourth reason against any ban on the possession of assault weapons by private persons is that this would infringe fundamental moral rights in addition to the right to self-defense. Todd C. Hughes and Lester H. Hunt argue that the right of individuals to autonomy, to control their own lives and be the instruments of their own acts of will, implies a right to bear arms.

> Today, the very idea that the possession of a gun—a mere technological device prized by hobbyists and lunatics—is a right, like freedom of speech, freedom of religion, and the right against self-incrimination, strikes many peope as silly. Nevertheless, such a conclusion is more or less forced upon us by a range of interpretations of the autonomy constraint, including some very plausible ones. To begin with the obvious: since this constraint is a guarantee against interference, all versions of it create a certain presumption in favor of liberty, and bans on firearms place limits on liberty. (Hughes and Hunt 2000, p. 6)

And Lance K. Stell argues against the prohibition of owning a gun from the moral right to equality, or more specifically the right to the equal protection of the laws.

> Despite the fact that no human being is invulnerable to assault, individual vulnerability to it is not equal. Some people are smaller, weaker, or of lesser interest to society's elite than others. Other things being equal, assaulting them has a lesser cost. Recognizing a

> fundamental right to equalizers eliminates the social discount. Therefore, if fundamental rights should, as far as reasonably possible, have equal value to their possessors, then the state has a duty not to prohibit possession of "equalizers"....[and]... a gun ban would enrich assaulters and disproportionately impoverish smaller, weaker, less well-connected potential victims of assault by reducing the costs of assaulting them. (Stell 2001, p. 31)

Even granted the cogency of arguments such as these, even fundamental moral rights are not absolute. Exceptions are permissible when they are necessary for some morally compelling reason. And because preventing mass shootings is a morally compelling state interest, it might well be that a ban on the private possession of assault weapons is morally justified.

Until we can diminish the attractiveness of violence and eliminate the causes of violent crime, both long-term and uphill battles, the threat of mass shootings will remain in our country. Hence, the strongest reason for a ban on the possession of assault weapons by private citizens is that this is a necessary and practicable means of preventing mass shootings. This is a morally compelling reason for state action because they violate the rights to life and person security of the victims and inflict serious harms upon third parties. However, any such prohibition would infringe the constitutional right to keep and bear arms. The strongest reason not to infringe this legal right is that keeping and bearing arms is often necessary for self-defense. This is also a morally compelling reason because, given the fact that one must be alive in order to exercise or enjoy any of one's rights, the moral right to self-defense is presumably the most important of all human rights. Fortunately, because under present circumstances in our society, individuals are almost never attacked by large groups of criminals, assault weapons are not necessary for self-defense. Therefore, on balance, the constitutional right to keep and bear arms ought to permit a ban on the private possession of assault weapons, but not on other arms more useful for defending oneself from criminal violence.

9 The Death Penalty

Although many states have abolished capital punishment, the death penalty is still in force, especially for murder, in other states and for kidnapping under federal legislation. The Supreme Court has considered a number of cases challenging the death penalty as violating the Eight Amendment that prohibits cruel and unusual punishments, it has never ruled that the death penalty is unconstitutional per se. However, public debate over its morality continues and many argue that it ought to be completely eliminated from the United States legal system. Ought criminals to have a constitutional right against the death penalty?

There are several plausible reasons why criminals, even those convicted for the most serious crimes, ought to have a constitutional right against the death penalty. First, the death penalty violates the moral law. The Sixth Commandment, accepted by Jews, Christians and Moslems alike as morally authoritative, reads simply "Thou shalt not kill." However, H. Wayne House points out that in other passages God commands killing. He reconciles this apparent inconsistency as follows:

> When a person argues against capital punishment based on the Sixth Amendment, he or she is ignoring the division between individual and governmental morality. No person is permitted to murder or kill another. But God has established governmental authority and given it the responsibility for punishing crime—applying, if necessary, the death penalty. (House 1997, p. 425)

And John P. Conrad also insists that the mandate against killing people must be qualified.

> No one questions the right of a person to kill in self-defense, and the law tends to be indulgent in allowing this defense. Except for the most adamantly uncompromising pacifists, the duty of the soldier to fight and kill in defense of his country or in a just war has always been accepted by theologians and moral philosophers. (Conrad 1983, p. 80)

And whether capital punishment is another exception to the moral law that prohibits killing remains controversial.

A second plausible reason why criminals ought to have a constitutional right against the death penalty is that it is inevitably cruel. Justice Douglas, concurring in *Furman v. Georgia*, reports that "It has been assumed in our decisions that punishment by death is not cruel, unless the manner of execution can be said to be inhuman and barbarous." (Supreme Court 1972, p. 427) This might possibly be said today but even though every attempt is made to make execution by the electric chair painless, these efforts often fail and the execution is then excruciating. Moreover, with many appeals and interminable delays, any criminal on death row suffers great anxiety while waiting for death or perhaps life. On the other hand, life imprisonment, the obvious alternative to the death penalty, is doubtless cruel to a considerable degree and many argue that any suffering inherent in execution by the electric chair is not excessive.

A third reason for a constitutional right against the death penalty is that in current practice it is discriminatory. Justice Douglas also reports that:

> The President's Commission on Law Enforcement and administration of Justice recently concluded: Finally there is evidence that the imposition of the death sentence and the exercise of dispensing power by the courts and the executive follow discriminatory patterns. The death sentence is disproportionately imposed and carried out on the poor, the Negro, and the members of unpopular groups. (Supreme Court 1972, pp. 249–250)

However, Justice Powell, dissenting, replies that:

> The possibility of racial bias in the trial and sentencing process has diminished in recent years. The segregation of our society in decades past, which contributed substantially to the severity of punishment for interracial crimes, is now no longer prevalent in our society. Likewise, the day is past when juries do not represent the minority group elements of the community. The assurance of fair trials for all citizens is greater today than at any previous time in our history. Because standards of criminal justice have "evolved" in a manner favorable to the accused, discriminatory imposition of capital punishment is far less likely today than in the past. (Supreme Court 1972, p. 450)

But how much less likely? Some argue that there remains enough discrimination in the application of the death penalty to call for a constitutional right to protect criminals from unjust treatment. However, H. Wayne House insists that:

> Inequities in the application of the death penalty exist, but they are reasons for revamping our criminal justice system, not eliminating capital punishment. If the death penalty is eliminated because of such inequities, then all punishments should have to be eliminated because few, if any, are fairly applied. (House 1997, p. 427)

But perhaps discrimination in the application of the death penalty is more serious than in the application of lesser penalties.

A fourth reason why criminals ought to hae a constitutional right against the death penalty is that it is irremediable. Justice Brennen, concurring in *Furman v. Georgia*, reports:

> Apart from the common charge, grounded on the recognition of human fallibility, that the punishment of death must inevitably be inflicted upon innocent men, we know that death has been the lot of men whose convictions were unconstitutionally secured in view of later, retroactively applied, holdings of the Court. The punishment may itself have been unconstitutionally inflicted…, yet the finality of death precludes relief. (Supreme Court 1972, p. 290)

In a study assessing the danger of mistaken executions, Hugo Adam Bedau found that between 1973 and 1997 at least 48 people have been released from prison with significant evidence of their innocence after serving time on death row. (Bedau 1997, p. 345) And Raymond Paternoster notes that in another study Bedau and Radeler reported that there have been 350 instances between 1900 and 1982 of persons who were erroneously convicted of potentially capital crimes. (Paternoster 1991, p. 264) With the more recent use of DNA evidence, we will discover an even greater number of innocent persons to have been sentenced to death. Given this evidence, the fact that there can be no remedy provided to one who has been wrongly executed is a strong reason to establish a constitutional right of criminals against the death penalty.

Finally, criminals ought to have a constitutional right against the death penalty because capital punishment violates human dignity. In Kantian terms, it treats the criminal as a mere means, not an end in himself. Although Justice Douglas declined in *Furman v. Georgia* to hold that the death penalty is unconstitutional, he did assert that it inevitably violates the humanity of the executed person.

> Death is truly an awesome punishment. The calculated killing of a human being by the State involves, by its very nature, a denial of the executed person's humanity. The contrast with the plight of a person punished by imprisonment is evident. The person in prison does not lose "the right to have rights." A prisoner retains, for example, the constitutional rights to the free exercise of religion, to be free of cruel and unusual punishments, and to treatment as a "person" for purposes of due process of law and the equal protection of the laws. A prisoner remains a member of the human family….An executed person has indeed "lost the right to have rights."…In comparison with other punishments today, then, the deliberate extinguishment of human life by the State is uniquely degrading to human dignity. (Supreme Court 1972, pp. 290–291)

H. Wayne House questions this line of reasoning.

> First of all, does capital punishment treat individuals as objects to be used for society's benefit without regard to the interests or rights of the criminal? On the contrary, those who would seek to "cure" and "heal" people without receiving their consent treat them as less than human. On the other hand, to punish criminals because they "deserve" it is to respect them as morally responsible persons created in God's image who knew better and therefore earned this punishment. (House 1997, p. 423)

But does even the person who has committed the most monstrous crime deserve to die? Granted the moral importance of human dignity, it is hard to define human dignity with precision or to judge its relevance to capital punishment with confidence.

There are, of course, plausible arguments on the other side of this controversy. Some suggest that the death penalty ought to be retained to reduce the cost of enforcing the criminal law. They argue that it will be much less expensive to execute a condemned criminal promptly than to keep him in prison for the remainder of his or her life. However, executions are seldom, if ever, prompt. Justice Marshall, concurring in *Furman v. Georgia*, responds as follows:

> As for the argument that it is cheaper to execute a capital offender than to imprison him for life, even assuming that such an argument, if true, would support a capital sanction, it is simply incorrect. A disproportionate amount of money spent on prisons is attributable to death row. Condemned men are not productive members of the prison community, although they could be, and executions are expensive. Appeals are often automatic, and courts admittedly spend more time and money on death cases. At trial, the selection of jurors is likely to become a costly, time-consuming problem in a capital case, and defense counsel will reasonably exhaust every possible means to save his client from execution, no matter how long the trial takes. ...When all is said and done, there can be no doubt that it costs more to execute a man than to keep him in prison for life. (Supreme Court 1972, pp. 357–358)

Although plausible, this reason is invalid as our legal system currently functions.

A second reason why criminals ought not to have a constitutional right against the death penalty is that capital punishment inculcates civic virtue and reduces socially harmful reactions by the citizens. As Justice Brennan reports in *Furman v. Georgia*:

> The infliction of death, the States urge, serves to manifest the community's outrage at the commission of the crime. It is, they say, a concrete public expression of moral indignation that inculcates respect for the law and helps assure a more peaceful community. Moreover, we are told, not only does the punishment of death exert this widespread moralizing influence upon community values, it also satisfies the popular demand for grievous condemnation of abhorrent crimes and thus prevents disorder, lynching, and attempts by private citizens to take the law into their own hands. (Supreme Court 1972, p. 303)

Others argue that, quite the contrary, the execution of criminals put a stamp of approval upon the killing of human beings so that it brutalizes the citizens.

However, Ernest van den Haag challenges this traditional and still popular argument.

> Beccaria wrote: "Laws that punish homicide...commit murder themselves" by imposing the death penalty. The laws thereby give "an example of barbarity." Beccaria advocated life imprisonment (which meant lifelong imprisonment then) for murder because "the death of a criminal is...a less efficacious method of deterring others than the continued example of

> man…as a beast of burden [in] perpetual slavery…in chains and fetters, in an iron cage…." These conditions of imprisonment would not be tolerated today. It is hard to see wherein Beccaria's life imprisonment would be less barbaric than the death penalty. I should think it more so. (Van den Haag 1983, p. 241)

Granted that life imprisonment is much less barbaric today than in Beccaria's time, whether the infliction of the death penalty inculcates civic virtue or a disregard for the value of human life remains in doubt.

A third reason why criminals ought not to have a constitutional right against the death penalty is that capital punishment incapacitates the most dangerous criminals so that they cannot commit further crimes. Justice Brennan, concurring in *Furman v. Georgia*, reports that:

> The State's primary claim is that death is a necessary punishment because it prevents the commission of capital crimes more effectively than any less severe punishment. The first part of this claim is that the infliction of death is necessary to stop the individuals executed from committing further crimes. (Supreme Court 1972, p. 300)

However he continues as follows:

> The sufficient answer to this is that if a criminal convicted of a capital crime poses a danger to society, effective administration of the State's pardon and parole laws can delay or deny his release from prison, and techniques of isolation can eliminate or minimize the danger while he remains confined. (Supreme Court 1972, pp. 300–301)

And Justice Marshall, concurring, adds that: "There is also a substantial body of data showing that the existence of the death penalty has virtually no effect on the homicide rate in prisons. Most of the persons sentenced to death are murderers, and murderers tend to be model prisoners." (Supreme Court 1972, p. 352) Thus, although the death penalty is the most effective way to incapacitate convicted criminals, it is not clear that it is necessary for this important state interest.

A fourth reason why criminals ought not to have a constitutional right against the death penalty is that capital punishment is needed to deter potential criminals. Justice Brennan, concurring in *Furman v. Georgia*, reports that: "The more significant argument is that the threat of death prevents the commission of capital crimes because it deters potential criminals who would not be deterred by the threat of imprisonment." (Supreme Court 1972, p. 301) However, Justice Marshall, also concurring, cites the statistical evidence of Thorsten Sellin, one of the leading authorities on capital punishment, that the death penalty has no significant deterrent effect. (Supreme Court 1972, pp. 348–350 Nevertheless, Ernest van den Haag insists that there are two quite satisfactory non-statistical indications that the death penalty has a greater deterring effect than life imprisonment. First:

> Life in prison is still life, however unpleasant. In contrast, the death penalty does not just threaten to make life unpleasant—it threatens to take life altogether. The difference is perceived by those affected. We find that when they have a choice between life in prison and execution, 99 % of all prisoners under sentence of death prefer life in prison. (Van den Haag 1983, p. 68)

And Second:

If we were quite ignorant about the marginal deterrent effects of execution, we would have to choose—like it or not—between the certainty of the convicted murderer's death by execution and the likelihood of the survival of future victims of other murderers on the one hand, and on the other his certain survival and the likelihood of the death of new victims. I'd rather execute a man convicted of having murdered others than to put the lives of innocents at risk. (Van den Haag 1983, p. 69)

Raymond Paternoster reports that although the vast and sophisticated statistical evidence shows that the death penalty has no deterrent effect in general, some argue that it is still necessary to protect the police. Someone committing a a crime with a penalty of life imprisonment has nothing to lose by killing an arresting officer if the penalty for murder is similarly merely life imprisonment. (Paternoster 1991, p. 227) However, he also reports that: "It would appear, then, from the research of both Sellin and Bailey that law enforcement personnel are no safer in jurisdictions that retain and use the death penalty to punish those who deliberately kill police officers than in those who impose some other penalty." (Paternoster 1991, p. 229) Moreover, in response to those who argue that a noncapital sanction does not offer sufficient protection against murderers who may kill correctional staff or other inmates while in prison, he points out that convicted murderers are very unlikely to commit another murder. (Paternoster 1991, p. 236) In the end, it is not easy to determine either whether the death penalty is a more effective in deterring potential criminals than life imprisonment or if so, whether to a significant degree.

A fifth reason why condemned criminals ought not to have a constitutional right aginst the death penalty is that death is just retribution for the most serious crimes. Justice Marshall, dissenting in *Gregg v. Georgia*, explains:

There remains for consideration, however, what might be termed the purely retributive justification for the death penalty—that the death penalty is appropriate, not because of its beneficial effects on society, but because the taking of the murderer's life is itself morally good.…The decision that capital punishment may be the appropriate sanction in extreme cases is an expression of the community's belief that certain crimes are themselves so grievous an affront to humanity that the only adequate response may be the penalty of death. (Supreme Court 1976, p. 239)

However, In *Furman v. Georgia* he had asserted that: "Punishment as retribution has been condemned by scholars for centuries, and the Eighth Amendment itself was adopted to prevent punishment from becoming synonymous with vengeance." (Supreme Court 1972, p. 343) Although retribution may sometimes degenerate into mere revenge, Ernest van den Haag insists that they are not synonymous.

Revenge is a private matter, a wish to "get even" with a person one feels has injured one, whether or not what the person did was legal. Unlike revenge, retribution is legally threatened beforehand for an act prohibited by law. It is imposed by due process and only for a crime, as threatened by law. Retribution is also limited by law. (Van den Haag 1983, p. 246)

Nevertheless, he recognizes that: "Retribution is hard to define. It is harder still to determine the punishments that should be exacted by "just deserts" once the *lex talionis* is abandoned." (Van den Haag 1983, p. 247) And Raymond Paternoster suggests that "responsibility for crime is not anchored solely in the individual, that society bears some blame, and that the determination of culpability cannot be made with any degree of precision because there are so many factors to consider." (Paternoster 1991, p. 261) How, then, can one tell whether any crimes are so serious as to justify the death penalty?

How well do these pro and con arguments survive critical examination? Let us begin with the negative arguments. It is simply not true that death penalty reduces the cost of law enforcement; quite the contrary. Capital punishment probably has negligible effect upon civic virtue or brutalizing society. Although the death penalty completely incapacitates the most dangerous criminals, it is probably not necessary for this purpose. It is possible that the death penalty is just retribution for the most serious crimes, but it is doubtful that judges and juries can reliably estimate what any given criminal really deserves. And it is possible that the death penalty deters potential criminals to a slight degree, but whether this is sufficient to outweigh the arguments in favor of a constitutional right against the death penalty depends upon the strength of these arguments.

The death penalty may or may not be against the moral law. There are exceptions to the moral principle that killing is morally wrong and whether capital punishments is such an exception is precisely the issue in this debate. Although current methods of execution often inflict excruciating pain, whether this is excessive enough to constitute cruelty remains controversial. And one cannot determine whether the death penalty violates human dignity until one has a fuller understanding of the nature of human dignity and how it is relevant to punishment for violations of the criminal law. However, there can be no doubt that the death penalty is discriminatory as currently practiced in the United States, and it is doubtful that such discrimination can be eliminated, or even greatly reduced, in our multicultural society where the gap between rich and poor is growing not diminishing. Crucially, there is reliable evidence that many innocent persons are given the death sentence so that the fact that the death penalty is irremediable is a very strong reason why criminals ought to have a constitutional right against the death penalty. On balance, the relevant considerations favor this controversial right.

10 Overview

Several illuminating patterns concerning the moral foundations of constitutional rights are visible in this chapter. Some concern the moral reasons to establish or extend a constitutional right. The first and most obvious is the existence of an analogous moral human right. Thus, the constitutional right to life and the constitutional right to freedom of speech are grounded, in part, upon the moral human rights to life and freedom of speech. Another, although probably less strong, reason is the existence of an analogous right in international human rights law because presumably each nation state has a moral obligation to conform to and uphold international law. Examples are the constitutional rights to free speech and equal protection of the law that protect the rights to freedom of expression and equal protection of the law in global and most regional human rights law. Establishing a constitutional right can also be justified when this is necessary to protect a human right with a different content. Thus, the constitutional right to habeas corpus serves to protect the human right to liberty, and probably other human rights as well. A fourth reason to establish or extend a constitutional right is that this would serve to preserve or improve democracy. The constitutional right to free speech is grounded in part upon this consideration, and a constitutional right to education might be similarly justified because only an educated citizen can exercise her right to vote responsibly.

One can also discern patterns concerning the most important reasons to limit or recognize exceptions to a constitutional right in the previous pages. Thus, it might be unjustified to extend the constitutional right to life to unborn children because, given the nature of rights, they are incapable of possessing any right. And a reason not to extend the right to vote to a young person under the age of eighteen would be that they are typically incapable of exercising this right responsibly. Third, a reason not to establish or extend a constitutional right is that it would infringe a conflicting human right. Thus, a reason not to recognize a constitutional right to affirmative action might be that this would violate the human right to equal protection of the law. On the other hand, a reason for a constitutional right to affirmative action on behalf of seriously disadvantaged groups might be that this is required by distributive or remedial justice. Finally, a reason for limiting or recognizing an exception to a constitutional right is that this is necessary for some morally compelling state interest. What makes some purpose morally, not merely legally, compelling is usually that a state must pursue it in order to possess legitimate authority or to fulfil some essential state duty to its subjects.

Unfortunately, no clear patterns emerge concerning how one should balance these reasons against one another. The moral weight of each depends upon the circumstances so that no hierarchy of relevant considerations exists. This may be one reason why it is appropriate for courts to sit in judgment upon the general rules enacted by legislatures.

References

Arneson, Richard J. (2000). Disability, Discrimination and Priority. In Americans with Disabilities: Exploring Implications of the Law for Individuals and Institutions, Leslie Pickering Francis and Anita Silver (eds.). Routledge. New York & London.

Baker, C. Edwin (2009). Autonomy and Hate Speech. In Extreme Speech and Democracy, Ivan Hare and James Weinstein (eds.). Oxford University Press. Oxford.

Bedau, Hugo Adam (1997). Innocence and the Death Penalty: Assessing the Danger of Mistaken Executions. In The Death Penalty in America—Current Controversies, Hugo Adam Bedau (ed.). Oxford University Press. New York.

Bickenbach, Jerome E. (2000). The ADA v. the Canadian Charter of Rights. In Americans with Disabilities: Exploring the Implications of the Law for Individuals and Institutions, Leslie Pickering Francis and Anita Silvers (eds.). Routledge. New York and London.

Blackstone, Sir William (1902). Commentaries on the Law of England, Book I, William Draper Lewis (ed.). Rees Welsh & Company. Philadelphia.

Butler, Halle I. (1997). Educated in the Classroom or on the Streets: the Fate of Illegal immigrant Children in the United States. Ohio State Law Journal 58: 1473–1498.

Conrad, John P. (1983). The Purpose of Punishment. In Earnest van den Haag and John P. Conrad, The Death Penalty: A Debate. Plenum Press. New York and London.

Crooker, Constance Emerson (2003). Gun Control and Gun Rights. Greenwood Press. Westport CT.
Doherty, Brian (2008). Gun Control on Trial: the Supreme Court Battle Over the Second Amendment. Cato Institute. Washington DC.
Dworkin, Ronald (2009). Foreward. In Extreme Speech and Democracy, Ivan Hare and James Weinstein (eds.). Oxford University Press. Oxford.
European Court of Human Rights (2004). Vo. v. France. Application no. 53924/00.
Goodwin, Liu (2006). Education, Equality, and National Citizenship. Yale Law Journal 116: 330–411.
Grandrath, Lora L. (1996). Note: Illegal Immigrants and Public Education: Is there a Right to the 3 Rs? Valparaiso University Kaw Review 30:749–810.
Hafetz, Jonathan (2011). Habeas Corpus after 9/11: Confronting America's New Global Detention System. New York University Press. New York & London.
Hamilton, Alexander (1961). The Federalist, Jacob E. Cooke (ed.). Meridian Books. New York.
Hayduk, Ron (2005). Democracy for All: Restoring Immigrant Voting Rights in the United States. Routledge. New York and London.
House, H. Wayne (1997). The New Testament and Moral Arguments for Capital Punishment. In the Death Penalty in America—Current Controversies, Hugo Bedau (ed.). Oxford University Press. New York and Oxford.
Hughes, Todd C. and Hunt, Lester H. (2000). The Liberal Basis of the Right to Bear Arms. Public Affairs Quarterly 14:1–25.
Kessler, Raymond G. (1984). The Political Functions of Gun Control. In Firearms and Violence: Issues and Public Policy, Don B. Kates Jr. (ed.). Ballinger Publishing Company. Cambridge MA.
Kleck, Gary (2001). Guns and Violence. In the Gun Control Debate: You Decide, Lee Nisbet (ed.). Prometheus Books. Amherst NY.
Koper, Christopher S. (2004). Updated Assessment of the Federal Assault Weapons Ban: Impacts on Gun Markets and Gun Violence 1994–2003. Document No. 204431. Department of Justice. Washington DC.
Koper, Christopher S. (2013). America's Experience with the Federal Assault Weapons Ban, 1994–2004. In Reducing Gun violence in America: Informing Policy with Evidence and Analysis, Daniel W. Webster and Jon S. Vernick (eds.). Johns Hopkins University Press. Baltimore MD.
Madison, James (1961). The Federalist, Jacob E. Cooke (ed.). Meridian Books. Cleveland and New York.
Maki, Jennifer L. (2005). The Three Rs: Reading, 'Riting, and Rewarding Illegal Immigrants: How Higher Education has Acquiesced in the illegal Presence of Undocumented Aliens in the United States. William and Mary Bill of Rights Journal 13:1341–1374.
Oakes, Jeannie (2010). Schools That Shock the Conscience: What Williams v. California Reveals About the Struggle for Education on Equal Terms Fifty Years after Brown. In Quality Education as a Constitutional Right, Teresa Perry et. al. (eds). Beacon Press. Boston.
Parekh, Bhikhu (2012). Is There a Case for Banning Hate Speech? In the Content and Context of Hate Speech: Rethinking Regulation and Responses, Michael Hertz and Peter Molnar (eds.). Cambridge University Press. Cambridge and New York.
Paternoster, Raymond (1991). Capital Punishment in America. Lexington Books. New York.
Rawls, John (1971). A Theory of Justice. Harvard University Press. Cambridge MA.
Rawls, John (1993). Political Liberalism. Columbia University Press. New York.
Roemer, John E. (2003). Defending Equality of Opportunity. The Monist 86:261–282.
Rubio-Marin, Ruth (2000). Immigration as a Democratic Challenge: Citizenship and Inclusion in Germany and the United States. Cambridge University Press. Cambridge.
Sadurski, Wojcich (1991). Freedom of Speech and Its Limits. Kluwer Academic Publishers. Dordrecht.

Stell, Lance K. (2001). Gun Control and the Regulation of Fundamental Rights. Criminal Justice Ethics 20:28–33.
Sunstein, Cass R. (1999). Democracy and the Problem of Free Speech. The Free Press. New York.
Supreme court (1866). Ex. Parte Milligan. 71 U.S. 2.
Supreme Court (1938). Missouri ex. rel. Gaines v. Canada. 305 U.S. 337.
Supreme Court (1942). Chaplinsky v. New Hampshire. 315 U.S. 568.
Supreme Court (1950). Johnson v. Eisentrager. 339 U.S. 736.
Supreme Court (1954). Brown v. Board of Education. 347 U.S. 483.
Supreme Court (1965). Griswold v. Connecticut. 381 U.S. 479.
Supreme Court (1971). Graham v. Richardson. 403 U.S. 365.
Supreme Court (1972). Furman v. Georgia. 408 U.S. 238.
Supreme Court (1973a) Roe v. Wade. 410 U.S. 113.
Supreme Court (1973b). San Antonio Independent School District v. Rodriguez. 411 U.S. 1.
Supreme Court (1973c). Sugarman v. Dugall. 413 U.S. 634.
Supreme Court (1976). Gregg v. Georgia. 428 U.S. 153.
Supreme Court (1982). Phyler v. Doe. 457 U.S. 202.
Supreme Court (1990). Cruzan v. Mo. Health Dept. 497 U.S. 261.
Supreme Court (1992a) R. A. V. v. City of St. Paul, Minnesota. 505 U.S. 377.
Supreme Court (1992b) Planned Parenthood of Southeastern Pa. v. Casey. 508 U.S. 833.
Supreme Court (2003). Lawrence v. Texas. 539 U.S. 558.
Supreme Court (2004a). Rasul v. Bush. 542 U.S. 446.
Supreme Court (2004b). Hamdi v. Rumsfeld. 542 U.S. 507.
Supreme Court (2006). Hamdan v. Rumsfeld. 548 U.S. 557.
Supreme Court (2008a). Boumediene v. Bush. 553 U.S. 723.
Supreme Court (2008b). District of Coljmbia v. Heller. 554 U.S. 570.
Supreme Court (2013). United States v. Windsor. 570 U.S. ___ slip opinion.
Supreme Court (2015). Obergefell v. Hodges. 576 U.S. ___ slip opinion.
Van den Haag, Earnest (1983). The Purpose of Punishment. In Earnest van den Haag and John P. Conrad, The Death Penalty: A Debate. Plenum Press. New York and London.
Veatch, Robert M. (1986). The Foundations of Justice: Why the Retarded and the Rest of Us Have Claims to Equality. Oxford University Press. New York and Oxford.
Vizzard, William J. (2000). Shots in the Dark: The Policy, Politics, and Symbolism of Gun Control. Rowman & Littlefield. Boulder CO.
Waldron, Jeremy (2012). The Harm in Hate Speech. Harvard University Press. Cambridge MA.
Weinstein, James (1999). Hate Speech, Pornography and the Radical Attack on Free Speech Doctrine. Westview Press. Boulder CO.
Wellman, Carl (1995). Real Rights. Oxford University Press. New York & Oxford.
Wellman, Carl (2011). The Moral Dimensions of Human Rights. Oxford University Press. New York.
Westfall, David (1982). Beyond Abortion: The Potential Reach of a Human Rights Amendment. American Journal of Law and Medicine 8:97–136.
Wheeler, Samuel C. (1997). Self-Defense: Rights and Coerced Risk-Acceptance. Public Affairs Quarterly 11:431–443.
Wheeler, Samuel C. (2001). Gun Control and Fundamental Rights. Criminal Justice Ethics 20:19–24.
Wolfson, Nicholas (1997). Hate Speech, Sex Speech, Free Speech. Praeger. Westport CT.

Chapter 6
Associations

Abstract This chapter provides a critical examination of the reasons for and against several actual or proposed constitutional rights of associations of private persons. These are the rights of Indian Tribes to partial sovereignty, of political parties to closed primaries, of labor unions to closed shops, of business corporations to spend funds for political purposes, of private clubs to deny membership because of race or sex, of universities to take affirmative action for African-Americans in admissions, and of the press to publish the content of classified government documents. Such reasons concern either the members of the association or the association as a whole.

Many kinds of associations, organized groups of private persons, possess constitutional rights. Religious organizations, newspapers and television stations, business corporations and labor unions, political parties and political actions groups come readily to mind. Politicians, jurists and moral philosophers often disagree about whether some established or proposed associational right is justified. It will be illuminating to examine a variety of such controversies.

1 Indian Tribes

Indian Tribes living on a reservation in the United States presumably have retained some portion of their original sovereignty. In *The Cherokee Nation vs. Georgia*, Chief Justice Marshall, delivering the opinion of the Supreme Court, asserted:

> So much of the argument as was intended to prove the character of the Cherokees as a state, as a distinct political society, separated from others, capable of managing its own affairs and governing itself, has, in the opinion of the majority of the judges, been completely successful. They have been uniformly treated as a state from the settlement of our country. (Supreme Court 1831, p. 16)

And in a following decision Marshall explained that:

> These articles are associated with others, recognizing their title to self government. The very fact of repeated treaties with them recognizes it, and the settled doctrine of the law of nations is, that a weaker power does not surrender its independence—its right to self-government, by associating with a stronger, and taking its protection. (Supreme Court 1832, pp. 560–561)

C. Wellman, *Constitutional Rights -What They Are and What They Ought to Be*,
Law and Philosophy Library 115, DOI 10.1007/978-3-319-31526-3_6

Generalizing these decisions to apply beyond the Cherokee Nation, one can conclude that Indian Tribes have a constitutional right to residual sovereignty. But whether Indian tribes living within the United States ought to possess any sovereign powers is controversial.

One reason why they ought to have a constitutional right to residual sovereignty is to rectify past wrongful treatment of Indian tribes. Patrick Macklem reminds us that European powers who settled in North America declared the land vacant and thus acquired sovereignty over the territory of what is now the United States by discovery. They displaced the Indian nations who occupied the land and thus treated their sovereignty differently than they would have treated the sovereignty of any European nation state. This clearly violated the formal principle of equality, the principle that all potential recipients of a distribution be treated as equals unless there is a valid reason for differential treatment. (Macklem 1993, p. 1357) Therefore:

> A justification of Indian government moved by formal equality considerations arises from a desire to rectify past unequal distribution of sovereignty. Formal equality supports the recognition of Indian forms of government because it places Indian nations in the position they would have been in had they been treated as formal equals. (Macklem 1993, p. 1362)

And presumably a constitutional right to sovereignty would recognize their right of self-government most effectively.

Another reason why Indian tribes ought to have a constitutional right to residual sovereignty is that this would help them to achieve substantive equality in the United States. Macklem explains that the principle of the substantive equality of peoples requires a scrutiny of the actual effects of laws and practices on the social and economic conditions of individuals and groups. (Macklem 1993, p. 1360) He then argues as follows:

> Indian nations in North America constitute identifiable communities that have been and continue to be oppressed by a variety of social and economic forces. ...A commitment to substantive equality suggests that the state attempt to remedy the oppression experienced by Indian nations. More specifically, the state ought to remove alien forms of economic, social, political, and legal organization that have been imposed on Aboriginal societies. (Macklem 1993, p. 1361)

A constitutional right to sovereignty, even if limited, would enable them to organize their own institutions in a way that would reflect their own cultures and traditions.

A third reason why American Indian Tribes ought to have a constitutional right to residual sovereignty is that this would honor the treaties our government has made with them.

Chief Justice Marshall observed in *Worcester v. Georgia* that:

> The constitution, by declaring treaties already made, as well as those to be made, to be the supreme law of the land, has adopted and sanctioned the previous treaties with the Indian nations, and consequently admits their rank among those powers who are capable of making treaties. The words "treaty" and "nation" are words of our own language, selected in our diplomatic and legislative proceedings, by ourselves, having each a definite and well understood meaning. We have applied them to Indians, as we have applied them to the other nations of the earth. (Supreme Court 1832, pp. 559–560)

Thus by making treaties with the Indian tribes, the United States has recognized them as sovereign nations. These treaties are legally binding upon the United States because *Pacta sunt servanda*, agreements must be kept, is a fundamental principle of international law. And they are morally binding also because this legal principle reflects the underlying moral principle that one who has made a promise has a moral obligation to keep that promise. Conferring a constitutional right to residual sovereignty upon Indian tribes is the only way the United States can keep the promises implicit in its many treaties with them.

A fourth reason why Indian tribes ought to have a constitutional right to residual sovereignty is to enable them to preserve their Native American cultures and ways of life. Granted that Indian tribes are under the guardianship of the United States, the federal government is incapable of guarding their traditional social and legal institutions because it reflects the alien traditions and values of the majority of citizens in our country. On the other hand, as Patrick Macklem observes:

> The internal aspect of sovereignty aptly describes the good at issue in questions involving the recognition of Indian forms of government in North America. Indian government is a means by which indigenous peoples can assert some degree of control over the form, content, and direction of their distinct individual and collective lives. (Macklem 1993, p. 1347)

The value of the collective institutions of Indian tribes ultimately rests on the fact that they shape and give content and value to the lives of the individuals living in each reservation. Moreover, it is essential that each Indian tribe retain its own residual sovereignty because the cultures and forms of life of Indian tribes vary considerably.

As one would expect, there are also reasons why Indian tribes ought not to have a constitutional right to residual sovereignty. First, tribal sovereignty can conflict with the duty of the United States to protect the individual Indians. In *United States v. Kagama*, Justice Miller explains the constitutional and moral ground of this duty.

> These Indian tribes are the wards of the nation. They are communities dependent upon the United States….From their very weakness and helplessness, so largely due to the course of dealing of the Federal Government with them and the treaties in which it has been promised, there arises the duty of protection, and with it the power. (Supreme Court 1886, pp. 383–384)

However, Indian tribes, exercising their sovereign power, may preserve traditional customs and institutions that seriously disadvantage individual Indians under contemporary conditions. Thus, respecting tribal sovereignty might prevent the federal government from fulfilling its duty to protect members of an Indian tribe from social or economic harm.

Another reason why Indian tribes ought not to have any constitutional right to residual sovereignty is that this would disrupt the territorial application of United States federal and state sovereignty. Sovereignty as defined in international law is essentially territorial. Internal sovereignty is the right of a nation state to make and enforce laws governing all those within its defined territory, and external sovereignty is its right against interference in its domestic affairs. The United States Constitution confers limited sovereign powers upon the federal government and confers all other governing powers upon the states. This leaves no other sovereign powers to be exercised by Indian tribes or any other internal bodies. (Supreme Court 1886, pp. 379–380) Nor should any such powers be permitted. National sovereignty is justified only when it protects all those subject to its jurisdiction from serious harms or the violation of their human rights. But to exempt any persons or groups living within its territory from its internal sovereignty would weaken its ability to enforce its laws, the laws that protect its inhabitants. Hence, internal sovereignty ought to apply to all parts of the territory of any nation state.

A third reason why Indian tribes ought not to have any constitutional right to residual sovereignty is that this would permit them to violate several important civil rights that protect fundamental human rights. Vine Deloria, Jr. and Clifford M. Lytle sum up the current situation as follows:

> As the Supreme Court noted in *Talton v. Mayes*, 165 U.S. 376 (1895), the powers of local self-government as exercised by Indians existed prior to the Constitution and neither were created by nor sprung from the Constitution. Hence, Indians have the power to define their own offenses and prosecute those who violate tribal laws without complying with the dictates of the U. S. Constitution. (Deloria, Jr. and Lytle 1983, p. 229)

Most important of these rights are probably the Fourteenth Amendment rights to due process and the equal protection of the laws that hold only against the states and the federal government, not Indian tribes. However, either the federal government or the states, or both, ought to be able to protect these rights of individual Indians because these protect moral human rights invaluable to all persons.

Not all of these pro and con reasons ought to be taken seriously. I doubt that the residual sovereignty of Indian tribes does very much to rectify past injustices or, given the power of Congress over Indian tribes, to protect them from future unjust treatment by the United States. Although it is important for the United States to honor treaties made with other nation states, Indian tribes no longer constitute independent states with the power to make or keep treaties. Hence, it is not clear how relevant the doctrine of *Pacta sunt servanda* remains. However, it does remain important for the Indian tribes to preserve their Native American cultures and this is a reason to recognize some residue of their original sovereignty. On the other side of the issue, the residual sovereignty of Indian tribes does not in practice often disrupt the effectiveness of the United States in exercising its internal sovereignty throughout its territory. But tribal sovereignty, limited as it is, can and sometimes does conflict with the duty of the United States to protect individual Indians from social or economic harms and to protect them from the violation of several of their civil and human rights. On balance, I conclude that Indian tribes ought not to have any constitutional right to residual sovereignty.

2 Political Parties

In *California Democratic Party v. Jones*, the Democratic, Republican, Libertarian and Peace and Freedom parties of California joined in claiming a constitutional right to closed primaries, primaries in which only a member of the party has the power to vote for its candidates for election. Although the Supreme Court ruled against them, this does not settle the question of whether political parties ought to have a constitutional right to closed primaries. Let us examine the most plausible arguments for and against such a right.

First, closed primaries are necessary to avoid voter confusion. In *Tashjian v. Republican Party*, the Republican Party of Connecticut argued that in an open primary "It would be difficult for the general public to understand what a candidate stood for who was nominated in part by an unknown amorphous body outside the party, while nevertheless using the party name." (Supreme Court 1986, p. 220) In order one to identify a candidate who would reliably represent the policies of the party one favors, it is necessary that only members of that party be eligible to vote in its primary election. However, there is no litmus test for the sincerity of candidates for office and no guarantee that they seriously intend to keep the promises they make to win election. Hence, voter confusion is present whether primaries are open or closed.

Another reason why primary elections ought to be closed is to preserve the diversity of viewpoints and breadth of information they provide to the public. When primaries are open to members of other parties and even independents who do not belong to any party, candidates must move, or at least pretend to move, toward the middle ground in order to appeal to the widest range of primary voters. Hence, what is most distinctive of each party's platform tends to go unmentioned in their speeches and advertisements. In closed primaries, the differences between the party platforms and the information to support these distinctive policies will be emphasized by the candidates. This will tend toward a better educated public, something essential to any successful democracy. But although the diversity of viewpoints and breadth of information provided to the public is of great importance, the public is provided with many other sources of views and information so that it need not rely upon political parties, hardly the most reliable informants.

A third reason why political parties ought to have a constitutional right to closed primaries is to prevent the dilution or misrepresentation of the views of the party. Only when the candidates need not appeal to independent voters or voters who belong to opposing parties, can they advocate the unadulterated party platform. As Justice Marshall explained in *Tashjian*, the nature of the interest of the Republican Party of Connecticut is the freedom to associate for the advancement of beliefs and ideas, an interest protected by the First Amendment right to freedom of speech. (Supreme Court 1986, p. 214) Because of the right to freedom of speech is essential to democratic government, political parties ought to have a constitutional right to closed primaries to protect their freedom of speech.

A fourth reason why political parties ought to have a constitutional right to closed primaries is to prevent raiding, a practice in which outsiders enter a party primary to vote for a weak candidate who can be defeated in the general election or a candidate who will not firmly adhere to the party's policies. But this undermines the integrity of the electoral process and the right of members of the party to associate to advance their own political preferences and oppose policies they reject. (Supreme Court 1986, pp. 214 & 219)

A fifth reason why political parties ought to have a constitutional right to closed primaries is to protect the responsibility of party government. (Supreme Court 1986, p. 222) The party that wins the majority of seats will have a controlling power in the legislature and often the administration also. In order to ensure that the members of the majority party govern according to the wishes of those who elected them, it is necessary that they depend for continuation in power upon their reelection by those with the same interests, the members of their own party and no others. Hence, closed primaries are essential to the democratic integrity of the party system.

A final reason why political parties ought to have a constitutional right to closed primaries is to ensure the existence of a loyal opposition, a minority party motivated to challenge abuses of power and limit serious practical misjudgments by the majority party. This will be true only if the viewpoints and policies of the two major parties are significantly different, and this in turn requires closed primaries so that crossover voters in the primary election cannot force them to adopt similar positions to lure independent voters in the subsequent general election.

There are, of course, reasons not to confer a constitutional right to closed primaries on political parties. First, closed primaries violate the right to privacy of citizens because they require them to register as party members in order to vote in the party's election of its candidates. Thus, they make public information about the political preferences of those who wish to exercise their democratic right to vote. However, as the Supreme Court recognized, party affiliation is not the most confidential of information about oneself and it should be possible to devise a close primary in which voter registration would not be made public. (Supreme Court 2002, p. 17 slip opinion)

A second reason why political parties ought not to have a constitutional right to closed primaries is that they decrease voter participation. Open or blanket primaries increase voter participation because they offer more choices, in the primary of one's choice as well as in the general election, and thus more incentives to exercise one's franchise. (Supreme Court 2002, pp. 16–17 slip opinion) Because closed primaries prohibit choosing to vote in any primary unless one is a registered party member, it reduces the incentive to vote. This in turn makes it less likely that the final outcome will represent the will of the entire body of citizens. But California's introduction of a blanket primary, the most open of all primary systems, did not significantly increase voter participation.

A third reason against closed primaries is that they remove an incentive to reconsider long-standing party policies that no longer fit changed circumstances or may have been unwise when originally adopted. Open or blanket primaries force candidates to adjust their policies to attract crossover voters who may be critical of some of the more extreme or unjustified planks in the party platform. (Supreme Court 2002, p. 15 slip opinion) Closed primaries, on the other hand, tend to perpetuate a party rigidity harmful to the general welfare and even to the party itself.

A fourth reason why political parties ought not to have a constitutional right to closed primaries is that they produce candidates who do not represent the preferences and interests of the majority of the electorate. Because candidates in closed primaries need not appeal to crossover voters they do not move toward more moderate positions that better represent the entire body of citizens. (Supreme Court 2002, pp. 1415 slip opinion) Therefore, if elected in the general election, they will not fully represent the will of the people as the ideal of democracy demands. However, in the long run this seems to be a self-correcting defect because unrepresentative candidates typically fail to win a majority of vote so that unrepresentative parties with an eye on the next election tend to move toward the middle.

A fifth reason against any constitutional right to closed primaries is that they increase the partisanship of the candidates and in turn those elected to govern. Because candidates in a closed primary do not need to appeal to more moderate independent voters and may be forced to appeal to more radical factions within their own party, only firmly partisan candidates can win in a closed primary. If they are subsequently elected to public office in the legislature or administration, they will tend to be uncompromising and thus to make effective government more difficult. As Justice Marshall reported in Tashjian: "We have previously recognized the danger that 'splintered parties and unrestrained factionalism may do significant damage to the fabric of government'." (Supreme Court 1986, p. 223)

Finally, political parties ought not to have a constitutional right to closed primaries because closed primaries "disenfranchise" many citizens in safe districts. (Supreme Court 2002, pp. 15–16 slip opinion) A safe district is one in which the candidates nominated by one party almost always win in the general election. Although members of other parties or independent voters are not literally disenfranchised because they can still vote, their votes are of no real value because they do not affect the outcome of the general election. This is contrary to the moral right of everyone subject to the jurisdiction of a government to have an effective voice and vote in selecting those who govern.

In my estimation, the most important reason why political parties ought to have a constitutional right to closed primaries is that closed primaries are necessary, or at least conducive, to responsible government. Because they do not permit unaffiliated persons to vote in the primary election by which the party selects its candidates, it tends to result in the choice of candidates strongly committed to the party platform and, if elected to office, to carry out its policies in legislation and administration. And because officeholders know that they will be held responsible by only members of their own party in a future closed primary, party loyalty is typically strong.

Another very important reason in favor of closed primaries is that they are necessary to prevent hedging, crossover voting for candidates likely to lose in the general election or whose views differ from those of the party. As the Supreme Court recognized in *Jones*:

> Representative democracy in any populous unit of government is unimaginable without the ability of citizens to band together in promoting among the electorate candidates who espouse their political views. The formation of national political parties was almost concurrent with the formation of the Republic itself. (Supreme Court 2002, p. 6 slip opinion)

But hedging infringes the right of citizens to associate for this purpose because crossover voters often vote for candidates whose views significantly depart from those of most party members or those who will be unable to promote those views because they will be defeated in the general election.

The strongest moral reason why political parties ought not to have a constitutional right to closed primaries is probably that they deprive citizens in safe districts of an effective vote. Anyone who is not a registered member of the majority party cannot vote for or against its candidates for nomination in the general election. Although one can vote in the general election, one's vote against a nominee of the majority party or for any other nominee will make absolutely no difference to the result. Democracy requires that all those subject to a government have a say in selecting those who govern, and justice requires that the vote of each subject counts equally with that of every other subject. However, not very many districts are securely safe, and a safe district often becomes competitive over time.

The strongest practical reason why political parties ought not to have a constitutional right to open primaries is that closed primaries increase partisanship. Hence, the nominees who are elected to public office are far too often uncompromising and unwilling to cooperate with those who represent the other national party. When different parties control the two houses of the legislature or when one party dominates both houses but the governor or president belongs to the other party, this leads to a stalemate so that pressing public problems cannot be effectively solved. In effect, the government cannot govern in any reasonable manner. Fortunately, eventually a frustrated public will demand legislative and executive action and threaten to vote recalcitrant official out of office.

Although there are weighty reasons on both sides of this question, to my mind the reasons for closed primaries slightly outweigh those against them. Effective governance in a democracy requires political parties to propose a coherent set of policies and select candidates prepared to carry them out in legislative and executive action. And elected officials can best be held responsible for advancing the party platform by knowing that there reelection will depend upon the members of their own party and no others. This in turn requires closed primaries to prevent raiding by crossover voters. Although weighty, the strongest reasons against closed primaries are less harmful to democratic governance and in the long run tend to be reduced by a changed public opinion. With considerable hesitation, I conclude that political parties ought to have a constitutional right to closed primaries.

3 Labor Unions

Because an unemployed individual worker is at the mercy of any large business firm offering to hire him or her on its own terms, workers organize labor unions to bargain collectively on their behalf. Recognizing this reality of the labor market, Congress passed the Wagner Act of 1935 to correct the inequality of bargaining power between employees who do not possess full freedom of association or actual liberty of contract and employers who are organized in the corporate or others forms of association. Both in order to maximize its bargaining power and because the Wagner Act required any collective bargaining agent to represent all the workers in the relevant unit, labor unions stove to negotiate closed shop agreements. These are contracts in which the employer agrees to hire only members of the labor union that represents its employees. Although the Wagner Act permitted closed shops and even encouraged them, Congress became convinced that labor unions were abusing their power and subsequently passed the Taft-Hartley Act of 1947 that prohibited closed shops. It also prohibited a number of allegedly unfair labor practices. Whether this establishes a fair balance between the power of employers and employees is obviously controversial. Hence, one may well ask whether labor unions ought to have a constitutional right to closed shops.

The traditional justification for closed shops is that they are necessary to establish a fair bargaining position of workers contracting with employers. As the Supreme Court recognized in NLRB v. Jones:

> Long ago we stated the reason for labor organizations. We said that they were organized out of the necessities of the situation; that a single employee was helpless in dealing with an employer; that he was dependent ordinarily on his daily wage for the maintenance of himself and family; that, if the employer refused to pay him the wages he thought fair, he was nevertheless unable to leave the employ and resist arbitrary and unfair treatment; that the union was essential to give laborers opportunity to deal on an equality with their employer. (Supreme Court 1937, p. 33)

And closed shops are necessary because if employers are permitted to hire workers who are not union members, employers will still be in a position to exploit their employees. Although it was probably true that historically union shops were necessary to counter the power of employees, one may wonder whether closed shops are still needed now that labor unions have become firmly established and widely respected. Moreover, minimum wage laws today limit the power of employers to pay their employees as little as they wish. Social security programs, especially unemployment insurance and those offering services to obtain alternative work, render workers less vulnerable when negotiating with employers. And United States law now prohibits a variety of unfair labor practices by employers. Nevertheless, unions can reply that unless employees are required to be union members and thereby committed to join in any strike or other union action against a recalcitrant employer, they will not be strong enough to insist upon fair contractual conditions for their members.

A second reason why unions ought to have a constitutional right to closed shops is that closed shops are necessary to protect the human rights of employees. Article 23 of the United Nations *Universal Declaration of Human Rights* of 1948 reads:

1. Everyone has the right to work, to free choice of employment, to just and favorable conditions of work and to protection against unemployment.
2. Everyone, without any discrimination, has the right to equal pay for equal work.
3. Everyone who works has the right to just and favorable remuneration ensuring for himself and his family an existence worthy of human dignity, and supplemented, if necessary, by other means of social protection.
4. Everyone has the right to form and join trade unions for the protection of his interests.

Additional human rights of workers are included in the International Labour Organization's *Declaration on Fundamental Principles and Rights at Work* of 1988. These fundamental moral rights are not always respected by employers and are not adequately protected by United States law. Only labor unions with the strength of closed shops can effectively supplement their legal protection.

A third reason why labor unions ought to have a constitutional right to closed shops is that these are necessary to prevent free-riding, benefiting from the actions of labor unions without joining in these actions. Charles Hanson, Sheila Jackson and Douglas Miller report as follows:

> Much the most common argument in favour of the closed shop is that 'he who benefits should pay'. In other words, because all employees in a particular firm benefit from collective bargaining through a trade union, all should be compelled to contribute to the cost of the union. (Hanson et al. 1988, p. 12)

Presumably they should do this by joining the union and paying its dues. However, the United States Supreme Court reasoned that closed shops were not necessary to prevent free riders, employees who receive the benefits of union representation but are unwilling to contribute their fair share of financial support to such union. Congress did this in the Taft-Hartley Act by prohibiting closed shops but requiring agency shops, union security agreements that require all employees to pay union dues but do not require them to be union members. (Supreme Court 1988b, pp. 747–749) Unions can insist that this is not sufficient to avoid free-riding. Union members contribute more than their dues to the collective bargaining from which all workers benefit. By joining the union they also promise to stand together with the other members of the union in the event of a strike or other union action against their employer. Hence, when push comes to shove, closed unions really are necessary to prevent free-riding.

A fourth reason why unions ought to have a constitutional right to closed shops is that they are necessary to ensure that workers have a high level of skills. Stuart White argues that:

> In the long run, it will be increasingly difficult for firms in the advanced capitalist countries to retain a competitive edge while pursuing older, mass-production strategies, and it is therefore imperative that the governments of these countries orient their economies toward

> the adoption of the newer, flexible systems strategies....In this economic context, trade unions have a critically important—indeed, indispensable—role to play in facilitating skills acquisition. (White 1998, pp. 341–342)

However, trade unions may not always play this role, for they have a strong motive to protect their current members, who may lack the newest technical skills, from being displaced by younger workers better oriented to this technological age.

A fifth reason why unions ought to have a constitutional right to closed shops is that these are necessary to enable unions to act responsibly. Charles Hanson, Sheila Jackson and Douglas Miller explain this reasoning as follows:

> Then there is the view that the closed shop encourages 'responsible' unionism. It is said that it gives union organisers a sense of security and enables them to devote themselves to the long-term interests of the members instead of collecting subscriptions and trying to persuade reluctant employees to join. Trade unionists are, therefore, less militant and aggressive, the emergence of rival unions is prevented and employers can rely on collective agreements being kept, because union negotiators have more authority over their members. (Hanson et al. 1988, p. 13)

Finally, unions ought to have a constitutional right to closed unions to ensure that they are strong and secure enough to effectively promote valuable social and political causes. As W. E. J. McCarthy explains:

> Trade unions can argue that they have important political as well as economic effects. That they assist in the redistribution of power as well as income. That they make possible a wider dispersal of authority at work; it may be said in their favour that they make possible the development and maintenance of effective industrial democracy. (McCarthy 1964, p. 238)

And Stuart White claims that:

> In almost any capitalist society strong unions will be necessary to achieve a balance of interest representation in the political process and, thereby, to help secure the enactment of legislation that may be vital to basic opportunity (e.g., minimum wage laws or wage councils, state-sponsored training programs, welfare programs, health and safety legislation. (White 1998, p. 339)

No doubt unions with closed shop agreements could, and probably would, promote moral ideals such as these. However, they are not the only, and perhaps not the most important, organizations to do so.

There are, of course, reasons why labor unions ought not to have a constitutional right to closed shops. First, closed shops violate the right to freedom of contract. They often prevent employers from hiring any worker they wish and prevent workers from accepting employment with the firm they prefer. The right to freedom of contract is important to individuals because it enables them to freely pursue their individual best interests. And it is valuable to the public because it is essential to market efficiency in any economy. Hence, the majority report of the British Royal Commission of 1867 concluded:

> Thus the law must recognize the right of the individual labourer to dispose of his labour, and the right of the employer to dispose of his productive powers, for, the interest of the public will be best consulted by allowing each of these parties to do what he thinks best for

> himself without further interest of the law than may be necessary to protect the rights of others. (McCarthy 1964, p. 187)

Some would reply that unions also serve the public interest and protect other individual rights.

Second, labor unions ought not to have a constitutional right to closed shops because closed shops violate the human right to freedom of association. Article 20 of the *Universal Declaration of Human Rights* reads: "1. Everyone has the right to freedom of assembly and association. 2. No one may be compelled to belong to an association." Thus, the human right of freedom of association implies the right not to join a trade union equally with the right to join. Now the right of workers to join together to form a union is of great importance to employees because only in union is there sufficient strength to negotiate favorable working conditions with their employers. But why is the right not to join a trade union so important to any worker seeking employment? Although one might have religious or equally serious moral objections to the policies of a trade union, this is not usually the case. But getting a job is vitally important to any unemployed worker, and many believe that closed shops deprive such persons of the opportunity to gain employment. The result has been the enactment of right to work laws in many states. These often follow the example of Florida's right to work law that reads in part:

> The right of persons to work shall not be denied or abridged on account of membership or non-membership in any labor union or labor organization, provided that this clause shall not be construed to deny or abridge the right of employees, by and through a labor organization or labor union, to bargain collectively with their employer. (Hanson et al. 1988, p. 145)

However this language is misleading, for such laws do nothing to require employers to hire any worker seeking employment or to require state or federal agencies to provide more positions for those seeking work. As Hanson *et. al.* observe, right to work laws might more accurately be called "voluntary union membership laws." (Hanson et al. 1988, p. 144) Therefore, in the end one must weigh the importance of the right to associate as members of a union with maximum strength against the right not to associate with the majority of employees of an employer by whom one wishes to become employed.

Third, unions ought not to have a constitutional right to closed unions because closed unions can and do abuse their power. Because closed unions have a monopoly of control over their members they are in a position to coerce their members unjustly. Twelve years after the Wagner Act, that permitted closed shops, the House of Representatives Committee on Education and Labor asserted:

> For the past 14 years, as a result of labor laws ill-conceived and disastrously executed, the American workingman has been deprived of his dignity as an individual....His whole economic life has been subject to the complete domination and control of unregulated monopolists....He has been denied any voice in arranging the terms of his own employment....In short, his, mind, his soul, and his very life have been subject to tyranny more despotic than one would think possible in a free country. (Aaron 1987, pp. 167–168)

Convinced that the trade unions had become too strong, Congress passed the Taft-Hartley Act that prohibited closed unions. However, it may well be that a better response to the abuse of power by unionists would have been to enact a comprehensive bill of rights for individual employees as Hartley originally intended. (Aaron 1987, p. 168)

Fourth, unions ought not to have a right to closed shops because closed shops reduce the incentives of union leaders to promote the needs of the members of their union. This is because they face no challenge from non-union workers who might be hired to displace union members. Stuart White reports that critics argue that the closed shop "reduces the incentive of union leaderships to make unions attractive to workers, and may thus lead to a unionism that is more attuned to the aspirations of union leaders than to the needs of ordinary members." (White 1998, p. 347) On the other hand, closed shops strengthen the union leaders when they negotiate agreements with employers providing working conditions beneficial to their members.

Fifth, labor unions ought not to have a constitutional right to closed shops because the closed shop has extremely harmful economic effects. Stephen Dunn and John Gennard sum up the view of free-market economists as follows:

> Its coercive effect is identified in restriction of output, resistance to technological change, retention of outdated skill differentials, shortage of skilled labour, embargoes on the goods and services of non-union firms and damaging use of the strike weapon. The result is escalating production costs, uncompetitive pricing, depressed profit margins and closures. (Dunn and Gennard 1984, p. 2)

However, this view may exaggerate the harmful effects of closed shops, and in a competitive economy unions ought to be free to pursue the interests of their members in every legally permissible manner. (McCarthy 1964, p. 191)

Upon reflection, it seems to me that none of the pro or con reasons is conclusive. The strongest arguments for closed shops is that they are necessary to provide a fair bargaining position between employers and employees, to protect the human rights of workers and to avoid free-riding. But as long as employees are permitted to form labor unions and employers are required to negotiate with the union formed by the majority of its workers, labor unions may well be able to bargain fairly and to protect the human rights of all employees. To be sure some free-riding would remain, but an agency shop where non-union employees would be required to pay union dues would reduce the seriousness of this injustice. Considering the strongest arguments on the other side of the issue, although closed shops would limit the right to freedom of contract and the right not to associate, these limits are probably not very serious because employers retain considerable power to negotiate agreements with their employees and workers retain the option of either joining the union or seeking employment elsewhere. And the ability of closed unions to abuse their power could and should be prohibited by enacting a bill of workers' rights. On balance, I conclude that labor unions ought to have a constitutional liberty-right to negotiate closed shop agreements with employers, but that they ought not to have any claim-right against employers to require them to agree to closed shops.

4 Business Corporations

In the Federal Elections Campaign Act of 1971 and more recently in the Bipartisan Campaign Reform Act of 2002, Congress has attempted to limit both contributions to candidates for public office and expenditures for political purposes from a variety of sources. Both acts have been challenged in the courts, especially provisions limiting spending by corporations. Although the legal debate has focused on whether corporate campaign finance may be limited, a number of serious moral issues remain unresolved. One of the most fundamental is whether business corporations ought to have a constitutional right to spend funds either by a contribution to a candidate or an expenditure for a political message.

There are several highly plausible reasons why business corporations ought to have such a right. (1) Business corporations ought to have a constitutional right to spend funds for political purposes in order that its members can exercise their constitutional and human right to association. As the Supreme Court reasoned in *Buckley:*

> The constitutional right of association explicated in NAACP v. Alabama stemmed from the Court's recognition that effective advocacy of both public and private points of view, particularly controversial ones, is undeniably enhanced by group association. Subsequent decisions have made clear that the First and Fourteenth Amendments guarantee "freedom to associate with others for the common advancement of political beliefs and ideas…." (Supreme Court 1976, p. 15)

However, individuals do not join together to form or purchase stock in a business corporation in order to advance their political beliefs or ideas. They join a for-profit association in order to make money. Hence, the relevance of their right to freedom of association to spending corporate funds for political purposes is dubious. In any event, the members of a business corporation have many other ways to associate for political purposes.

(2) Business corporations ought to have a constitutional right to spend funds for political purposes because this is implied by their right to freedom of expression. As the Supreme Court asserted in *Citizens United*, to prohibit corporations from using their general treasury funds for electioneering communications or advocating the election or defeat of a candidate is a clear violation of the constitutional provision that "Congress shall make no law…abridging the freedom of speech." (Supreme Court 2010, p. 1 slip opinion) The exercise of this constitutional right ought to be fully protected in order to protect the highly valuable human right to free speech of the members of the corporate body. However, Justice Brennen, concurring in *Austin*, observed that "A stockholder might oppose the use of corporate funds drawn from the general treasury—which represents, after all, his money—in support of a particular political candidate." (Supreme Court 1990, p. 670) Thus, protecting the right to free speech of some members of the corporation might, and often would, violate the right to free speech of other members. Although the human right to free speech is a right of individual human beings only, in United States law corporations are legal persons. Is that sufficient to justify a corporate right to freedom of political

speech? Business corporations pay corporate income taxes and might appeal to the revolutionary principle "No taxation without representation." Because business corporations are taxed as corporations, they ought to have a constitutional freedom of spending funds to determine who will represent them in the government. But in the end it is the shareholders who pay corporate taxes and they can spend their profits to influence the elections that determine who represents them.

Finally, (3) business corporations ought to have a constitutional right to spend funds for political purposes in order to serve the justifying purpose of the right to freedom of speech. This is maximizing the amount of information and diversity of viewpoints needed to create an educated public in a democracy. As the Supreme Court reasoned in *Buckley*:

> A restriction on the amount of money a person or group can spend on political communication during a campaign necessarily reduces the quantity of expression by restricting the number of issues discussed, the depth of their exploration, and the size of the audience reached. This is because virtually every means of communicating ideas in today's mass society requires the expenditure of money. (Supreme Court 1976, p. 19)

Moreover, corporate speech expresses a distinct and vitally important point of view because of the tremendous importance of business corporations in the nation's economy

There are also several plausible reasons why business corporations ought not to have a constitutional right to spend funds for political purposes. (1) Contributions to a candidate or expenditures for political advertising threaten to corrupt public officials. John Samples reports that:

> Some have compared campaign contributions to bribes by noting that such donations benefit the recipients. That abstraction obscures an important distinction between bribes and donations. Unlike bribes, contributions can be spent legally only on political activity: getting out the vote, persuading voters by advertising, building campaign organizations, and other activities connected to elections. (Samples 2006, pp. 85–86)

And the Supreme Court in *Buckley* denied that expenditures for political purposes threaten actual corruption of public officials.

> Unlike contributions, such independent expenditures may well provide little assistance to the candidate's campaign, and indeed may prove counterproductive, The absence of prearrangement and coordination of an expenditure with the candidate or his agent not only undermines the value of the expenditure to the candidate, but also alleviates the danger that expenditures will be given as a quid pro quo for improper commitments from the candidate. (Supreme Court 1976, p. 47)

Moreover, the danger that either contributions to or expenditures on behalf of a candidate will actually corrupt public officials is limited by the criminal laws prohibiting most forms of political corruption.

(2) Business corporations ought not to have a constitutional right to spend funds for political purposes because large contributions to a candidate or expenditures on his or her behalf create the appearance of corruption. The mere appearance of corruption undermines democracy because it causes distrust of the government and lowers voter turnout. In *Buckley* the Supreme Court asserted that: "Of almost equal

concern as the danger of actual quid pro quo arrangements is the impact of the appearance of corruption stemming from public awareness of the opportunities for abuse inherent in a regime of large individual financial contributions." (Supreme Court 1976, p. 27) On the other hand, John Samples argues that: "Distrust of the federal government and low voter turnout do not justify limiting spending on politics. Neither one is inherently bad or caused by money in politics….In fact, most citizens have a high opinion of their nation, if not of the Federal government." (Samples 2006, p. 129)

A more moderate argument is that (3) business corporations ought not to have a constitutional right to spend funds for political purposes because their large contributions have undue influence on legislation. Mark Green describes the current situation as follows:

> Of course, much of the $3 billion contributed to candidates in 2000 came because donors knew the candidate, believed in the candidate's philosophy, liked his/her personality, looks, religion, or race. The problem, however, is that the system is also flooded with a Niagara of contributions from economic interests seeking a return. And getting one. (green 2002, p. 161)

He then reports the political contributions of several large corporations and the subsequent legislation favorable to each. However, correlation is not necessarily causation. Anthony Gierzynsk takes a more balanced viewpoint.

> There is little evidence that money influences the votes of lawmakers on the floor of the U.S. House. But there is evidence that contributions are related to the activity of lawmakers during the legislative process—in committees, where the details of the bills are written—and in issues that do not seem to concern large segments of the population. (Gierzynski 2000, p. 9)

Hence, there is some uncertainty about how serious the problem of improper influence is in our country today.

(4) Business corporations ought not to have a constitutional right to spend funds for political purposes because their massive contributions and expenditures distort the marketplace of political ideas. As the Supreme Court opined in *Austin*:

> Regardless of whether this danger of "financial quid pro quo" corruption…may be sufficient to justify a restriction on independent expenditures, Michigan's regulation aims at a different type of corruption in the political arena: the corrosive and distorting effects of immense aggregations of wealth that are accumulated with the help of the corporate form and that have little or no correlation with the public's support for the corporation's political ideas. (Supreme Court 1990, pp. 659–660)

But why should public support be an appropriate measure of the desirability of a political contribution or communication? As Justice Scalia, dissenting in *Austin*, argued:

> Those Founders designed, of course, a system in which popular ideas would ultimately prevail, but also, through the First Amendment, a system in which true ideas could readily become popular. For the latter purpose, the calibration that the Court today endorses is precisely backwards. To the extent a valid proposition has scant public support, it should have wider, rather than narrower, public circulation. (Supreme Court 1990, p. 693)

Unfortunately, in *Austin* the Supreme Court did not explain why preventing deviation from public opinion is a compelling state interest.

(5) Business corporations ought not to have a constitutional right to spend funds for political purposes because such a right would give them an unfair advantage regarding political influence. Anthony Gierzynski explains that:

> An unequal distribution of money in elections leads to unequal political influence by diminishing the role of elections, which in turn makes the interest group system more important, and, by biasing that interest group system to favor the financially advantaged interests. (Gierzynski 2000, p. 15)

And the Supreme Court in *Austin* recognized that:

> State law grants corporations special advantages—such as limited liability, perpetual life, and favorable treatment of the accumulation and distribution of assets—that enhance their ability to attract capital and to deploy their resources in ways that maximize the return on their shareholders' investments. These state-created advantages not only allow corporations to play a dominant role in the nation's economy, but also permit them to use "resources amassed in the economic marketplace" to obtain "an unfair advantage in the political marketplace." (Supreme Court 1990, pp. 493–494)

Hence, there is an important state interest in denying corporations this unfair advantage in order to equalize the political influence of all citizens. But Justice Scalia, dissenting in *Austin*, argued that:

> But the concept that government may restrict the speech of some elements of our society in order to enhance the relative voice of others is wholly foreign to the First Amendment, which was designed "to secure the widest possible dissemination of information from diverse and antagonistic sources," and "to assure unfettered interchange of ideas for the bringing about of political and social changes desired by the people." (Supreme Court 1990, p. 685)

Restricting corporate speech might also appear to be political discrimination against the shareholders in business corporations and thus foreign to the Fourteenth Amendment. Finally, John Samples suggests that equality as a Madisonian ideal is equality before the law, not equality of wealth or equality of political influence. (Samples 2006, p. 163)

To my mind, most of the pro and con reasons are either dubious or weak. The strongest reason why business corporations ought to have a constitutional right to spend funds for political purposes is that this would enable them to greatly increase the money needed to convey relevant information and diverse viewpoints to a wider range of voters and that the corporate message conveys a distinct perspective that it is important for the public to hear. The strongest reason why business corporations ought not to have a constitutional right to spend funds for political purposes is that this would give them an undue influence on the legislative process, the influence of special interests rather than the interests of the public in general. Although there may be some truth in the slogan that: "What is good for General Motors is good for America." On balance, it seems to me that the former reason outweighs the latter. Hence, I conclude that business corporations ought to have a constitutional right to spend funds for political purposes.

5 Private Clubs

Black's Law Dictionary defines a club as "A voluntary, incorporated or unincorporated, association of persons for common purposes of a social, literary, investment, political nature, or the like." Clubs typically admit new members selectively and exclude persons they consider incompatible with their common purpose. The legal, and moral, question is whether their right to deny membership is unlimited. There have been a number of court cases in which clubs have claimed the right to exclude all African-Americans or women. This claim is most plausible in the case of a private club. A private club is one in which its meetings and facilities, if any, are open only to its members or their guests. Ought private clubs to have a constitutional right to deny membership because of race or sex?

There are several reasons why private clubs ought to have a constitutional right to deny membership because of race or sex. (1) Their right to deny membership is implied by their constitutional right to freedom of association. Lois M. McKenna reports that:

> The constitutional right of freedom of association guarantees unfettered association between individuals. This right allows association in intimate settings, as in the fellowship between family members, and in "expressive" settings in which groups practice free speech. Freedom of association also extends to truly private organizations, permitting fraternization without interference. Yet, implicit in the right to choose one's associates is the prerogative to exclude others, which may result in discriminatory acts. (McKenna 1989, p. 1061)

One, but not the only, moral ground of this constitutional right is the human right to freedom of association asserted in Article 20 of the *Universal Declaration of Human Rights*. Private clubs often claim that this right is important for their purposes. For example, the General Secretary of Rotary International testified that the exclusion of women results in an aspect of fellowship enjoyed by the present male membership and that it enables Rotary to operate effectively in foreign counties with varies cultures and social norms. (Supreme Court 1987, p. 541) However, no constitutional or human right is absolute. A government might be justified in limiting the right to freedom of association of private clubs if this were really necessary for some morally compelling state interest.

(2) Private clubs ought to have a constitutional right to deny membership because of race or sex in order to protect the constitutional right to privacy of their members. Justice Goldberg in *Bell v. Maryland* asserted that:

> Prejudice and bigotry in any form are regrettable, but it is the constitutional right of every person to close his home or club to any person or choose his social intimates and business partners solely on the basis of personal prejudices including race. These and other rights pertaining to privacy and private association are themselves constitutionally protected liberties. (Supreme Court 1964, p. 313)

And our constitutional right to privacy serves to give legal protection to the fundamental human right to privacy. Article 12 of the *Universal Declaration of Human Rights* reads: "No one shall be subjected to arbitrary interference with his privacy, family, home or correspondence…" However, as the Supreme Court reasoned in *Rotary*:

> In determining whether a particular association is sufficiently personal or private to warrant constitutional protection, we consider factors such as size, purpose, selectivity, and whether others are excluded from critical aspects of the relationship….The evidence in this case indicates that the relationship between Rotary Club members is not the kind of intimate and private relation that warrants constitutional protection. (Supreme Court 1987, p. 546)

And the same can be said of many other private clubs. Thus, the analogy between one's home and one's private club presupposed in most appeals to the right to privacy is suspect.

(3) Private clubs ought to have a constitutional right to deny membership because of race or sex in order to encourage, or at least not discourage, the formation and activities of these personally and socially valuable organizations. Individual citizens will feel more at home in clubs where they are not forced to associate with members who make them feel uncomfortable. Their discomfort may be a result of their racial or sexual prejudices, but may arise from mere unfamiliarity or inhibitions. Hence, many individuals will be more willing to join clubs that exclude African-Americans or women and more highly motivated to be active in their services to society. The Rotary International Board of Directors issued a statement that said in part:

> We find it incredible that a voluntary organization such as a Rotary which each year provides more than $300 million worth of services to improve communities, which sends each year 10,000 young people on international exchanges, and which is immunizing the world's children against polio—all done without regard to race, sex, creed, or nationality—be likened to commercial business establishments. (Rogers 1988, p. 120)

Commenting on recent Supreme Court cases decided against private clubs, Lois M. McKenna, a more neutral observer, asserted that:

> These decisions do not imply, however, that all organizations should be subject to regulation concerning their membership policies, or that clubs are negative influences. Social organizations provide support and comfort, and are mediums for the members' self-expression. Groups develop as a result of common concerns, and reflect cultural developments. Throughout history, social organizations have played a useful role in promoting social change, reform, and filling social and cultural voids. (McKenna 1989, pp. 1089–1090)

Presumably, the government ought not to undermine the formation and activities of private clubs that contribute so much to the personal wellbeing of their citizens and the welfare of society as a whole. However, regarding the exclusion of women, Deborah I. Rhode suggests that: "The issue is not simply whether single-sex associations are beneficial, but whether experiences of commensurate value are available in mixed environments with fewer social costs." (Rhode 2010, p. 246) The same can be said of the relative value of single-race compared with mixed-race associations.

There are also strong reasons why private clubs ought not to have a constitutional right to deny membership because of race or sex. (1) They ought not to have any such right because this would permit private clubs to engage in racial and sexual discrimination and thereby to violate the rights to equal treatment of non-white and female applicants for admission. First, there is the constitutional right to the equal protection of the law. Second, there is the human right to equality before the law asserted by the *Universal Declaration of Human Rights* in Article 7 that reads in part: "All are equal before the law and are entitled without any discrimination to equal protection of the law…." Finally, there is the more general moral right to equitable treatment that holds against all others, not merely the legal authorities. This is the moral right not to be treated worse than others who are similarly situated without a just-making reason. (Wellman 1982, pp. 138–147) Thomas H. Sawyer describes one of the costs of perpetuating the all-white male private club as follows:

> America is considered a free country by most….Yet today, the concept of inherent racial, religious or gender inequality survives in the bylaws and admission policies of private clubs that can reject a black, Jew or female applicant with no more justification than "no___ allowed." The use of classifications is psychologically harmful to any group being discriminated against. (Sawyer 1993, pp. 202–203)

This psychological harm is one, but only one, of the grounds of our laws prohibiting wrongful discrimination. However, it is not obvious how to balance these rights to equitable treatment against the rights to freedom of association and privacy claimed by private clubs.

(2) Private clubs ought not to have a constitutional right to deny membership because of race or sex because this would permit them to violate the moral right to equal opportunity of non-white and female applicants. While the rights to equal treatment are negative rights, rights not to be unjustly discriminated against, the right to equal opportunity is a positive right. It is best conceived as the right to have available a combination of circumstances or set of conditions as favorable to living a worthwhile human life as those available to others in one's society. (Wellman 1990, pp. 22–30) The relevance of this right to private clubs was recognized by the Supreme Court in *Club Association*.

> It is hereby found and declared that the city of New York has a compelling interest in providing its citizens an environment where all persons, regardless of race, creed, color, national origin or sex, have a fair and equal opportunity to participate in the business and professional life of the city, and may be unfettered in availing themselves of employment opportunities….One barrier to the advancement of women and minorities in the business and professional life of the city is the discriminatory practices of certain membership organizations where business deals are often made and personal contacts valuable for business purposes, employment and professional advancement are formed. (Supreme Court 1988a, pp. 5–6)

Some might reply that although equal opportunity may be a moral ideal for any society, strictly speaking there is no moral right to equal opportunity. Hence, it is merely a desirable government interest rather than a compelling one.

(3) Private Clubs ought not to have a constitutional right to deny membership because of race and sex because this would undermine the social ideal of racial and

sexual integration. The unity and cohesiveness of any society is weakened by segregation. Integration is a socially important goal because it helps its members to agree on mutually beneficial policies and to carry them out with minimal resistance. Thomas H. Sawyer observes that:

> Private clubs are often indistinguishable in their operation from public restaurants, pools, golf courses, tennis courts, rod and reel clubs open to the public. Yet, by establishing the policies outlined in the *Cornelius* case, many groups (not just white males) can escape social integration mandated by court decisions and legislation. To the extent that there is a national policy of promoting integration (race and gender) for its own sake, this policy is undermined by the maintenance of a system in which any group can, in effect, purchase the right to maintain segregation. (Sawyer 1993, p. 204)

However, some insist that forced integration is counterproductive because it reinforces racial and sexual prejudice by adding resentment against coercion.

Finally, (4) private clubs ought not to have a constitutional right to deny membership because of race and sex because this is unnecessary and would permit injustice. A democratic legal system ought to establish a constitutional right only when this is necessary to prevent unjust legislation or the serious abuse of administrative power. This is because establishing a constitutional right transfers ultimate authority from legislators, elected by and accountable to the people, to unelected judges. Those private clubs that ought to be entitled to deny membership because of race and sex do not need any additional constitutional right to do so because they can appeal to their existing constitutional rights to freedom of association and privacy. Moreover, to establish a constitutional right of private clubs as such to deny membership because of race or sex would enable many of them to do so unjustly. This is because justice requires that similar cases be treated similarly and dissimilar cases be treated dissimilarly. Private clubs are very different in size, purpose, range of activities and the prestige and power of their members. These are relevant differences and imply that private clubs ought to be treated differently regarding the permissibility of their admission practices.

Everything considered, ought private clubs to have a constitutional right to deny membership because of race or sex? The case for such a right rests primarily on the rights to freedom of association and privacy of their members. But it is not clear that these rights are applicable to clubs with many members and in which political advocacy plays no significant role in their defining purposes. In any event, these rights are not absolute and are probably often outweighed by the state interests in eliminating racial and sexual discrimination and providing equal opportunity to all citizens. Thus, given the very different characteristics of private clubs, a constitutional right to deny membership because of race or sex is not necessary for those clubs that ought to be permitted to do so and would unjustly fail to treat relevantly different private clubs differently. Therefore, private clubs ought not to have a constitutional right to deny membership because of race or sex.

6 Universities

Affirmative action, in the legally relevant sense, is action taken to remedy wrongful discrimination. Thus it is positive action, such as offering scholarships to applicants from low-income families, in contrast to negative action, merely not discriminating in any wrongful way. It is typically preferential, advantageous to one class of persons and disadvantageous to others. Hiring a female in a predominantly male firm would prevent an equally qualified male from obtaining that position. The legality and morality of preferential affirmative action has been and still is highly controversial. Because the legal and moral issues are most explicit in a series of court cases concerning the admission policies of institutions of higher education, I will ask "Ought colleges and universities to have a constitutional right to preferential affirmative action in favor of African-Americans in their admissions procedures?" To simplify my exposition I will use "universities" to refer to both colleges and universities.

There are several reasons against any constitutional right to preferential affirmative action. One reason is that this seems to violate the *International Convention on the Elimination of All Form of Racial Discrimination*. Article 1.1 defines "racial discrimination" in terms of "any distinction, exclusion, restriction or preference based on race, colour, descent, or national or ethnic origin." This would seem to rule out any affirmative action that gives preferential treatment to African-Americans. And Article 2.1 imposes an obligation upon all State Parties to eliminate all racial discrimination. What gives great moral force to this legal obligation is that racial discrimination violates the principle of equality under law that protects many fundamental human rights. However, Paragraph 10 of the *General Comment No. 18: Non-discrimination* of the Human Rights Committee reads in part:

> The Committee also wishes to point out that the principle of equality sometimes requires States parties to take affirmative action in order to diminish or eliminate conditions which cause or help to perpetuate discrimination prohibited by the Covenant....Such action may involve granting for a time to the part of the population concerned certain preferential treatment in specific matters as compared with the rest of the population.

Thus, according to the most authentic interpretation of the *International Convention*, it does not in fact rule out preferential affirmative action. But the Committee on Human Rights does not explain how some preferential treatment based on race can be required by, much less consistent with, strict equality under law. Moreover, many worry that once established, policies of preferential affirmative action will be hard to eliminate and will persist long after they are no longer needed.

Another reason why universities ought not to have a constitutional right to affirmative action now might be that such programs are no longer necessary. Granted that for the major portion of the history of our nation, the white majority has discriminated against African-Americans in grossly unjust ways, some argue that today the integration of our schools and businesses has reduced racial discrimination to a minimal level. However, there is considerable anecdotal and statistical evidence that serious racial discrimination still exists. A more plausible argument is that there are alternative programs that are more just than ones that give preferential treatment on a racial basis. Carl Cohan insists that:

> In sum, race preference gives to those who don't deserve and doesn't giive to those who do. It gives more to those who deserve less, and less to those who deserve more. These failings are inescapable because the preferences in question are grounded not in earlier injury but in physical characteristics that cannot justly serve as grounds for advantage or disadvantage. (Cohen and Sterba 2003, p. 33)

He concludes that it would be better to abandon preferential affirmative action and use alternative programs designed to "compensate most those who were injured most, and compensate least, or not at all, those who were injured least, or not at all. (Cohen and Sterba 2003, p. 30)" However, James P. Sterba, among others, reply that there are serious disadvantages, both moral and practical, to the existing alternative programs. (Cohen and Sterba 2003, p. 272)

Thus, it seems that preferential affirmative action is still needed in our society.

A third argument against preferential affirmative action is that it inhibits progress towards the moral ideal of a color-blind society. Because it conceives of the social problem to be solved as racial discrimination and the solution to consist in racial preference, it perpetuates the discriminatory racial attitudes that engender social injustice. However, Richard Wasserstrom believes that the attempt to achieve a color-blind society is premature. Because all discussion about race in our society must employ our concepts and our categories of racial identity, they do necessarily to some degree invoke the commitments of the racist ideology which first gives them their meaning and applicability. And affirmative action programs should be seen as a means of overcoming this ideology. (Wasserstrom 1995, pp. 167–168)

A fourth reason advanced against permitting preferential affirmative action is that it is bad for those preferred. In his *Bakke* opinion, Justice Powell admits that: "Second, preferential programs may only reinforce common stereotypes holding that certain groups are unable to achieve success without special protection based on a factor having no relationship to individual worth." (Supreme Court 1978, p. 298) And after listing ten ways in which he believes that preferential affirmative action is bad for those preferred, Carl Cohen asserts:

> These consequences of preference I will explain—but its worst consequences, with which I will begin, are the injuries it inflicts upon the racial minorities preferred, *creating widespread* resentment, *reinforcing stereotypes*, and *humiliating its purported beneficiaries* in the eyes of their classmates, colleagues, workmates, teachers—and even in their own eyes. (Cohen and Sterba 2003, p. 320)

Because he recognizes the force of this objection, James P. Sterba concludes that preferential affirmative action programs are justifiable only when they are limited to candidates who are or soon will be qualified for the programs into which they are admitted. (Cohen and Sterba 2003, pp. 262–263)

The strongest reason not to permit preferential affirmative action seems to be that it violates the moral principle of equality. Carl Cohen formulates this principle as follows: "All the members of humankind are equally ends in themselves, all have equal dignity—and therefore all are entitled to equal respect from the community and its laws." (Cohen and Sterba 2003, p. 24) He is aware that this does not require the same treatment for all persons. For example, citizens have rights and responsibilities that non-citizens do not have. Hence, it is morally permissible to permit citizens to vote but deny the vote to other persons. However, different treatment by the society requires special moral justification, and race or nationality cannot serve as justification for unequal treatment. (Cohen and Sterba 2003, pp. 23–24) However, James W. Nickel advances an equally strong refutation:

> The defect in this charge is that it mistakenly assumes that race is the justification for preferential treatment. This is only apparently so. If preference is given to blacks because of past discrimination and present poverty, the basis for this preference is not that these people are black but rather that they are likely to have been victimized by discrimination, to have fewer benefits and more burdens than is fair, to be members of an underrepresented group, or to be the sorts of persons that can help public institution meet the needs of those who are now poorly served. (Nickel 1975, p. 550)

Accordingly, the crucial question is whether any such reasons do in fact justify preferential affirmative action. But before we turn to the critical examination of these and similar reasons we should consider one last reason against preferential affirmative action.

This reason not to permit racial preferential affirmative action is that it is reverse discrimination. It is racial discrimination against whites and therefore wrong for precisely the same reason that racial discrimination against African-Americans was and still is wrong. As Justice Powell observed in *Bakke*: "Third, there is a measure of inequity in forcing innocent persons in the respondent's position to bear the burden of redressing grievances not of their making. (Supreme Court 1978, p. 298)" This certainly seems to be true. But what is wrongful discrimination in the morally and legally relevant sense? It is treating one person or some class of persons worse than the treatment provided to others who are similarly situation without a sufficient justification. The question remains whether there are any reasons sufficient to justify the measure of inequity involved in preferential affirmative action programs that threat white persons worse than black persons.

One reason to permit racial preferential affirmative action in education, especially higher education, is that it promotes the diversity. This justification was first recognized by the Supreme Court in *Bakke*:

> The fourth goal asserted by petitioner is the attainment of a diverse student body. This clearly is a constitutionally permissible goal for an institution of higher education. Academic freedom, though not a specifically enumerated constitutional right has been viewed as a special concern of the First Amendment. The freedom of a university to make its own judgments as to education includes the selection of its student body. (Supreme Court 1978, pp. 311–312)

In Grutter v. Bollinger, Justice O'Connnor explained the educational benefits as follows:

> These benefits are substantial. As the District Court emphasized, the Law School's admission policy promotes "cross-racial understanding," helps to break down racial stereotypes, and "enables [students] to better understand persons of different races." These benefits are "important and laudable" because "classroom discussion is livelier, more spirited, and

> simply more enlightening and interesting" when the students have "the greatest variety of backgrounds.'...In addition...numerous studies show that student body diversity promotes learning outcomes, and "better prepares students for an increasingly diverse workforce and society, and better prepares them as professionals." (Supreme Court 2003, pp. 17–18 slip opinion)

However, Carl Cohen inserts doubt that "racial diversity has any measurable impact upon the quality of learning or teaching in a university" and insists that even if it did, this "would carry very little weight in a just society." (Cohen and Sterba 2003, p. 39) And John Kekes asserts that the attempt to justify racial preferential affirmative action is arbitrary because. "No effort is made to contribute to diversity by according preferential treatment to religious fundamentalists, and feminists, political conservatives, defenders of the desirability of American primacy in international affairs, or to those who advocate research into genetic racial differences." (Kekes 1995, p. 200) Although most experts believe that the educational benefits of racial diversity are considerable, it is not clear that they are sufficient to outweigh the injustice of reverse discrimination.

A second reason to permit racial preferential affirmative action is to cultivate leaders seen to be legitimate in order to preserve their legitimacy. Justice O'Connor argued as follows:

> In order to cultivate a set of leaders with legitimacy in the eyes of the citizenry, it is necessary that the path to leadership be visibly open to talented and qualified individuals of every race and ethnicity. All members of our heterogeneous society must have confidence in the openness and integrity of the educational institutions that provide this training....Access to legal education (and thus to the legal profession) must be inclusive of talented and qualified individuals of every race and ethnicity, so that all members of our heterogeneous society may participate in the educational institutions that provide the training and education necessary to succeed in America. (Supreme Court 2003, pp. 332–333)

Arguably racial preferential affirmative action, at least in higher education, is justified because it contributes to the seen legitimacy of the leaders of our society. However, one may wonder to what extent it serves this important purpose. The seen legitimacy of the leaders in our society depends upon a wide variety of factors, only one of which is the racial integration of our professional schools. Hence, this is probably an important but not compelling state interest.

A third reason to permit racial affirmative action in education is that this would contribute greatly to the public welfare. James W. Nickel explains that:

> On this approach a program using preferential policies to increase educational and employment opportunities would be seen as one means of promoting the public welfare by eliminating poverty and its attendant evils and by eliminating the sort of inequality that leads to resentment and strife. Extreme poverty is objectionable to one who is concerned with utility because of what it involves, namely unmet needs and suffering, and because of what it leads to, namely crime, family strife, lack of self-respect and social discontent. (Nickel 1975, p. 541)

On the other hand, John Kekes argues that preferential programs in education damage our society because by giving preference to less qualified persons they undermine teaching, research and knowledge upon which the welfare of society so deeply depend. (Kekes 1995, pp. 202–203) This objection can be met if, with Sterba, preferential affirmative action is limited to reasonably well qualified African-Americans. Thus, given the importance of education for success in our society, it would seem that the utility of racial affirmative action in education might well be great enough to justify such programs.

A fourth reason to permit racial affirmative action is to provide a more just redistribution of benefits in our society. James W. Nickel explains this appeal to distributive justice as follows:

> Programs using preferential policies are also conceived as a means of promoting the redistribution of income and other important benefits. This approach would claim that the justification for such programs lies in the reduction of distributive inequalities that they bring about. Since good educations lead to good job, and good jobs provide income, security and status, altering the ways in which educations and jobs are distributed so as to give a bigger share to the previously deprived is one way of bringing about redistribution, A concern with distributive justice is a concern with whether people have fair shares of benefits and burdens. Distributive justice does not require that all people have the same income or equally good jobs. The requirement is rather that that benefits and burdens be distributed in accordance with relevant considerations such as the rights, deserts, merits and needs of the recipients. (Nickel 1975, p. 539)

Since African-Americans have not in the past and still do not receive their fair share of the benefits distributed to persons in our society, they have a moral right to a more fair redistribution of benefits. Presumably this is a means of promoting the equal protection of the law, not a violation of that bsasic moral principle.

A fifth justification for preferential affirmative action concerning African-Americans is as just compensation for past racial discrimination. African-Americans have for decades suffered great harms from racial discrimination in our society. Although there is no way to compensate those now deceased, our society can and should rectify as far as possible the harms unjustly imposed on our living African-American compatriots. However, Carl Cohen argues that affirmative action on the basis of race is both over-inclusive and under-inclusive; it favors many who have not suffered serious racial discrimination and fails to compensate many who have been victims of past racial discrimination. (Cohen and Sterba 2003, pp. 29–30) One reply to this charge is that because individual African-Americans have suffered racial discrimination because of their race, they have a group-right to compensation and that therefore, preferential treatment for all and only members of their group is entirely appropriate. There is serious question as to whether there really are any moral group-rights, and in *Bakke* the Supreme Court affirmed that: "It is settled beyond question that the 'rights created by the first section of the Fourteenth Amendment are, by its terms, guaranteed to the individual. The rights established are personal rights.'" (Supreme Court 1978, p. 289) A second reply to this charge of a mismatch between those who benefit from racial affirmative action and those who have suffered from past racial discrimination is that there is a very high correlation between being an African-American and having suffered from past racial discrimination. Hence, because law must use general classifications and there is a high correlation between membership in the class of African-Americans and the class of those who have suffered racial discrimination, administrative convenience can justify using race as a basis for compensation for past racial discrimination. (Nickel 1975, pp. 550–552) Still, not everyone would grant that administrative convenience carries sufficient moral weight to justify affirmative action programs that often fail to favor those who deserve compensation and do favor those who do not deserve it.

A sixth reason to permit racial preferential affirmative action programs in education is that they will prevent, or at least greatly reduce present and future racial discrimination in our society. James Sterba reminds us that:

> It is also important to distinguish between remedial affirmative action that seeks to compensate for past discrimination (which we have been discussing) and remedial affirmative action that simply attempts to put an end to present discrimination. With regard to the latter form of affirmative action, there is no need to prove that those who benefit from the affirmative action are those who were discriminated against in the past. (Cohen and Sterba 2003, p. 259)

Richard Wasserstom explains how preferential affirmative action programs would serve this purpose. They will provide role models of successful African-Americans, bring them into relationships of greater power, authority and status with members of the dominant white group, reduce the differences in the experiences and understandings of those who are black and those who are white, and put blacks in positions where they are more likely and better able to serve the needs of their fellow African-Americans. He concludes that:

> In the light of all this, the defense of programs of preferential treatment that I offer is that they are at least presumptively justifiable because of their causal role in weakening the existing system of racial disadvantage whose existence and effects make a person's blackness rather than whiteness have the kind of pervasively different, regularly deleterious social meanings and significance that it does have. (Wasserstrom 1995, p. 156)

Carl Cohen would not doubt respond that the existing system of racial disadvantage could and should be weakened by alternative programs that are racially neutral. (Cohen and Sterba 2003, pp. 303–304) The question, of course, is whether any such racially neutral programs would in fact be effective in preventing or reducing present and future racial discrimination.

Although not all of the arguments against preferential affirmative action for African-Americans survive critical examination, three carry significant moral weight. Affirmative action programs that give preferential treatment in education to African-Americans can and often do harm some of them in several ways. These harms should not be taken lightly. It is true that giving preferential treatment on the basis of race does seem to violate the moral principle of equality. But even Carl Cohen admits that this principle does permit different treatment for different classes of persons when, but only when, there is a morally relevant reason to do so. Hence, any affirmative action programs for African=Americans in education carry a very heavy burden of proof. The charge of reverse discrimination similarly imposes a heavy burden of proof because wrongful discrimination consists in treating one or more persons worse than other who are similarly situated without a sufficient justification. Accordingly, the moral permissibility of racial affirmative action depends upon the strength of the reasons for it.

Of the most plausible reasons in its favor, only three deserve to be taken seriously. Preferential affirmative action programs for African-Americans do promote the public welfare by reducing social harms such as abject poverty, wasted talents of the undereducated, and high crime in predominately black urban areas of our cities. Nevertheless, taken alone this might not be sufficient to justify the harms imposed upon innocent white citizens by these programs. However, the fact that these programs also tend to redistribute social benefits and burdens more justly supplements the moral force of the appeal to public welfare. Finally, to my mind the strongest justification for preferential affirmative action programs in education for African-Americans is not that they will compensate African-Americans for past racial discrimination, but that they will prevent, or at least significantly reduce, racial discrimination against them in the future. Because these three reasons together fully meet the burden of proof imposed by the reasons against racial preferential affirmative action, I conclude that universities ought to have a constitutional right to take preferential affirmative action for African-Americans in their admission policies.

7 The Press

The First Amendment to the *United States Constitution* reads in part: "Congress shall make no law…abridging the freedom of speech, or of the Press…." Here "the Press" is an umbrella term covering all the media of mass communication, especially newspapers, television and radio stations. Presumably the freedom of the Press to publish information, or misinformation, is not unlimited. It clearly does not include the freedom to publish libel or defamation. But does it include the freedom to publish the content of classified government documents? Although the Supreme Court rejected a request of the executive to issue an injunction prohibiting the publication of the Pentagon Papers, Justice Stewart suggested that there might be circumstances under which prior restraint would be legally justified. (Supreme Court 1971, pp. 714 & 730) Whatever the Supreme Court may decide in the future, what limits, if any, there ought to be on the freedom of the Press remains highly controversial, as the heated debate over the publication of documents leaked by Edward Snowden shows. Hence, let us ask "Ought the Press to have a constitutional right to publish the content of classified government documents?"

One reason to establish such a right is that this is required by the fundamental moral right to liberty of those who associate to form associations of mass communication. Their primary purpose is to communicate the news to the public, an entirely legitimate purpose. Hence whenever the content of a classified document is newsworthy, the Press has a moral liberty to publish it. However, the moral right to liberty is the right to act in any manner that is not morally wrong, and some might object that publishing the content of classified information is morally wrong because it is illegal. But the courts have to date failed to hold that this is so. Others might object that it is morally wrong because it harms the public interest. But whether this is true depends on the reasons against any such publication.

A second reason for the Press to have a constitutional right to publish the content of classified documents is to protect the civil liberties of the people. Madison's version of the speech and press clauses of the First Amendment reads: "The people shall not be deprived or abridged of their right to speak, to write or to publish their sentiments; and the freedom of the press, as one of the great bulwarks of liberty, shall be inviolable." (Annals of Congress 1789, p. 434) Morton H. Halperin and Daniel N. Hoffman confirm the need for this bulwark of liberty.

> The executive branch today has the capacity to conceal, for considerable periods of time, information that would significantly contribute to legitimate public debate on major issues….In some cases, moreover, the attempt to prevent or punish unwelcome disclosures has led to significant infringements of our civil liberties. (Halperin and Hoffman 1977, p. 24)

Surely it is imperative to protect our civil liberties. But it is also essential to protect our national security. How to balance these two great constitutional values remains to be decided.

A third reason why the Press ought to have a constitutional right to publish the content of classified documents is to enable it to inform the citizens about the real policies and hidden activities of their government. As Justice Black asserted in *New York Times v. United States*:

> In the First Amendment the Founding Fathers gave the free press the protection it must have to fulfill its essential role in our democracy. The press was to serve the governed, not the governors. The Government's power to censor the press was abolished so that the press would remain forever free to censure the Government. The press was protected so that it could bare the secrets of government and inform the people. (Supreme Court 1971, p. 717)

But, many will object, publishing some top secret documents would threaten our national security and weaken our relationships with other nations. However, Justice Stewart, also in *New York Times v. United States*, argues that:

> In the absence of the governmental checks and balance present in other areas of our national life, the only effective restraint upon executive policy and power in the areas of national defense and international affairs may lie in an enlightened citizenry—in an informed and critical public opinion which alone can here protect the values of a democratic government. For this reason, it is perhaps here that a press that is alert, aware, and free most vitally serves the basic purpose of the First Amendment. For without an informed and free press there cannot be an enlightened people. (Supreme Court 1971, p. 728)

And without an enlightened people there cannot be a government of the people, by the people, and for the people.

Finally, the Press ought to have a constitutional right to publish the content of classified government documents in order that the electorate can hold public officials fully accountable for their actions. Geoffrey R. Stone reports that:

> The classification system is a highly imperfect guide to the *need* for classification. The concept "reasonably be expected to harm the national security" is inherently vague and

> plastic. It is impossible to know from this standard how likely, imminent, or grave the potential harm must actually be. Moreover, the classification process is poorly designed and sloppily implemented. Predictably, the government tends to overclassify information. (Stone 2007, p. 11)

And Mark J. Rozell argues that:

> In addition, creating an environment in which secrecy and distrust are the norms runs the risk of government becoming an unchecked power. Executive privilege does not provide presidents the power to do whatever they want when they want, or to conceal information that might be politically embarrassing or disadvantageous in some other way. Instead our government is based the premise of accountability of actions. Without knowing what the executive branch is doing, no one can be held accountable. (Rozell 2010, p. 189)

Therefore, the Press ought to have a constitutional right to publish the content of classified documents in order that the electorate can know what their government is doing and hold public officials accountable for their actions.

These considerations must be weighed against the reasons why the Press ought not to have a constitutional right to publish the content of classified government documents. First, there is a better alternative. The executive branch can best be held accountable by requiring that the content of classified documents be made available to Congress. Its committees, especially those on national security and international relations can be trusted to keep this information confidential and thus avoid the risk that it will be revealed to our enemies and other government by open publication. Morton H. Halperin and Daniel N. Hoffman argue that this alternative would be ineffective:

> A member of Congress who is disturbed by secret information that he or she obtains is placed in a difficult position. Ordinarily, the support of colleagues for controversial measures is developed with the assistance of public speeches, public debate, and public exchanges with the executive branch. The nonpublic processes of informal consultation and bargaining among legislators work best when backed by the sanction of public support. (Halperin and Hoffman 1977, p. 98)

For example, when Ellsberg delivered a set of the Pentagon papers to William Fulbright, Chairman of the Senate Foreign Relations Committee, the senator was unable to use of this information. (Halperin and Hoffman 1977, pp. 11–12)

Another reason why the Press ought not to have a constitutional right to publish the content of classified documents is that this would distract the Executive Branch from the energetic performance of its constitutional duties. The Supreme Court recognized this as a reason to "afford Presidential confidentiality the greatest protection consistent with the fair administration of Justice." (Supreme Court 2004, p. 11 slip opinion) However, there may well be occasions when keeping the content of classified documents is not consistent with the fair administration of justice. Then justice dictates that the Press ought to have a constitutional right to publish that information.

A third reason why the Press ought not to have a constitutional right to publish the content of classified documents is that this would reduce the access of administrative officials to full and candid advice. Chief Justice Burger, in delivering the opinion of the Supreme Court in *United States v. Nixon*, explained:

> The expectation of the President to the confidentiality of his conversations and correspondence, like the claim of confidentiality of judicial deliberations, for example, has all the values to which we accord deference for the privacy of all citizens and, added to those values, is the necessity for protection of the public interest in candid, objective, and even blunt or harsh opinions in Presidential decision-making. A President and those who assist him must be free to explore alternatives in the process of shaping policies and making decisions and to do so in a way many would be unwilling to express except privately. These are the considerations justifying a presumptive privilege for Presidential communications. The privilege is fundamental to the operation of Government and inextricably rooted in the separation of powers under the Constitution. (Supreme Court 1974, p. 708)

Notice, however, that these considerations are claimed to justify only a presumptive, not an absolute, privilege of privacy. Hence, Chief Justice Burger added: "But this presumptive privilege must be considered in the light of our historic commitment to the rule of law." (Supreme Court 1974, p. 709) Hence, this reason against recognizing a right of the Press to publish the content of classified documents will be inapplicable, or at least significantly weakened, when the Executive Branch is acting illegally or in any other way undermining the rule of law.

A fourth reason why the Press ought not to have a constitutional right to publish the content of classified government documents is that this would often damage the relations of the United States with other nations. In 1796 the House of Representatives passed a resolution requesting information about negotiations between the United States of Great Britain. President Washington refused to comply with this request and explained that:

> The nature of foreign negotiations requires caution, and their success must often depend on secrecy, and even when brought to a conclusion a full disclosure of all the measures, demands, or eventual concessions which have been proposed or contemplated would be extremely impolitic; for this might have a pernicious influence on future negotiations, or produce immediate inconveniences, perhaps danger and mischief, in relation to other powers. (Richardson 1897, pp. 186–187)

And in *New York Times v. United States*, Justice Stewart argued similarly that:

> Other nations can hardly deal with this Nation in an atmosphere of mutual trust unless they can be assured that their confidences will be kept. And within our own executive departments, the development of considered and intelligent international policies would be impossible if those charged with their formulation could not communicate with each other freely, frankly, and in confidence. (Supreme Court 1971, p. 728)

Hence, the publication of classified government documents would often jeopardize the international relations of the United States. But some would reply that vital international relations are sustained primarily, if not exclusively, by shared national interests and can survive the disclosure of even the most embarrassing information.

Finally, the Press ought not to have a constitutional right to publish the content of classified government documents because such publication would very often endanger our national security. As William Rehnquist explained:

> The need for extraordinary secrecy in the field of weapons systems and tactical military plans for the conducting of hostilities would appear to be self-evident. At least those of my

generation and older are familiar with the extraordinary precautions taken against revelation of either the date or the place of landing on the Normandy beaches during the Second World War in 1944. The executive branch is charged with the responsibility for such decisions, and has quite wisely insisted that where lives of American soldiers or the security of the nation is at stake, the very minimum dissemination of future plans is absolutely essential. (Rehnquist 1971, p. 434)

Presumably our national security requires equal protection even when the United States is not engaged in a war. However, denying the Press the right to publish classified information in the name of national security may well be unjustified. Justice Black insisted that:

The word 'security' is a broad, vague, generality whose contours should not be invoked to abrogate the fundamental law embodied in the First Amendment. The guarding of diplomatic and military secrets at the expense of informed representative government provides no real security to our Republic. (Supreme 1971, p. 719)

And defenders of the Press could add that historically the Press has been highly responsible in refraining from publishing information that would seriously endanger our national security. Unfortunately, WikiLeaks, a new international online nonprofit journalistic organization, has not maintained this traditional restraint.

Of the reasons to establish a constitutional right of the Press to publish the content of classified government documents, only two are strong enough to be taken seriously: to enable the Press to inform the citizens about the real policies and hidden activities of their government and in order that the electorate can hold public officials fully accountable for their actions. There are also three strong reasons not to establish such a right: this would reduce the access of administrative officials to full and candid advice, damage the relations of the United States with other nations, and endanger our national security. Of these important considerations, the danger to our national security is the most imperative. Nevertheless, I believe that one must not forget the opinion of Justice Black that: "The guarding of diplomatic and military secrets at the expense of informed representative government provides no real security for our Republic." (Supreme Court 1971, p. 719) Why would it not provide real security? Because what is so precious that we ought to guard it is not merely the sovereignty of the United States, but its democratic institutions that enable us to live worthwhile lives. Thus, it would seem that the Press ought to have a constitutional right to publish classified information because this is essential to informing the citizens and to enable them to hold their government accountable.

On the other hand, our national security is also necessary to maintaining our democratic government. Therefore, I suggest that the Press ought to have a limited constitutional right to publish the content of classified government documents. What is required is a limitation analogous to the clear and present danger limit to the right to freedom of expression. The opinion of Justice Stewart in *New York Times v. United States* might provide this limitation when he observed that: "But I cannot say that disclosure of any of them will surely result in direct, immediate, and irreparable damage to our Nation or its people." (Supreme Court 1971, p. 730) In any event, my conclusion is that, everything considered, the Press ought to have a limited constitutional right to publish the content of classified government documents.

8 Overview

The reasons for and against any controversial constitutional right of an association can be divided into two distinct classes. There are reasons directly concerning the rights or welfare of individual persons, either members of the association or individuals affected by its actions, and reasons that in the first instance concern the rights or welfare of social collectivities, either the association itself or other social organizations including the society as a whole. For example, one reason why labor unions ought to have a constitutional right to closed shops is that closed shops are necessary to protect the human rights of their members, and a different reason is that closed shops are necessary to enable unions to act responsibly. One reason why business corporations ought to have a constitutional right to spend funds for political purposes is in order that its members can exercise their constitutional and human rights to associate for political purposes, and a different reason is to maximize the amount of information and diversity of viewpoints needed to create an educated public in a democracy. One reason why the Press ought to have a constitutional right to publish the content of classified government documents is that this is required by the moral right to liberty of those who form associations of mass communications, and a different reason is to enable the electorate to hold public officials accountable.

Similarly, one reason why Indian Tribes ought not to have a constitutional right to some residual sovereignty is that this would permit them to violate several civil rights of their members, and a different reason why they ought not to have such a right is that this would disrupt the application of United States federal and state sovereignty. One reason why political parties ought not to have a constitutional right to closed primaries is that closed primaries violate the right to privacy of their members, and a different reason why political parties ought not to have such a right is that closed primaries remove an incentive to reconsider long-standing policies that no longer fit the changed circumstances or were originally unwise. Finally, one reason why universities ought not to have a constitutional right to take preferential affirmative action for African-Americans is that this is often bad for those who are preferred, and a different reason is that this would inhibit progress toward the moral ideal of a color-blind society.

The significance of this difference consists in the fact that reasons directly concerning the rights or welfare of individual persons are more fundamental than reasons that in the first instance concern the rights or welfare of social collectivities. This is because the rights or welfare of collectivities are morally important only insofar as they make a difference to the individual persons that comprise them. For example, the value of democratic institutions lies in the ways in which they make the lives of those affected by them more secure and rewarding.

References

Aaron, Benjamin (1987). Rights of Individual Employees Under the act. In American Labor Policy: A Critical Appraisal of the National Labor Relations Act, Charles J. Morris (ed.). Bureau of National Affairs. Washington DC.

Annals of Congress (1789). 1:434.

Cohen, Carl and Sterba, James P. (2003). Affirmative Action and Racial Preference: A Debate. Oxford University Press. New York & Oxford.

Deloria, Jr., Vine and Lytle, Clifford M. (1983). American Indians, American Justice. University of Texas Press. Austin TX.

Dunn, Stephen and Gennard, John (1984). The Closed Shop in British Industry. Macmillan. London.

Gierzynski, Anthony (2000). Money Rues: Financing Elections in America. Westview Press. Boulder CO.

Green, Mark (2002). Selling Out" How Big Corporate Money Buys Elections, Rams Through Legislation, and Betrays Our Democracy. Harper Collins. New York.

Halperin, Morton H. nd Hoffman, Daniel N, (1977). Top Secret: National security and the Right to Know. New Republic Books. Washington DC.

Hanson, Charles et. al. (1988). The Closed Shop: A Comparative Study in Public Policy and Trade Union Security in Britain, the USA and West Germany. St. Martin's Press. New York.

Kekes, John (1995). The Injustice of Affirmative Action Involving Preferential Treatment. In The Affirmative Action Debate, Steven M. Cahn (ed.). Routledge. New York & London.

Macklem, Patrick (1993). Distributing Sovereignty: Indian Nations and Equality of Peoples. Stanford Law Review 45:1311–1368.

McCarthy, W. E. J. (1964). The Closed Shop in Britain. University of California Press. Berkeley CA.

McKenna, Lois M. (1989). Freedom of Association or Gender Discrimination? New York State Club Association v. City of New York. The /American University Law Review 38:1061–1092.

Nickel, James W. (1975). Preferential Policies in Hiring and Admissions: A Jurisprudential Approach. Columbia Law Review 75:534–558.

Rehnquist, William (1971). Executive Privilege. Statement Before the Subcommittee on Separation of Powers of the Committee on the Judiciary, U. S. Senate, 92nd Cong. 1st sess, July 1971.

Rhode, Deborah I. (2010). Association and Assimilation. In the First Amendment Freedom of Assembly and Petition: Its Constitutional History and the Contemporary Debate, Margaret M. Russell (ed.). Prometheus Books. Amherst NY.

Richardson, James (1897). A Compilation of the Messages and Papers of the Presidents, vol. 1. Bureau of National Literature. New York.

Rogers, Barbara (1988). Men Only: An Investigation into Men's Organizations. Pandora Press. London.

Rozell, Mark J. (2010). Executive Privilege: Presidential Power, Secrecy, and Accountability, 3rd edition. University of Kansas Press. Lawrence KS.

Samples, John (2006). The Fallacy of Campaign Finance Reform. University of Chicago Press. Chicago.

Sawyer, Thomas H. (1993). Private Golf Clubs: Freedom of Expression and the Rights of Privacy. Marquette Sports Law Review 3:187–214.

Stone, Geoffrey R. (2007). Top Secret: When Our Government Keeps Us in the Dark. Rowman & Littlefield. Lanham MD.

Supreme Court (1831). The Cherokee Nation v. The State of Georgia. 30 U.S. 1.

Supreme Court (1832). Worcester v. Georgia. 31 U.S. 575.

Supreme Court (1886). United States v. Kagama. 118 U.S. 375.

Supreme Court (1937). NLRB v. Jones. 301 U.S. 1.

Supreme Court (1964). Bell V. Maryland. 378 U.S. 226.

Supreme Court (1971). New York Times v. United States. 403 U.S. 713.
Supreme Court (1974). United States v. Nixon. 418 U.S. 683).
Supreme Court (1976). Buckley v. Valeo. 424 U.S. 1.
Supreme Court (1978). University of California Regents v. Bakke. 438 U.S. 265.
Supreme Court (1986). Tashjian v. Republican Party of Connecticut. 479 U.S. 208.
Supreme Court (1987). Board of Directors of Rotary International v. Rotary Club. 481 U.S. 537.
Supreme Court (1988a). New York State Club Association v. New York City. 487 U.S. 1.
Supreme Court (1988b). Communication Workers of America v. Beck. 487 U.S. 735.
Supreme Court (1990). Austin v. Mich. Chamber of Commerce. 494 U.S. 652.
Supreme Court (2002). California Democratic Party v. Jones. 530 U.S. 567 slip opinion.
Supreme Court (2003). Grutter v. Bollinger. 539 U.S.___ slip opinion.
Supreme Court (2004). Cheney v. United States Dist. Court for D.C. 542 U.S.___ slip opinion.
Supreme Court (2010). Citizens United v. Federal Elections Commission. 558 U.S. 310 slip opinion.
Wasserstrom, Richard (1995) Preferential Treatment, Color-Blindness, and the Evils of Racism and Racial Discrimination. In the Affirmative Action Debate, Steven M, Cahn (ed.). Routledge. New York & London.
Wellman, Carl (1982). Welfare Rights. Rowman and Littlefield. Totowa NJ.
Wellman, Carl (1990). Equal Opportunity. Journal of the British Society for Phenomenology 21:26–38.
White, Stuart (1998). Trade Unionism in a Liberal State. In Freedom of Association, Amy Gutmann (ed.). Princeton University Press. Princeton NJ.

Postscript

After two brief introductory chapters, the focus of this volume has been on legal and political debates about controversial constitutional rights. Some of these are established in the constitutional law of the United States and others are merely proposed rights. Because the detailed reasons for and against each of these rights may not suggest any coherent overall perspective, it may be useful to review the previous chapters to see what has been accomplished and to preview what should follow from them.

Several important theoretical theses have been asserted, and to some extent defended, in the previous chapters. (1) What defines constitutional law in the sense relevant to this examination is the way in which it allocates the sovereign power of a nation state. It may do this by means of a single fundamental document such as the *Constitution of the United States*, but it need not do so. For example, the constitutional law of the United Kingdom consists of several historically important documents such as the *Bill of Rights*, fundamental principles of the common law, and a few basic acts of Parliament.

(2) Constitutional law allocates the sovereign power of the nation state primarily by conferring power-rights upon the fundamental institutions, legislative, executive and judicial, of the nation and upon the public officials playing a variety of roles, such as enacting statutes or administering these laws, in these institutions. Hence, these governmental power-rights are the primary constitutional rights in any legal system. It is a mistake to think of the civil rights of private persons and the governmental powers of public officials as fundamentally different and independent in legal practice because most governmental powers are defining cores of rights.

(3) Constitutional rights, in the sense relevant to this volume, are best defined as rights conferred by the constitutional law of some nation state. In the United States, and presumably in other nation states, there are four distinct classes of constitutional rights: rights of constitutional institutions, rights of public officials, rights of private persons and rights of associations of private persons. In the United States, textbooks on constitutional rights typically limit themselves to civil rights, primarily the constitutional rights of private persons and with much less attention to the

C. Wellman, *Constitutional Rights -What They Are and What They Ought to Be*, Law and Philosophy Library 115, DOI 10.1007/978-3-319-31526-3 constitutional rights of associations. This is misleading because they omit the primary constitutional rights of governmental institutions and officials.

(4) To understand the nature of constitutional rights and their moral foundations it is best to consider all four species of constitutional rights together. This is because the primary function of civil rights is to limit governmental power-rights. Also, real law is law as it functions in the legal system, and these four classes of constitutional rights modify each other in judicial decisions, for example the power right of Congress to limit the publication of information or misinformation is limited by the civil right of private persons to the freedom of speech. Moreover, the moral justification of any constitutional right is essentially related to the justification of other constitutional rights. Thus, in judging any statute that limits the civil right to freedom of speech, the courts will consider the importance of free speech for our democracy and importance of the state interest Congress has a right to protect by legislation.

The previous chapters also provide some information about current practice in legal education, judicial decision and political debate. (1) In the United States, there are typically two sets of legal textbooks, one on civil rights and others on administrative law. However, In the United Kingdom, both civil rights and administrative law are usually treated together in the same textbooks on constitutional rights.

(2) The cited passages from decisions of the United States Supreme Court show that judges often appeal to moral reasons to interpret the content of some claimed constitutional right and sometimes to moral reasons to decide whether some claimed constitutional right exists. For example, judges consider alleged compelling state interests to define the limits of some established constitutional right or the importance of an informed public to decide whether the Press has a constitutional right to publish the content of classified government documents.

(3) There are many examples of ongoing political debates about what constitutional rights ought or ought not to be established in the United States. The most important pro and con arguments are described and assessed for their cogency and strength. Although these are only a sample of the contemporary controversies about constitutional rights in practical politics, they probably reveal most of the relevant reasons. At the very least, they indicate the kinds of reasons that are worth considering when one argues for or against some existing or proposed constitutional right.

The purpose of this volume is to make a contribution to the theory and perhaps the practice of constitutional rights, but at best it is a modest step forward in this important enterprise. First, what needs to be done to complete and improve the theory of what constitutional rights are? (1) Much more needs to be explained about the nature of law. The literature on this subject is vast, but disagreements abound. The resolution of these differences is a project requiring thought and the exchange of viewpoints between many jurists and philosophers of law.

(2) The special features of constitutional law also require much fuller explanation. Precisely what is a constitution? When does constitutional law take priority over other species of law and why? Among other species are statute law, common law, international law, and sometimes religious law.

(3) Similarly much more is required to explain the nature of rights. Although I advocate a Hohfeldian analysis of rights, others do not. One should consider carefully which sort of rights theory best explains the special features of legal rights, especially constitutional rights. Clearly, there is much theoretical work ahead.

Second, what needs to be done to complete and improve the theory of what constitutional rights ought to be? (1) One would like a useful classification, even better several classifications, of the kinds of reasons that are relevant to the justification of constitutional rights. This needs to be supplemented with some explanation of precisely why each kind of reason is a reason for or against establishing such a right.

(2) Most of the reasons to which judges or others appeal derive their moral force from more basic considerations. Hence, in order to understand moral reasoning concerning what constitutional rights ought to be one must describe the chain of reason from ultimate moral reasons to intermediate ones to conclusions about justifiable constitutional rights. This will require some explanation of why the most basic moral reasons are the ultimate ones.

(3) In the end, one must balance the reasons for any constitutional right against the contrary reasons. Hence, one needs some explanation of how one might assess the importance of any relevant pro or con reason. To what extend this depends upon present or long-term circumstances will be part of this explanation.

What implications for future practice, if any, are there in the previous chapters? (1) The second chapter explains why any adequate theory of constitutional rights needs to cover both civil rights of private persons or associations and governmental rights of institutions or public officials. However, in the United States legal textbooks on constitutional rights, and presumably classes in law schools, include only civil rights. Ought our legal education be reformed by adopting the United Kingdom practice of combining civil rights and administrative law in textbooks? Not necessarily. There are advantages to both practices. Our practice is more useful in the training of practicing lawyers because it results in greater specialization that enables a higher competence in legal details and past court cases. But academics who teach and write about constitutional rights ought to master the theory of all four species of constitutional rights.

(2) I doubt that judges could learn much, if anything, about how to reason about what the constitutional rights in our legal system are or how they ought to be defined. But in the event that they must decide some case involving one of the contested constitutional rights considered in this volume, they might find the pro and con reasons described here suggestive.

(3) Chapters three through six identify and assess the reasons for or against actual or proposed constitutional rights. They also reach conclusions about whether each of these ought to be recognized in United States law. Ought legislators and judges accept and act on these conclusions? Only occasionally. My competence is very limited and my practical wisdom imperfect. What they might well do is to reflect on my discussions, look for additional relevant considerations, and continue the debate in their own minds and in public forums. If any of these practical implications significantly influence the actions of my readers, I will be immensely gratified and more than a little surprised. It is probably just as well that we do not live in a Platonic republic where philosophers rule.

MIX
Papier aus verantwortungsvollen Quellen
Paper from responsible sources
FSC® C105338
FSC
www.fsc.org

If you have any concerns about our products,
you can contact us on
ProductSafety@springernature.com

In case Publisher is established outside the EU,
the EU authorized representative is:
Springer Nature Customer Service Center GmbH
Europaplatz 3, 69115 Heidelberg, Germany

Printed by Libri Plureos GmbH
in Hamburg, Germany